ACCOUNTS RECEIVABLE
PRACTICAL EXPERIENCE
USING QUICKBOOKS ONLINE

Step by step practical guide

STERLING LIBS FCCA, FCPA

Accounts Receivable Work Experience Using QuickBooks online

www.sterlinglibs.com

London, United Kingdom

ISBN: 978-1-911037-14-9

PRACTICAL WORK EXPERIENCE IN ACCOUNTANCY – ACCOUNTS RECEIVABLE

The role of the Accounts Receivable clerk involves providing financial, administrative and clerical support to the organisation. ensure their company receives payments for goods and services and records these transactions accordingly. An Accounts Receivable job description will include securing revenue by verifying and posting receipts and resolving any discrepancies.

This role requires the candidate to be organised and have a keen eye for detail to spot any issues that may arise.

You'll spend most of your time at your desk raising invoices and talking to clients.
This job is ideal for you if you want a career that offers room to move as there's plenty of scope for promotion once you've got some experience. Sales ledger clerks often graduate to work as a supervisor or manager and from there to credit controller and even financial controller.

For an Accounts Receivable role, an understanding of basic bookkeeping and accounting skills is required. Whilst a degree is not mandatory for this role, a degree in the following subjects: Finance or Economics, Accounting and Business studies would be beneficial for an Accounts Receivable career.

Having an AAT qualification (level 2-4) and ACCA Foundation stage will also be very beneficial for a career as an accounts receivable clerk.

Attention to detail and data entry skills, people and customer relations skills are important requirements for an Accounts Receivable job description. In this role, you will be interacting with employers and Customers on a daily basis, so it is imperative that you are able to interact on a professional manner at all times.

If you are looking for an Accounts Receivable role, this book will give you a good head start and help build your confidence and competence.

On page 1 of this book, you will find detailed job description of an Accounts Receivable clerk and please do also have a look at the table of contents of this book for the details of what is covered.

The Author can be contacted by sending an email to sterling@sterlinglibs.com

Your Role as an Accounts Receivable Clerk

Attention to detail and data entry skills, people and customer relations skills are important requirements for an Accounts Receivable job role. In this role, you will be interacting with employers and Customers on a daily basis, so it is imperative that you are able to interact on a professional manner at all times.

Table of Contents

WORKING AS AN ACCOUNTS RECEIVABLE CLERK **1**

Testing your practical accounting knowledge (17 Questions & Answers) 2

The professional code of ethics you are required to abide by as an accountant. 5

The key skills that can help you get and keep an accounting job 6

TASK 1: SETTING UP & GETTING STARTED **13**

Introduction to QuickBooks Online 13

Task 1a: Setting up the business in QuickBooks Online 13

Task 1a(i). Understanding the general layout of QuickBooks Online 19

Task 1a(ii). Understanding QuickBooks Online VAT Codes 22

Task 1a(iii). Understanding QuickBooks Online chart of accounts 25

Task 1b: Setting up Customers & Suppliers 30

Task 1b(i): Setting up Customers and corresponding opening balances 30

Task 1b(ii): Setting up Suppliers and corresponding opening balances 37

Task 1c: Setting up products & services 44

Task 1d: Setting up the fixed assets register 54

Task 1e: Setting up opening balances from the Trial balance 56

TASK 2: HOW TO DO BUDGETING IN QUICKBOOKS ONLINE **61**

TASK 3: DOING THE ACCOUNTS RECEIVABLE TASKS **65**

How to analyse a financial - Invoice. 85

Task 3b: Recording Customer receipts and a non-customer recept 86

3b(i) Recording customer receipts 87

3b.(ii) Recording non-customer receipts 90

Task 3c: How to update dishonoured cheques and returned goods. 94

Task 3d: How to collect outstanding debtor amounts – part of credit control. 102

TASK 4: JOURNAL ENTRIES AND DOUBLE ENTRY REVIEW **105**

Task 4a: Posting a journal on issue of share capital. 105

Task 4b: Double entry review. 106

Task 4b(i): Double entry to record a cash sale paid for by cash and bank transfer. 106

Task 4b(ii): Double entry to record a Credit sale. 107

TASK 5: HOW TO ENSURE SECURITY OF ACCOUNTING DATA 109

Task 5a: How to change your password in QuickBooks online. 109

Task 5b: How to add a new user in QuickBooks online. 110

ABOUT THE AUTHOR 113

NOTE TO THE READER

This step by step guide is designed to provide practical information on how to work as an Accounts Receivable clerk using QuickBooks Online accounting software.

Every effort has been made to make this book as complete and accurate as possible. However, no assurance is given that the information is comprehensive in its coverage or that it is suitable for dealing with your particular situation. Accordingly, the information provided should not be relied upon as a substitute for independent research. It is sold with the understanding that the publisher and author are not engaged in rendering any accounting, legal, or other professional advice nor do they have any responsibility for updating or revising any information presented herein.

No representation or warranty (express or implied) is given as to the accuracy or completeness of the information contained in this book, and, to the extent permitted by law, the Author/publisher, its members, employees and agents do not accept or assume any liability, responsibility or duty of care for any consequences of you or anyone else acting, or refraining to act, in reliance on the information contained in this book or for any decision based on it. If legal or other expert assistance is required, the services of a competent professional should be sought.

The author and publisher cannot warrant that the material contained herein will continue to be accurate nor that it is completely free of errors when published. Readers should verify statements before relying on them.

Purpose

This book is information only and has been prepared for general guidance for those who are interested in learning how to work as an Accounts Receivable clerk as described in the job description of an Accountant on page 1 of this book and is current at the time of publication.

About this book

This book is a step by step guide designed to provide practical information on how to work as an accountant using QuickBooks online accounting software.

"If there is no price to pay, it's also not of value."
Albert Einstein

WORKING AS AN ACCOUNTS RECEIVABLE CLERK

If you choose to work as an Accounts Receivable Clerk, what are you most likely to be doing?

Job profile summary:

As an Accounts Receivable clerk, you will be fully accountable for the whole Sales ledger process, from sales orders through to invoices and Debtor account reconciliation.

Your main duties will include matching and coding invoices, ensuring your company receives payments for goods and services, and record these transactions accordingly and reconciling customer accounts.

You will generally work as part of the finance team; however, you may work independently in a smaller organisation.

In a nutshell, your role as an Accounts Payable Clerk is to provide a professional and efficient service to the finance function, monitoring how much is owed and collected to the company at all times and providing accurate financial information to the Finance Director or manager as needed.

Working hours:

Typical work hours are 9:00 am – 5:00 pm Monday to Friday.

Key responsibilities:

Your responsibilities will depend on the size of the company you work for, and they can include any or all of the following duties and responsibilities:

,

- *Matching, checking and coding invoices*
- *Working out VAT*
- *Processing staff expenses*
- *Setting up of new Customer accounts and maintaining existing account details*
- *Reconciliation of Customer accounts*
- *Sending invoices to Customers*
- *Collecting outstanding debts from customers*
- *Data entry*
- *Reviewing systems and processes and making improvements where necessary*
- *Raising Sales orders*
- Processing Customer invoices
- *Deal with purchase enquiries*
- *File invoices and statements*
- *Process staff expenses*
- Setting up standing orders and direct debits to receive money from Customers
- Doing other ad hoc administrative duties as and when needed.

Testing your practical accounting knowledge (17 Questions & Answers)

Question 1: Under what legal entities can businesses operate in the UK?

Answer: *Sole Trader, Partnership, Company Limited by Shares (LTD), Company Limited by guarantee (Charity), Community Interest Company (CIC), Limited Liability Partnership (LLP) Designated Activity Company, Public Listed Company (PLC)*

Question 2: What is a tax year and what is a financial year?

Answer: *A tax year in the UK is from the 6th of April the current year to the following 5th April next year.*
A financial year is a 12-month period commencing from the date the business starts trading or gets registered with Companies House (UK)

Question 3: What are the three key stages of the accounting cycle?

Answer: *Analysis stage, Recording stage and Reporting stage*

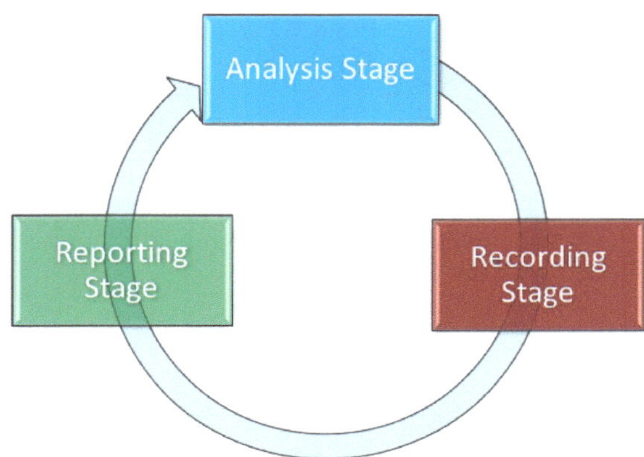

Question 4: Briefly describe what you should do at each of the three stages listed above.

Answer:

a. *Analysis Stage*
   - *Classification of financial documents*
   - *Checking that the correct values are reflected in the financial documents*
   - *Making sure that the documents are within the financial year date to which they relate to.*

b. *Recording stage*
   - *It is mostly about data entry*
   - *Using double-entry bookkeeping principles*

c. *Reporting stage*
   - *Checking for any errors in the nominal accounts*
   - *Making yearend/period end adjustments*
   - *Producing yearend/period end reports and statements for filing with government agencies (Companies House & HMRC in the UK)*

Question 5: What are the key steps in the sales ledger (Accounts Receivable process)

Answer:

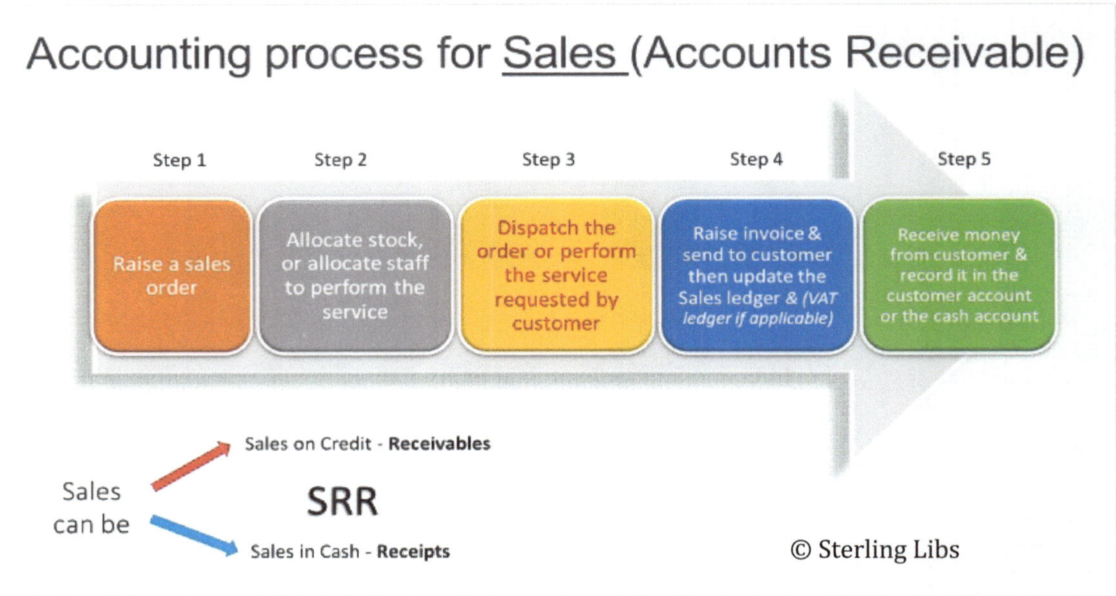

Question 6: What are the key steps in the purchase ledger (Accounts payable) process

Answer:

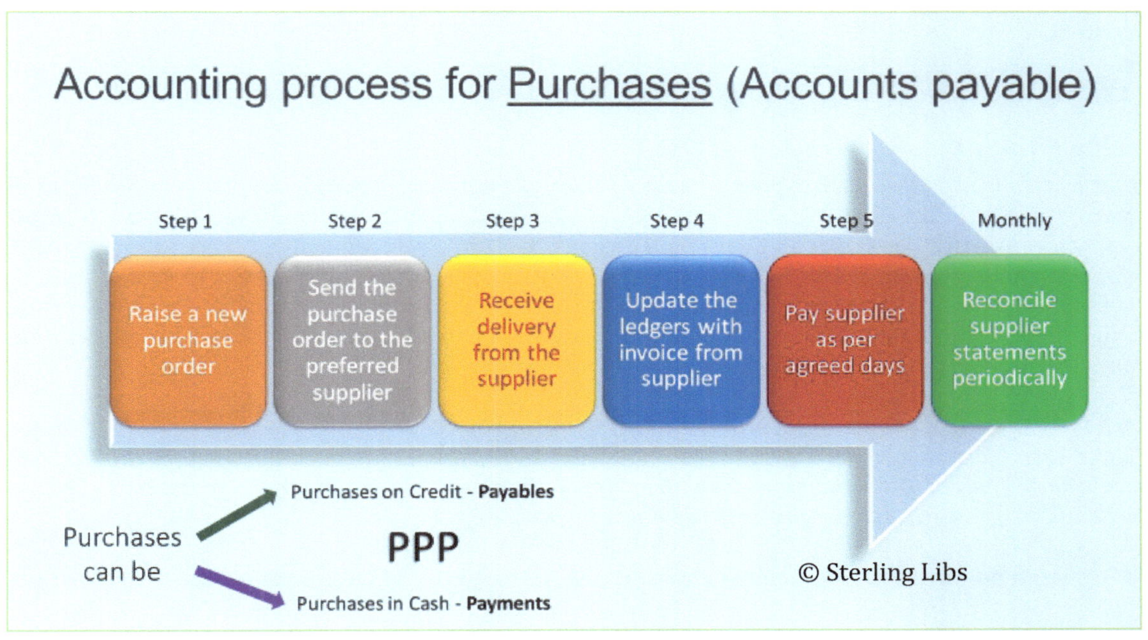

Question 7: When does a business need to register for PAYE in the UK?
Answer: *When it starts employing people/when it becomes an employer*

Question 8: When does a business have to register for VAT?

Answer: *Compulsory registration: You must register for VAT if your VAT taxable turnover is more than £85,000 (the 'threshold') in a 12-month period or if you expect to go over the threshold in a single 30-day period.*

Question 9: What is the current standard rate of VAT in the UK
Answer: *20%*

Question 10: What is the current rate of corporation tax in the UK?
Answer: *19% for tax year 2017/2018*

Question 11: What is normally done at the month end close process
Answer: *Three key steps are usually performed to manage the end-of-the-month accounting process successfully. They are:*

Description of the key steps	*What to do at each stage (the tasks)*
Key step 1: Checking the general ledger accounts for errors & making the necessary corrections	• *Correct the general ledger account errors including mispostings and inaccuracies.*
Key step 2: Doing Adjustments and Reconciliations	• *Financial adjustments, e.g. interest payments adjustments, prepayments, accruals and depreciation* • *Control account reconciliations: Debtors' control account, Creditors' control account, VAT control account, Bank account, Wages account etc.* • *Balance sheet reconciliation (Reconciliation of the Assets, Liabilities, Equity & Reserves)* • *Calculations of closing balances of the accounts after adjustments & reconciliations*
Key step 3: Reporting to senior management	• *Producing a profit & Loss statement and other various management reports if necessary.*

Question 12: Why is it important to do bank reconciliation?

Answer:
A bank reconciliation is used to compare your records to those of your bank, to see if there are any differences between these two sets of records for your cash transactions. The ending balance of your version of the cash records is known as the book balance, while the bank's version is called the bank balance. It is extremely common for there to be differences between the two balances, which you should track down and adjust in your own records. If you were to ignore these differences, there would eventually be substantial variances between the amount of cash that you think you have and the amount the bank says you actually have in an account. The result could be an overdrawn bank account, bounced checks, and overdraft fees. In some cases, the bank may even elect to shut down your bank account.

It is also useful to complete a bank reconciliation to see if any customer checks have bounced, or if any checks you issued were altered or even stolen and cashed without your knowledge. Thus, fraud detection is a key reason for completing a bank reconciliation. When there is an ongoing search for fraudulent transactions, it may be necessary to reconcile a bank account on a daily basis, in order to obtain early warning of a problem.

Question 13: Which government agencies do businesses in the UK need to submit accounts and returns to?

Answer:
Her Majesty's Revenue and Customs (HMRC) and Companies House.

Question 14: Which reports usually are submitted to the government agencies you have stated above?

Answer:

a) HMRC – *Tax returns, VAT Returns,*
b) Companies House - *Statutory annual accounts and annual returns*

Question 15: And who is legally responsible for submitting the reports you've stated above?

Answer: *The Director(s) of the company*

Question 16: What key competencies will help you work effectively as an accountant?

Answer:

a. Attention to detail
b. Analytical skills
c. Numerical skills
d. Communication skills and teamwork
e. Accounting software skills
f. Speed and accuracy

Question 17: What code of ethics are accountants expected to abide by?

Answer:

a. Integrity
b. Objectivity
c. Confidentiality
d. Professional competence and due care
e. Adopting professional behaviour

The professional code of ethics you are required to abide by as an accountant.

Under the Code of Professional Ethics, as an accountant, you must follow these five principles:

1. **Integrity.**

You must be straightforward and honest in all professional and business relationships.

2. **Objectivity.**

You must not compromise professional or business judgment because of bias, conflict of interest or the undue influence of others.

3. **Professional competence and due care.**

You must maintain professional knowledge and skill (in practice, legislation and techniques) to ensure that a client or employer receives competent professional service.

4. **Confidentiality.**

You must not disclose confidential professional or business information or use it to your advantage unless you have explicit permission to disclose it, or a legal or professional right or duty to disclose it.

5. **Professional behaviour.**

You must comply with relevant laws and regulations and avoid any action that may bring disrepute to the profession.

Professional Ethics | AAT. (n.d.). Retrieved from https://www.aat.org.uk/about-aat/professional-ethics

The key skills that can help you get and keep an accounting job

Skilled people in any profession are very valuable. So let me take this opportunity to talk to you about some of the skills you should look to develop at the early formative years of your accounting career.

Identifying the skills that lead to success in accounting will not only increase your job satisfaction but also make it easier for you to build your long-term career goals.

No matter how big a company ever gets, the need for an accounts department persists. Perhaps that focus is on auditing, maybe management or tax and finance related. Chances are, you will start in one of two career paths – technical or commercial.

Accounting requires certain hard skills, such as mathematics and expertise with accounting software. Thorough knowledge of relevant laws and regulations is necessary for many positions, too.

However, accounting also requires some soft skills that you might not learn in school but will help you land and keep a job.

Staying current with technology is perhaps the most significant pressure you will continuously face in your accounting and finance career. As technology impacts on the way you do your job as an accountant, make sure you stay abreast of the changes and train and retrain to keep your skills up to date

Here is a list of six accounting skills that you should look to hone in your career as a professional accountant. Your CV/resume, cover letter, job application will be scrutinised for these skills and even during your job interviews – if you make it that far. It will serve you well to be in possession of these skills in increasing measure as you progress in your accounting career.

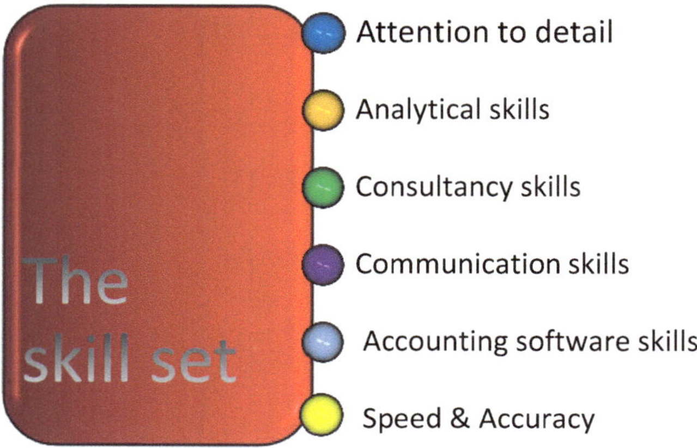

Let me elaborate a bit more on each skill above.

Attention to detail

Attention to detail is an essential requirement for a successful accounting career. The ability to notice an error, inconsistency or discrepancy can often lead to discovering other inaccuracies. On the other hand, missing a small detail can affect the integrity of the organisation's financial records and may have dire consequences. It is therefore quite essential that you should have a detail-oriented approach to your work to ensure that financial records conform to standards, laws and regulations.

Analytical Skills

As an accountant, you must be analytical when examining documents and financial processes. The use of critical thinking skills to determine ways to make the organisation more financially efficient will be required of any good accountant.
My experience in working with many businesses is that; the analytical skills help you develop ways to reduce costs, increase revenues, improve profits and eliminate waste.

You will also have to carefully evaluate financial performance and investigate financial investments at some point in your accountancy career as you keep growing and that my friend, will call for excellent analytical skills.

Hopefully, with the passage of time, you will be able to demonstrate this skill in greater measure.

Consultancy skills

The Accountant of the 21st century is more of a consultant than a person who merely deals with numbers. As a professional accountant of nowadays, you should also be a problem solver and possess sound judgement, and you shouldn't not jump to conclusions.

Good consultants study, consider the facts, ask questions, challenge the norm and then make a recommendation or a decision. They use their experience from previous assignments to solve new problems and challenges in your current assignment. They possess excellent written and oral communication skills as well as good listening skills. These are the kind of things you will be expected to do more of as the accountant of the 21st century because accounting software's are doing a lot more of what the traditional accountant of yesteryears used to do. So you need to evolve to what I would call – the Accounting consultant.

Communication skills

How are your written and verbal communication skills like?

You see, the accountant of the 21st century now interacts with a variety of people ranging from managers and directors to members of the accounting staff and various stakeholders in a business. You will meet people through the course of your work with a wide range of unique characteristics, not all of them pleasant or to your liking.
It is therefore important that train yourself to be able to clearly converse or correspond and to ask questions and discuss issues or discrepancies quite easily.
Also, accountants offer advice and make recommendations regarding the best financial business decisions. Therefore, being articulate and well presented will help a great deal here.

Accounting software skills

Gone are the days when accounting used to be done manually. Almost invariably, every business now uses some form of software to do their bookkeeping and accounts. From Excel to the more sophisticated ERP accounting software, accounting and financial analysis are now so much software based and the better you are in using any of these accounting software, the better you will be in your accounting career.

Accounting software all use the same basic principle of double entry, so if you are proficient in one, you will find it easy to learn any other accounting software relatively quickly.

I suggest therefore that you learn at least how to use one accounting software very well because that will act as a stepping stone for you learning other software should you change jobs and find that your new employer uses a different accounting software. At least know how to use one software proficiently.

Speed & Accuracy
You need to be conscious of the fact that accounting is a very dynamic profession and at times very highly pressured. If you are looking to be successful in your accounting career, you've got to develop a reputation for speed and dependability (producing accurate & trustworthy information).

Time is the currency of the 21st century. Business today is very, very dynamic. Employers are less and less patient with slow, incompetent employees because they recognise that customers will change suppliers overnight if someone else can serve them faster than the people they are currently dealing with.

So, your job, as you start developing your accountancy career is to develop a reputation for speed. Move fast on opportunities, move quickly when you see something that needs to be done. You've heard it said that whenever you want to get something done, give it to a busy man or woman.

Employees who have a reputation for moving quickly, attract more and more opportunities and possibilities to them and that is the kind of thing you want in the early years of your accountancy career development.

If you can combine your ability to determine your highest priority tasks with the commitment to getting it done quickly and accurately, you will find yourself progressing through your accounting career with flying colours and moving to the front/top of it. More and more doors and opportunities will open for you that you can't even imagine today.

One more thing – very, very important indeed.

Underlying all of the skills you will ever have is one very important and profound aspect of life you need to watch over. What am I talking about? Your attitude. That's right, has to do a lot with your quality of life and success in any career or profession.

Come to think it; you could be a genius as far as accounting is concerned and even have the most excellent and lofty practical experience there is to find. However, if you have a terrible attitude, you will realise soon or later that not many people would like to work with you or have dealings with you whatsoever. They would prefer keeping their distance from you. Is that good, you think, for your career? Not in the slightest if you ask me.

So, let me talk to you a little bit about attitude since it is such a crucial aspect of your job success as an accountant just as it is in any area of your life. Your attitude goes a long way in determining what company of people you will keep, what actions you will take, how successful you will be in your accounting career and above all, how much and how deep you will enjoy life. Something worth exploring, wouldn't you agree? Yes, of course.

Look, I can guarantee you that your current attitude is either helping you move forward or is making you lag behind in life. The good news though is this; your attitude is 100% under your control, and you can change it at any time to help support your career progression.

Your Life only gets better when you get better, and since there is no limit on how much better you can become, there is no limit on how much better your life can become. True? Well, judge for yourself.

Zig Ziglar once said; "*It's your attitude and not your aptitude that determines your altitude*".

Here then are some of the attitudes that I believe will help you make excellent progress in your accountancy career.

1. **Attitude of gratitude**

When you exude an attitude of gratitude at all times, you make people around you feel important. The truth is, everything you say or do that causes another person to feel better in any way also causes you to feel better to the same degree. Haven't you realised that when you encourage, inspire, motivate someone else, you feel motivated, inspired and encouraged yourself?

And guess what...

The converse is true when you degrade, insult and abhor someone else, you feel the same too!

The need for appreciation is a deep subconscious desire of every individual you meet. When you satisfy this need, you will by all accounts become one of the most popular people in that person's world, and what is the key to expressing gratitude and appreciation? Simple, just say 'thank you' on every occasion and mean it.

You say thanks in a whole host of different ways: by giving compliments, admiration, giving encouragement, by unconditionally accepting people for who they are, by smiling, giving a hug, a pat on the back....., all these actions communicate one message ;-well done 'buddy' I am really proud of you'. If you become a finance manager, you should do more of this with your juniors.

In fact, the best way to ensure your happiness is to assist others to experience their own. "Those who bring Sunshine to others cannot keep it from themselves" James Banie
Be a professional, happy, gregarious and friendly accountant. It will do you good.

2. **A forgiving attitude**

Jim Loehr & Tony Schwartz in their book; In the power of Full engagement, said: "*The richer and deeper the source of our emotional recovery, the more we refill our reserves and the more resilient we become.*"

You see, people are emotional beings. People decide emotionally then justify logically. Emotion comes first. So when we are hurt, our emotions immediately take over, and for some, this leads to prolonged periods of sulking and being grumpy, and they will justify it logically by saying that they are hurt. What they seem not to understand is that a lot of their emotional energy which could otherwise be expended in some other productive venture is being put to waste on destructive tendencies. So the faster they recover from any hurt through total and sincere forgiveness, the better for them.

I know it is not easy to forgive, but I also know that it is difficult to enjoy life in an accounting career if you are hurting from the inside.

So if there is anyone who has hurt you; whoever it is, or wherever it was, please forgive them. It could be your parent(s), your spouse, your close friend, your sibling, your pastor, teacher, work mate, it could be anyone and everyone really, whoever it is, find it in your heart to forgive and release them from the pain they have caused you. It's very noble, and it is an eternal act, which has both present and eternal rewards.

Forgiveness is a choice, and we all have to make that choice time and again if our relationships and careers are to be worth our time, effort and rewards thereof.
Be a forgiving accountant. Don't be a grumpy & bitter accountant.

3. **Courageous attitude**

Courage is a very admirable quality. Your boldness will help you get as much as you need in life. The bold move makes you seem larger and more powerful than you are. More than that, the bold draw attention and what draws attention, draws power. We simply cannot keep our eyes off the audacious, can we? We can't wait to see their next bold move.
Everyone admires the bold; no one honours the timid, isn't that true?

Better still...

A courageous person is an upward and forward-looking person, he/she faces the future without fear but with determination, not with doubt but with faith. He/she is willing to take great chances and reach for new horizons and remake the world around them. They recognise that there is more to their life than the ordinary, they take the status quo and turn it around. It is simply magnetic and very inspiring to be around them. The good news is that you can be one of those very courageous ones as well.

The courageous individuals teach us to have our horizons limitless. Ultimately if we are to be true to our past, we also have to seize the future every day, and courage will help us make the most of our; time, abilities (effort), and opportunities that will ultimately help us make the most of our lives and accounting career.

And...

No matter how bitter the raw, how stony the accountancy road, courage enables us to persevere, not to falter or grow weary but to demand, strive and shape a better accountancy career for yourself!
Simply refuse to give up on the idea of the forward and upward move but ultimate triumph, despite the most extreme odds that you will sometimes face during your accountancy career. In some circumstances, you will need a lot of courage to do the right thing that the code of ethics demands of you.

4. **A compassionate attitude**

Compassion makes you believable, it magnetises and magnifies the power of your faith and undeniably makes you very welcoming and attractive in the sight and hearts of many people. Compassion moves the heavens on your behalf and bestows upon you the invisible power of influence and force of accomplishment.

Compassion naturally leads you to be a giver; it enhances the quality of benevolence - one of the hallmark characteristics of the truly superior person.

When you give freely and generously of yourself to others or for a cause, you feel more valuable and happier inside.
Here is a principle to remember when it comes to benevolence and compassion: "The more you give of yourself to others without expectation of return, the more good things there are that will come back to you from most unexpected sources."

You will also realise that, over time, you are becoming more patient and understanding, less judgmental or demanding of others. You will feel peaceful, confident and pleasant to be around. In a nutshell, you become a better and finer person and more importantly a compassionate accountant.

Isn't that wonderful?

5. **Integrity**

Your Character is the most important thing that you develop in your entire life, and one of the cornerstones of your character is your integrity.

You develop integrity, and become a completely honest person, by practising telling the truth to yourself and others in every situation.

It is imperative that your relationships and accountancy career are based on the foundation of truth, and this can be done by developing the habit of living in truth with yourself and with everyone around you. Of course, this does not mean that you will always be right 100% of the time, it, however, emphasises the fact that you endeavour to tell the truth, as you see or know it.

Others will learn to know that they can confidently rely on you and your word (and that is very important for an accountant). Though they may not like what you say on certain occasions, they will still know that you always speak the truth. This goes a very long way to earn you a great reputation in your accounting career and form a very solid foundation for your integrity. Listen to what Shakespeare once wrote, "*To thine own self be true, and then it must follow, as the night the day, thou canst not then be false to any man*".

In this day and age with the advancement of technology, CCTV and satellite, you cannot afford to be careless about how you conduct yourself or how you treat others or do business. To be successful nowadays is largely determined by the number of people who trust you and who are willing to work with you or give you credit if you are a borrower or help you during difficult times etc. Trust is essential, and trust is earned not given, and you earn trust by being a person of integrity.

You must guard your integrity as a sacred thing, as the most important statement about you as an accountant.
As Brian Tracy once said; "Whenever you are in doubt about a course of action, simply ask yourself, Is this the right thing to do?" And then behave accordingly.

"Weakness of attitude becomes weakness of Character" – A. Einstein

6. A loving attitude

As Apostle Paul said in 1Corinthians 13:2-3 *"And though I have the gift of prophecy, and understand all mysteries, and all knowledge; and though I have all faith so that I could remove mountains,.....And though I bestow all my goods to feed the poor, and though I give my body to be burned, and have not Love, I am nothing."*

Without genuine, heartfelt love for the people in your life and the things you do, your relationships and success in life are doomed to fail.

Jesus Christ emphasised this point of love so much that He gave a new commandment: *"...Thou shalt love the Lord thy God with all thy heart, and with all thy soul and with all thy mind........, Thou shalt love thy neighbour as thyself"* Matthew 22:37-3

To love is a decision you make and should form a core part of your attitude in life and especially in your accounting career.
I think it is important to bear in mind what Jesus Christ said in the scripture above and also to embrace the Golden Rule: *"Do unto others what you would have them do unto you"*.

In closing on this aspect of attitudes of success in accountancy, I would like to say that; the way to a super attitude and hence a great accountancy career at any time of the day and at any day of the week is to trust in God with all your heart and lean not on your own understanding.

I am not being religious here, but simply stating the obvious and plain truth. If you don't believe me, try it your way or any other way and see how far you can go being successful and happy at the same time.

I hope you will forever resolve to be a grateful, forgiving, courageous, compassionate, trustworthy and loving accountant. I really do hope so.

Okay. I am done with that bit. Let's get to work, shall we?

Integrity

You must guard your integrity as a sacred thing, as the most important statement about you as an accountant.

As Brian Tracy once said; "Whenever you are in doubt about a course of action, simply ask yourself, is this the right thing to do?" And then behave accordingly.

"Start where you are. Use what you have. Do what you can". **Arthur Ashe**

TASK 1: SETTING UP & GETTING STARTED

Introduction to QuickBooks Online

QuickBooks is an accounting software package developed and marketed by Intuit. QuickBooks products are geared mainly toward small and medium-sized businesses and offer on-premises accounting applications as well as cloud-based versions that accept business payments, manage and pay bills, and payroll functions.

There are three versions of QuickBooks Online. A plan can be chosen to suit the requirements of the business. Each offering provides features relevant to the selected plan. Further details on the features available under each product version can be found at https://quickbooks.intuit.com/pricing/

Task 1a: Setting up the business in QuickBooks Online

The details you have been given about the business to set up in QuickBooks Online are as follows:

- **Company/Business name:** *Horizon Tristar Ltd*
- **Business address:** *77 Lee Road, London, SE3 9DE*
- **Financial year:** *Set to the 1st November last year*
- **Home currency:** *Depending on where you are doing this work experience from (country), Use the currency of that country as the home currency in QuickBooks Online (We will be using the British Pound in this tutorial)*
- **VAT information:** *Registered for VAT on the standard VAT scheme and the registration number is 843277159*
- **Director/Manager:** *Mr Terry Smith*
- **Opening balances** to be entered in QuickBooks online as of 1st January this year.

Let's get started.

Look at the links below and depending on which part of the world you are in, use the appropriate link to get started.

If you are based in the **United Kingdom (UK),** use/click on - https://quickbooks.intuit.com/uk/

If you are based in the **United States (US)**, use/click on - https://quickbooks.intuit.com

If you are based in the **European Union (EU),** use/click on - https://quickbooks.intuit.com/eu/

If you are based in **Australia,** use/click on - https://quickbooks.intuit.com/au/

For all the **Rest of the World**, use/click on - https://quickbooks.intuit.com/global/

For this work experience, I have opted to use the UK site, https://quickbooks.intuit.com/uk/ because I live in the UK. However, the software functionally is the same regardless of which part of the world you are based in. So, follow through with me.

Once you visit any of the sites above, the landing pages are quite similar, and there will be an offer for a free 30 day trial in almost all the sites - See figures 1 & 2 below.

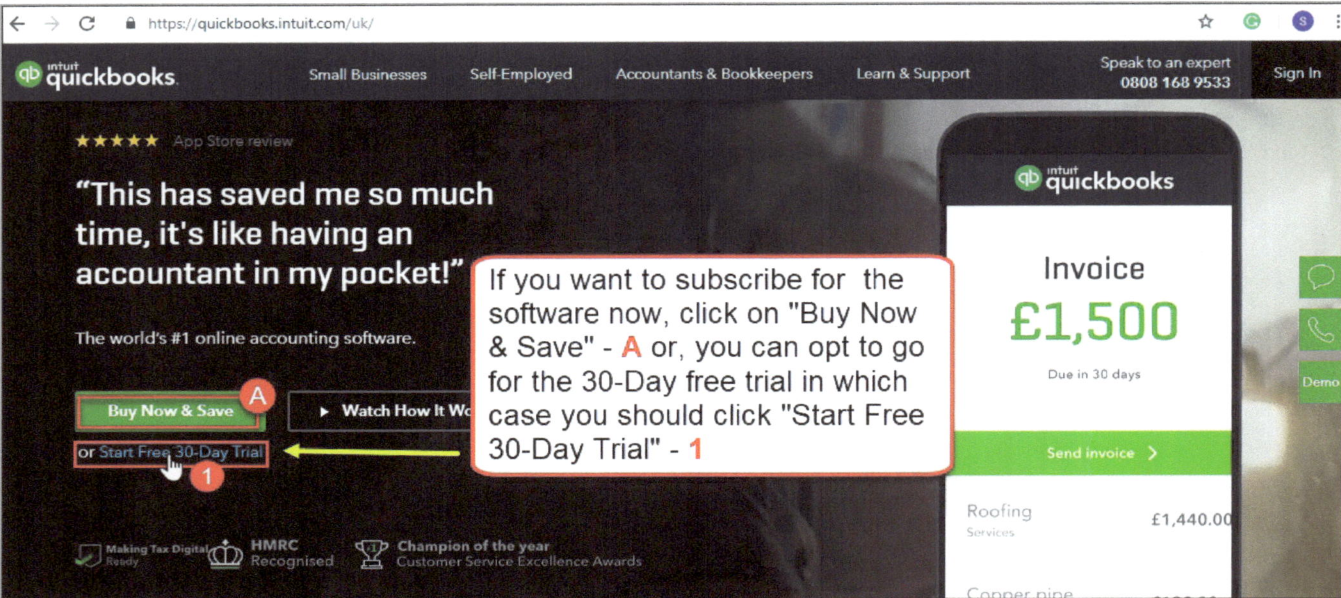

Fig. 1

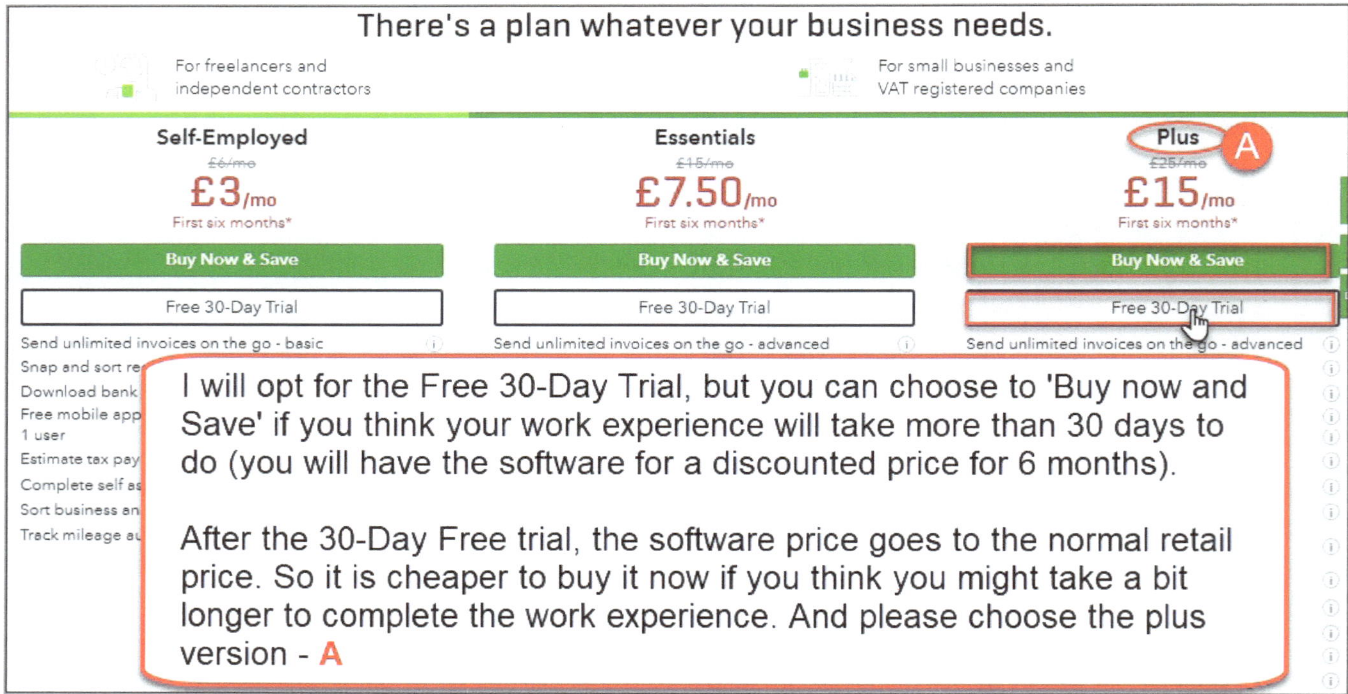

Fig. 2

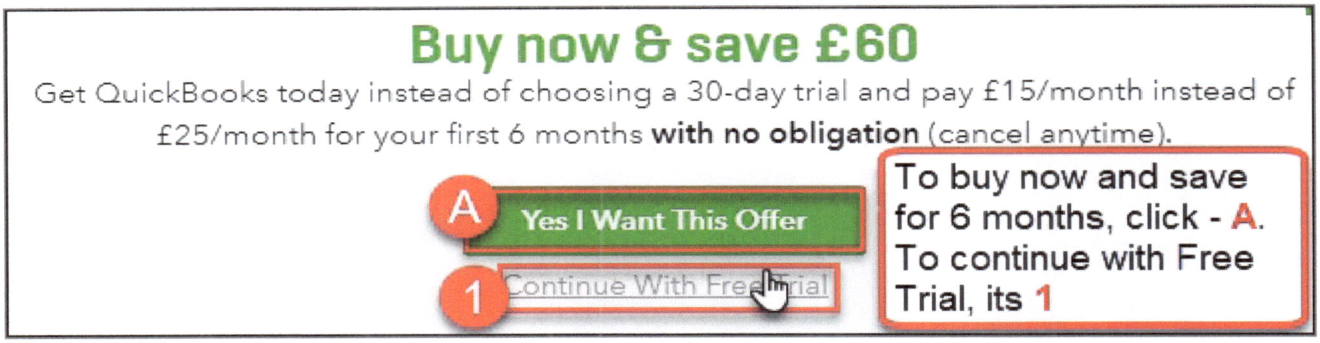

Buy now & save £60
Get QuickBooks today instead of choosing a 30-day trial and pay £15/month instead of £25/month for your first 6 months with no obligation (cancel anytime).
A
Yes I Want This Offer
1
Continue With Free Trial
To buy now and save for 6 months, click - A. To continue with Free Trial, its 1

Fig. 3

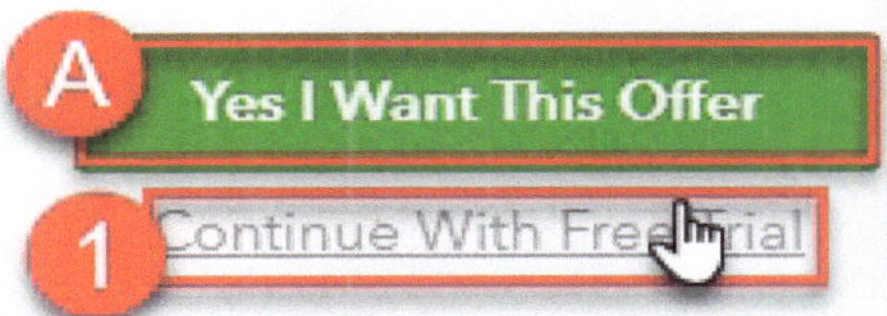

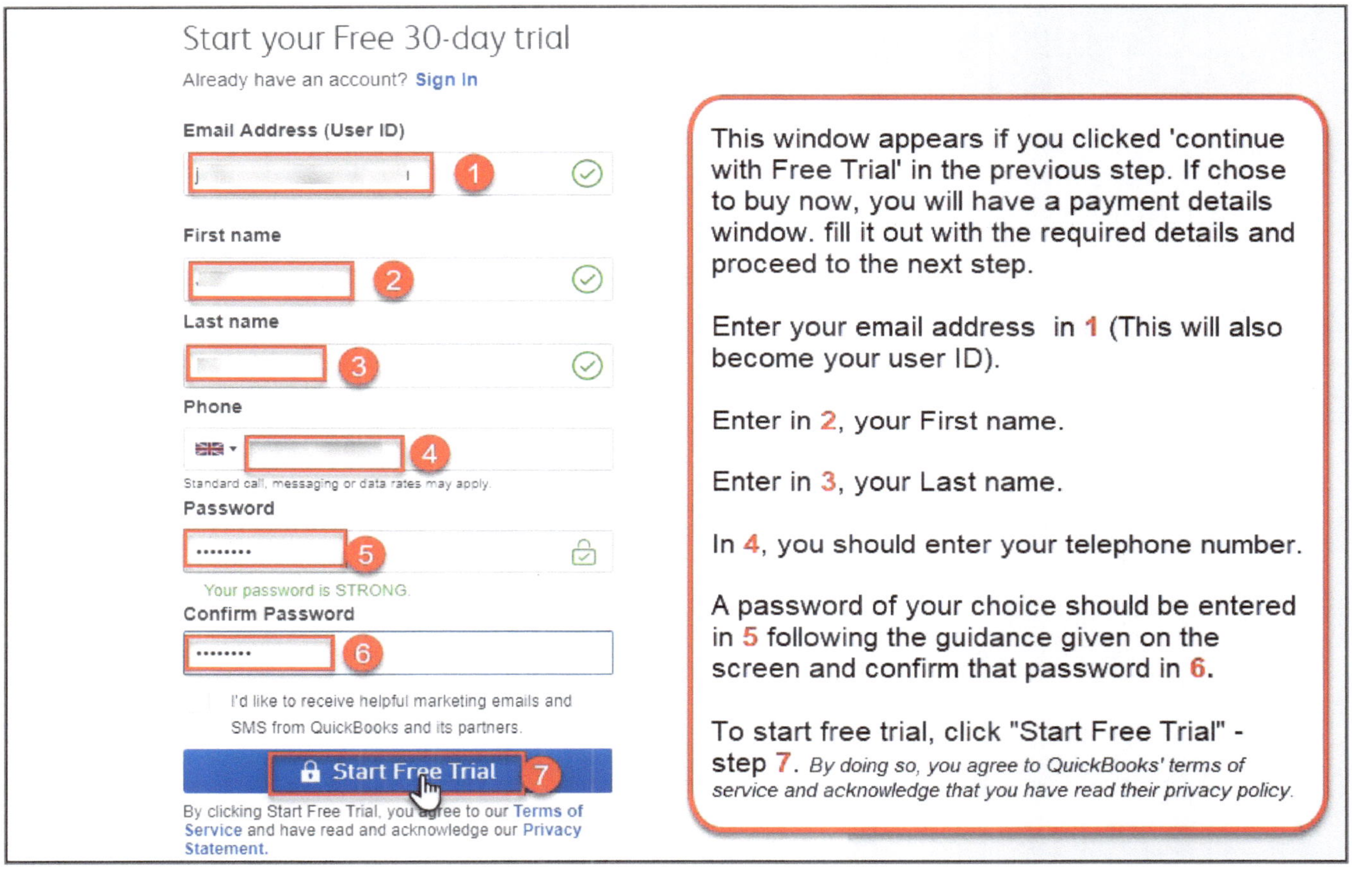

Start your Free 30-day trial
Already have an account? Sign In
Email Address (User ID)
1
First name
2
Last name
3
Phone
4
Standard call, messaging or data rates may apply.
Password
5
Your password is STRONG.
Confirm Password
6
I'd like to receive helpful marketing emails and SMS from QuickBooks and its partners.
Start Free Trial
7
By clicking Start Free Trial, you agree to our Terms of Service and have read and acknowledge our Privacy Statement.
This window appears if you clicked 'continue with Free Trial' in the previous step. If chose to buy now, you will have a payment details window. fill it out with the required details and proceed to the next step.
Enter your email address in 1 (This will also become your user ID).
Enter in 2, your First name.
Enter in 3, your Last name.
In 4, you should enter your telephone number.
A password of your choice should be entered in 5 following the guidance given on the screen and confirm that password in 6.
To start free trial, click "Start Free Trial" - step 7. By doing so, you agree to QuickBooks' terms of service and acknowledge that you have read their privacy policy.

Fig. 4

Creating your QuickBooks account
Configuring your account
Activating your features
Starting the set up wizard
Your QuickBooks account is now being created

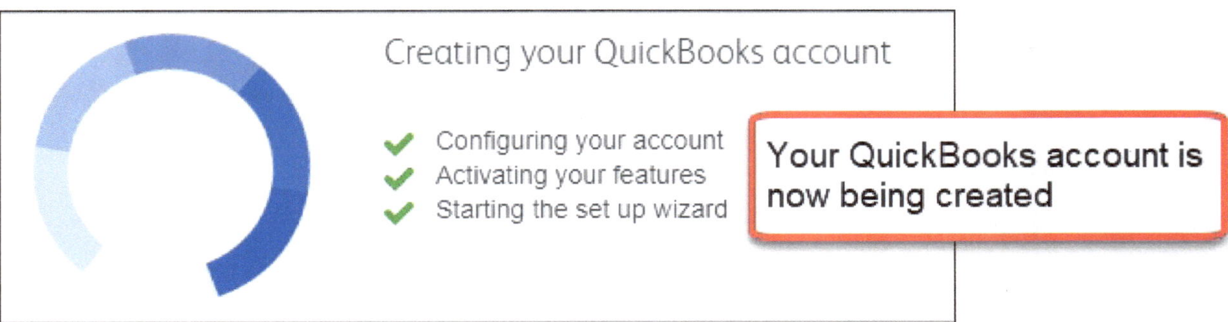

Fig. 5

intuit quickbooks
No two businesses are alike
We should know–we've seen a lot! Help us get to kn
What's your business called?
Horizon Tristar
1
What type of business do you have?
Private limited company
2
How long have you been in business?
1-2 years
3
I've been using QuickBooks Desktop and want to bring in my data.
4
Next
Enter in 1 the Company name: Horizon Tristar
From the drop down arrow list - 2, select - Private limited company, as the type of business
Select from the drop down arrow list - 3, a period of 1-2 years then click "Next" - 4 to proceed.

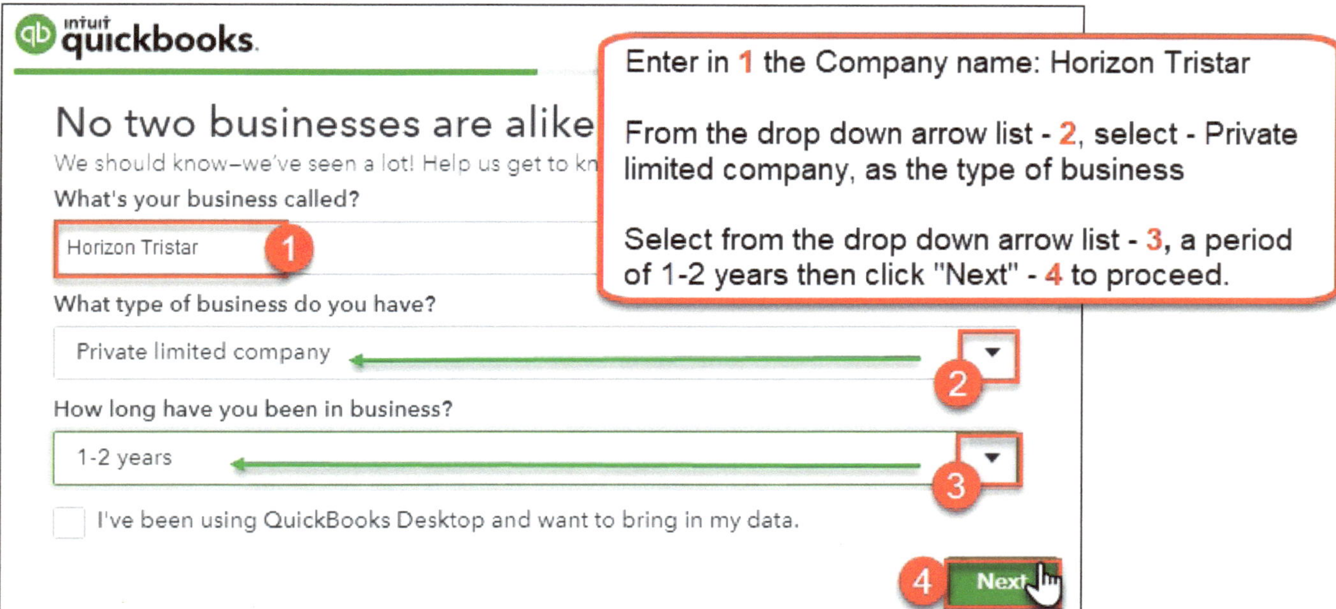

Fig. 6

intuit quickbooks
2 of 2
What would you like to do in QuickBooks?
This is just to get you started. You can always do more later.
Track your VAT
Track construction industry taxes
Track your retail sales
Send and track invoices
Manage your stock
Pay your employees
Track hour
1
Click on each of these items - 1 (you will see a tick on each item you click on)
Once that is done, click "All set" - 2.
Back
All set
2

Fig. 7

After you click "All set" as illustrated in the figure above, the home page appears. The Home page displays a summary of key information. A new file set up would display as in figure 8 (on the next page) with no transactions.

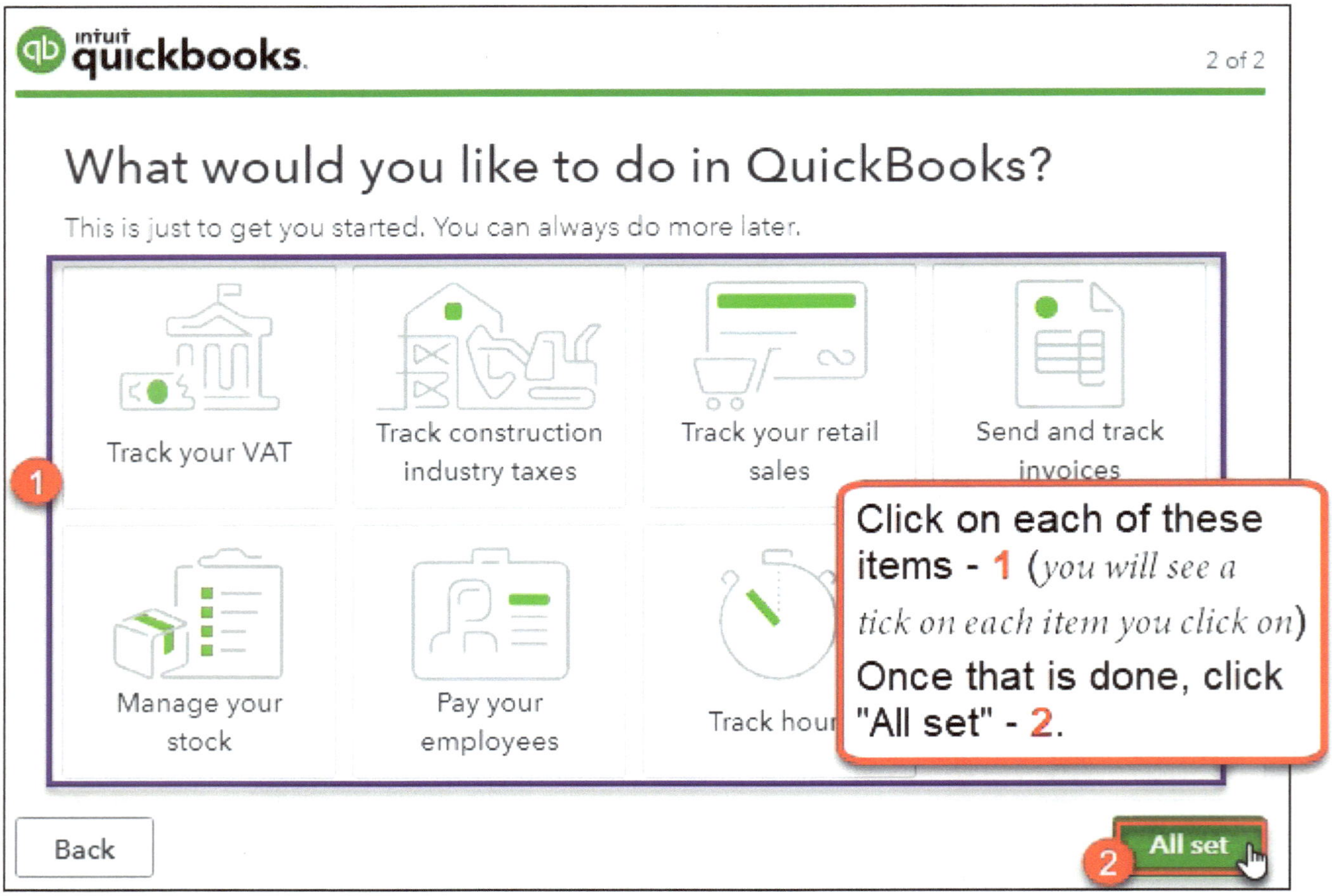

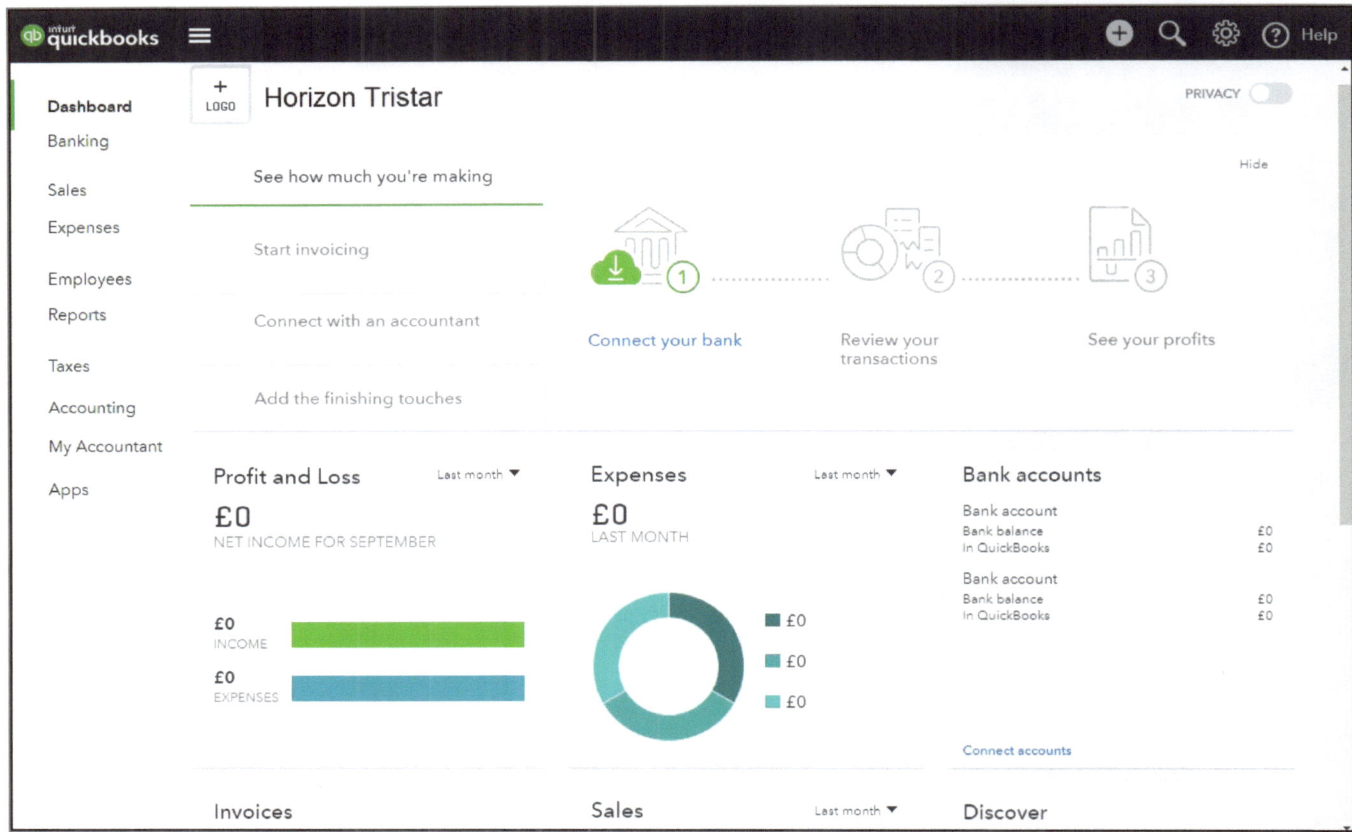

Fig. 8

To sign out of your QuickBooks online screen, see details on the figure below.

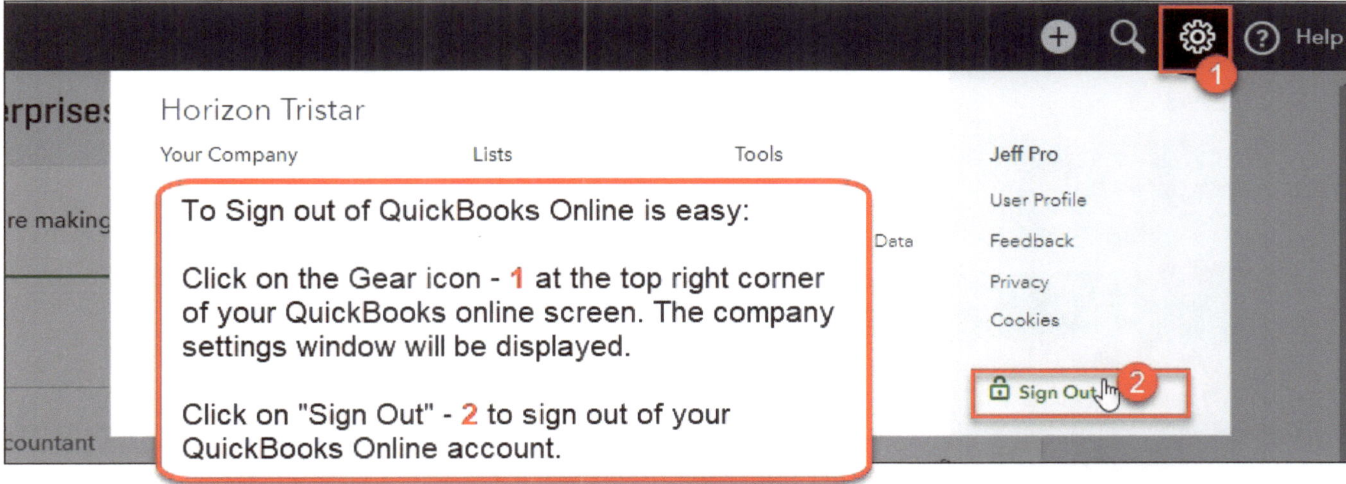

Fig. 9

This space is for notes

To sign back into your QuickBooks online account, follow the steps as illustrated in the figure below.

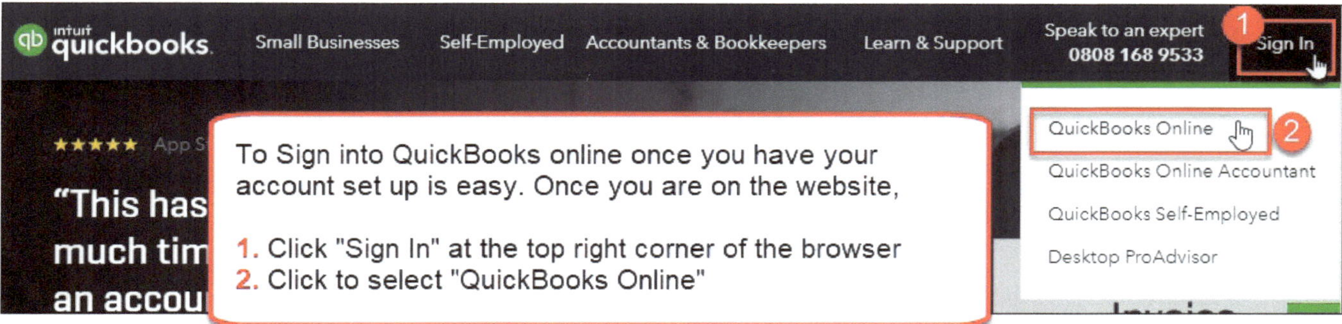

Fig.10

Fig. 11

Task 1a(i). Understanding the general layout of QuickBooks Online

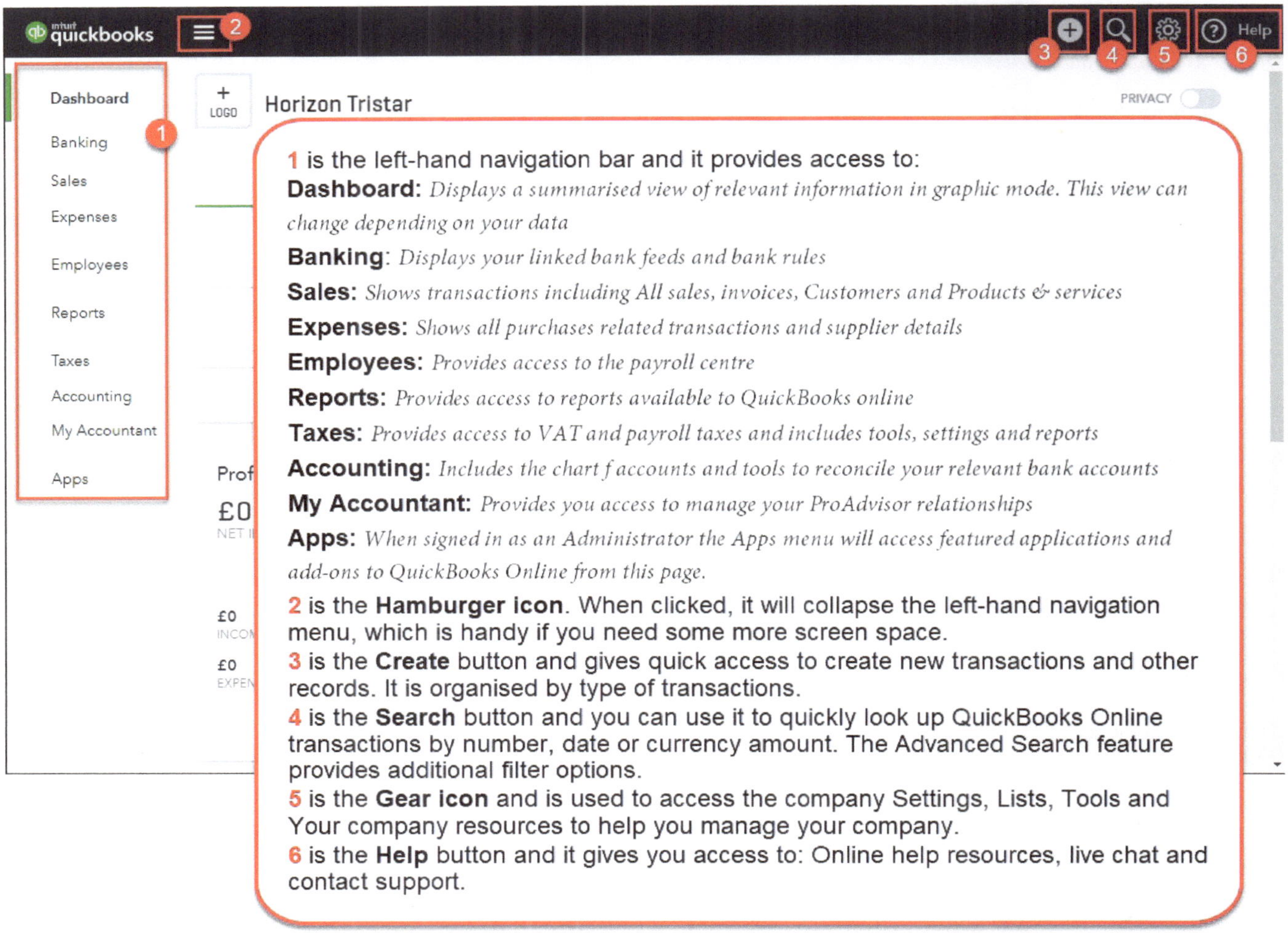

quickbooks
Help
Dashboard
Banking
Sales
Expenses
Employees
Reports
Taxes
Accounting
My Accountant
Apps
LOGO
Horizon Tristar
PRIVACY
1 is the left-hand navigation bar and it provides access to:
Dashboard: Displays a summarised view of relevant information in graphic mode. This view can change depending on your data
Banking: Displays your linked bank feeds and bank rules
Sales: Shows transactions including All sales, invoices, Customers and Products & services
Expenses: Shows all purchases related transactions and supplier details
Employees: Provides access to the payroll centre
Reports: Provides access to reports available to QuickBooks online
Taxes: Provides access to VAT and payroll taxes and includes tools, settings and reports
Accounting: Includes the chart f accounts and tools to reconcile your relevant bank accounts
My Accountant: Provides you access to manage your ProAdvisor relationships
Apps: When signed in as an Administrator the Apps menu will access featured applications and add-ons to QuickBooks Online from this page.
2 is the Hamburger icon. When clicked, it will collapse the left-hand navigation menu, which is handy if you need some more screen space.
3 is the Create button and gives quick access to create new transactions and other records. It is organised by type of transactions.
4 is the Search button and you can use it to quickly look up QuickBooks Online transactions by number, date or currency amount. The Advanced Search feature provides additional filter options.
5 is the Gear icon and is used to access the company Settings, Lists, Tools and Your company resources to help you manage your company.
6 is the Help button and it gives you access to: Online help resources, live chat and contact support.

Fig. 12

Let's move on and set up the company's financial year date.

Horizon Tristar
Your Company
Lists
Tools
Jeff Pro
Account and Settings
Manage Users
Custom Form Styles
Chart of Accounts
QuickBooks Labs
User Profile
Feedback
Privacy
Cookies
Sign Out
Audit Log
Click on the Gear icon - 1, to get to company settings,
Then,
Click on "Account and Settings" - 2.

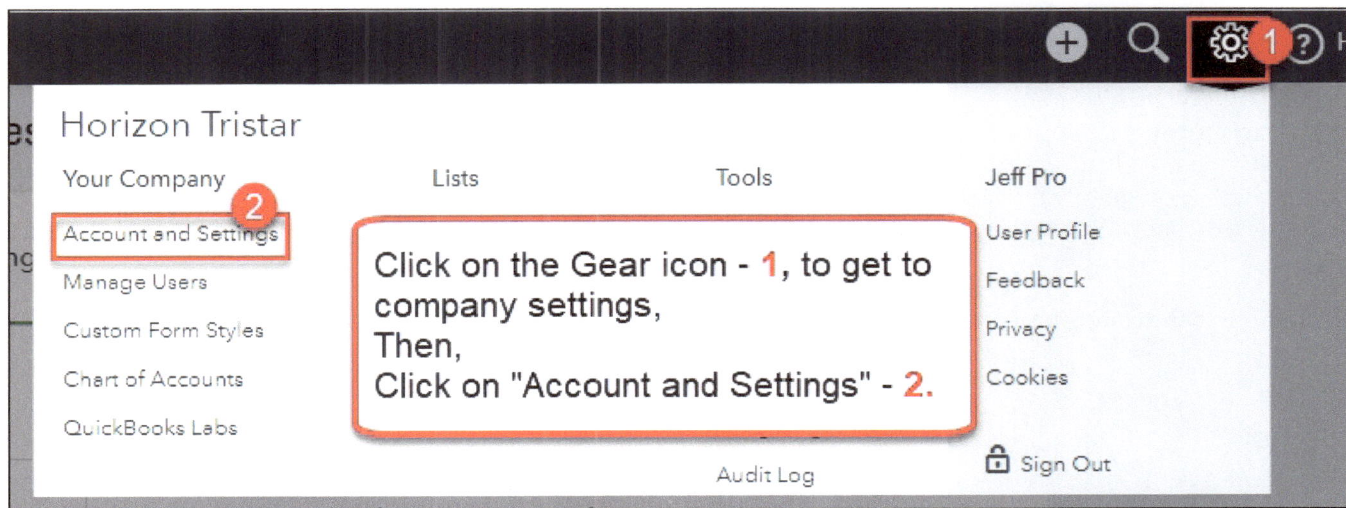

Fig. 13

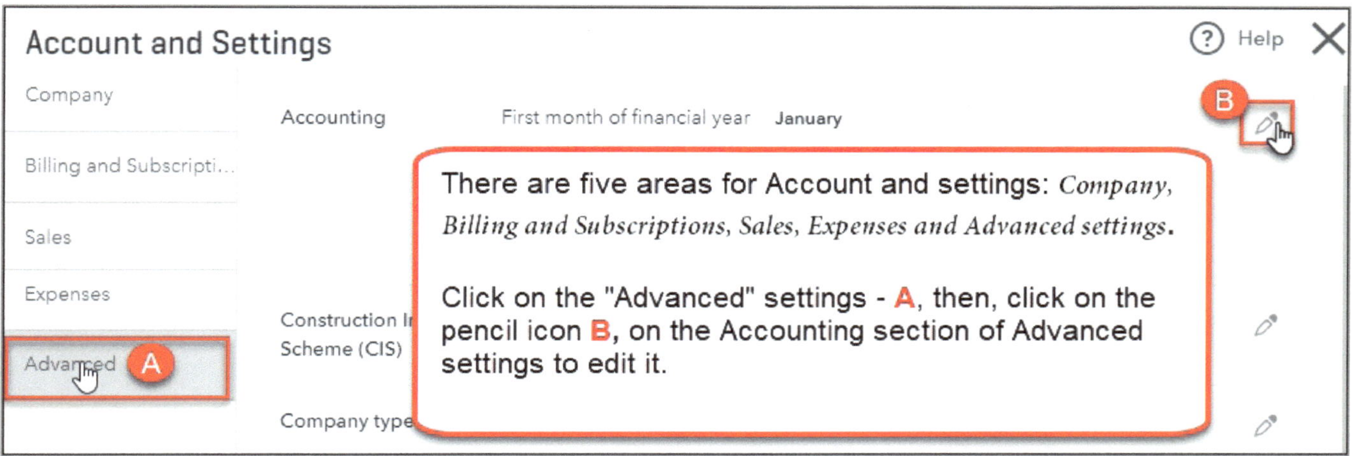

Fig. 14

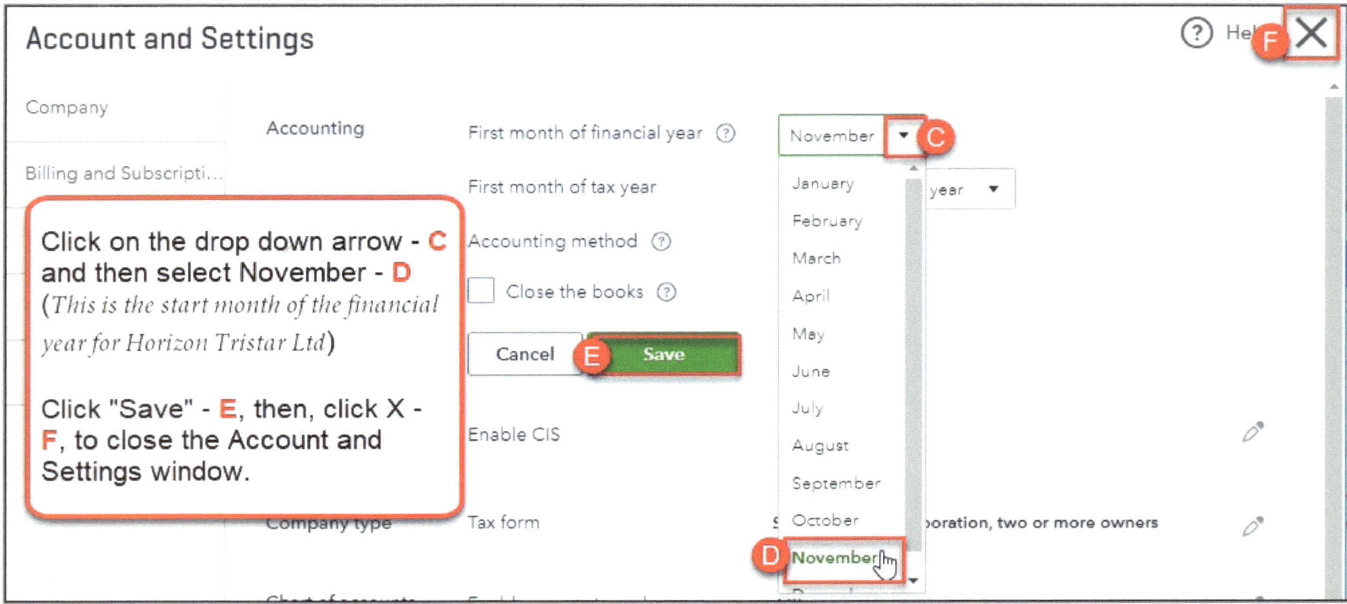

Fig. 15

Multicurrency

Trade nowadays is quite international, and that means having to deal with different currencies as a business buys and sells internationally. We are therefore going to set the multicurrency option in QuickBooks Online for Horizon Tristar Ltd.

To do so, go to the company settings – see figure 16 on the next page – see figure 16 on the next page

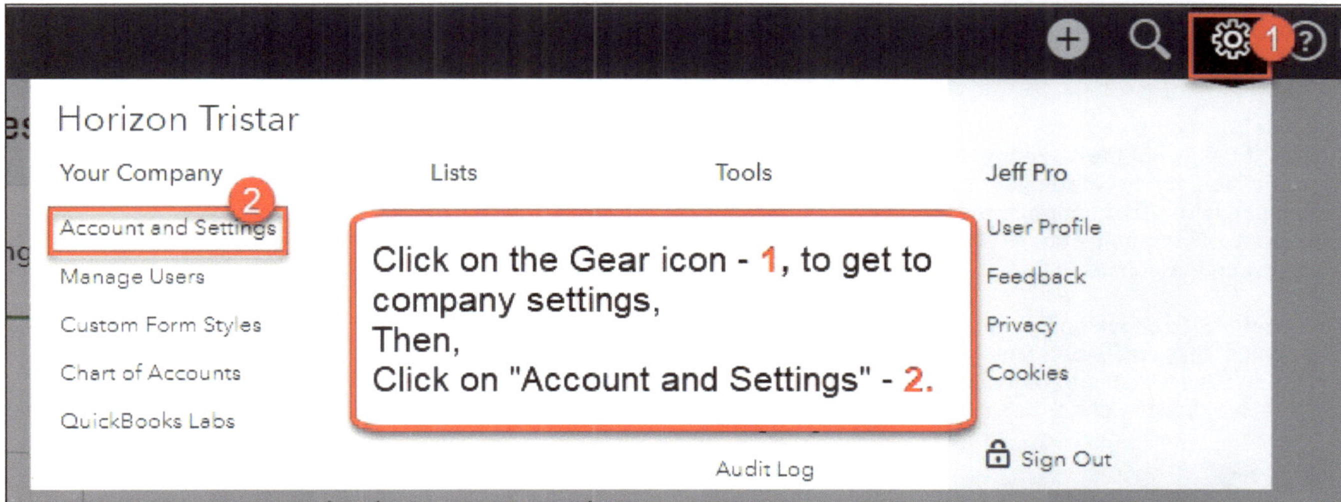

Fig. 16

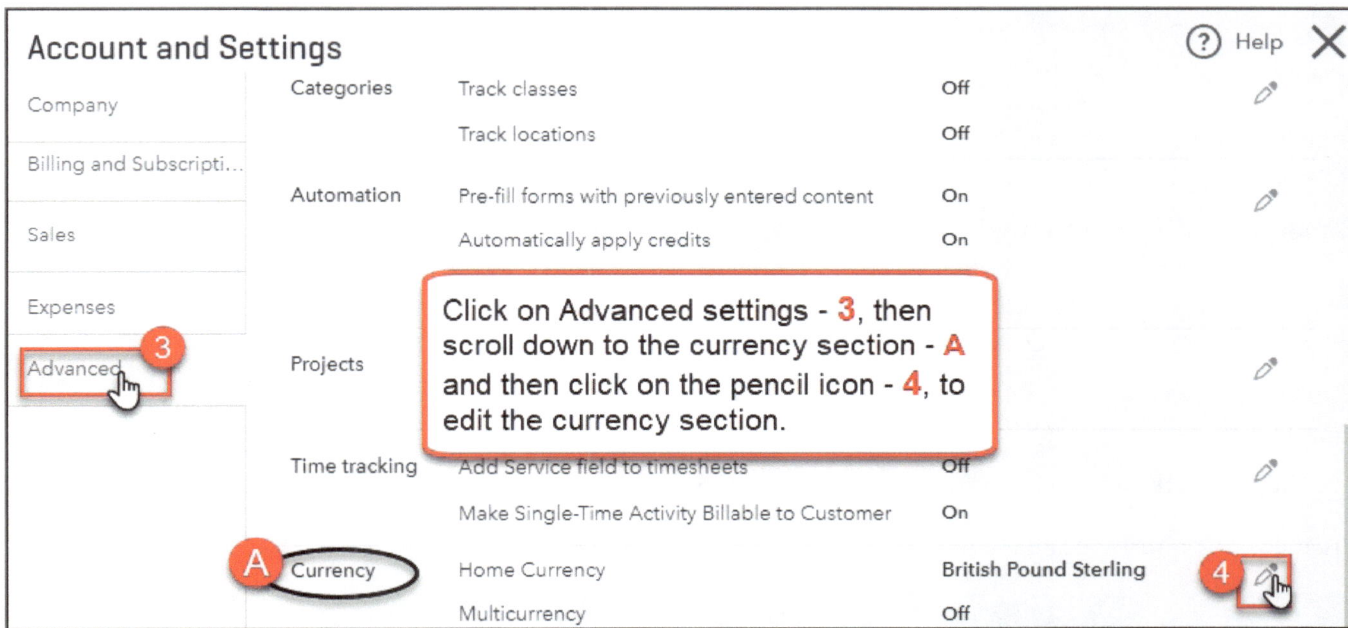

Fig. 17

This space is for notes

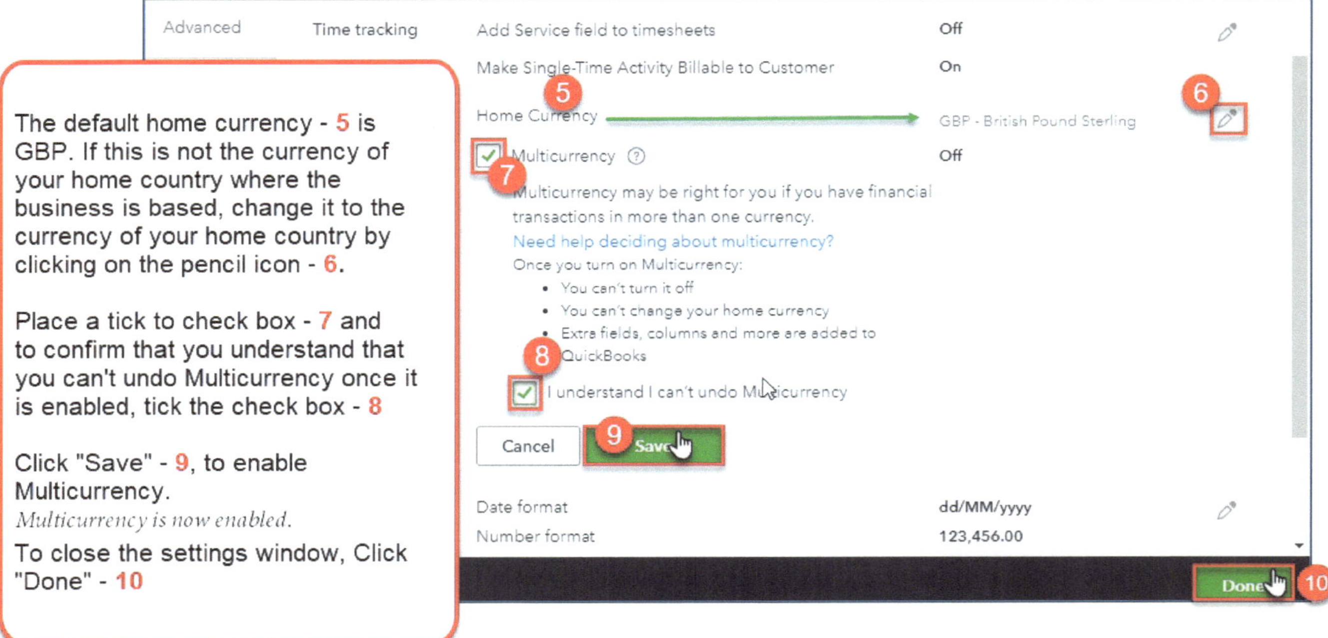

Fig. 18

The Multicurrency section of the set up is now done. Let's move next to looking at the VAT codes in QuickBooks Online.

Task 1a(ii). Understanding QuickBooks Online VAT Codes

Horizon Tristar Ltd is registered for VAT and therefore has to charge VAT at the standard rate on all its taxable goods and services.

To understand more about VAT rates, visit HMRC website on http://www.hmrc.gov.uk/vat/start/ to find out what rate of VAT applies in any particular set of circumstances.

To understand the VAT codes in QuickBooks Online, we have to first set up VAT in QuickBooks.

To do so, **Click on Taxes on the left navigation bar > then click on Set up VAT**

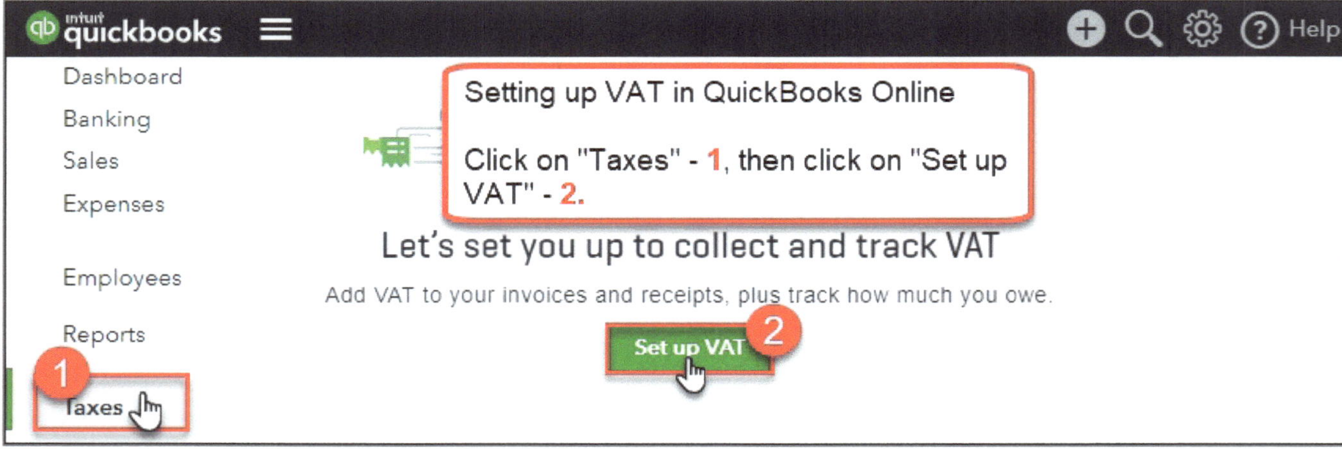

Fig. 19

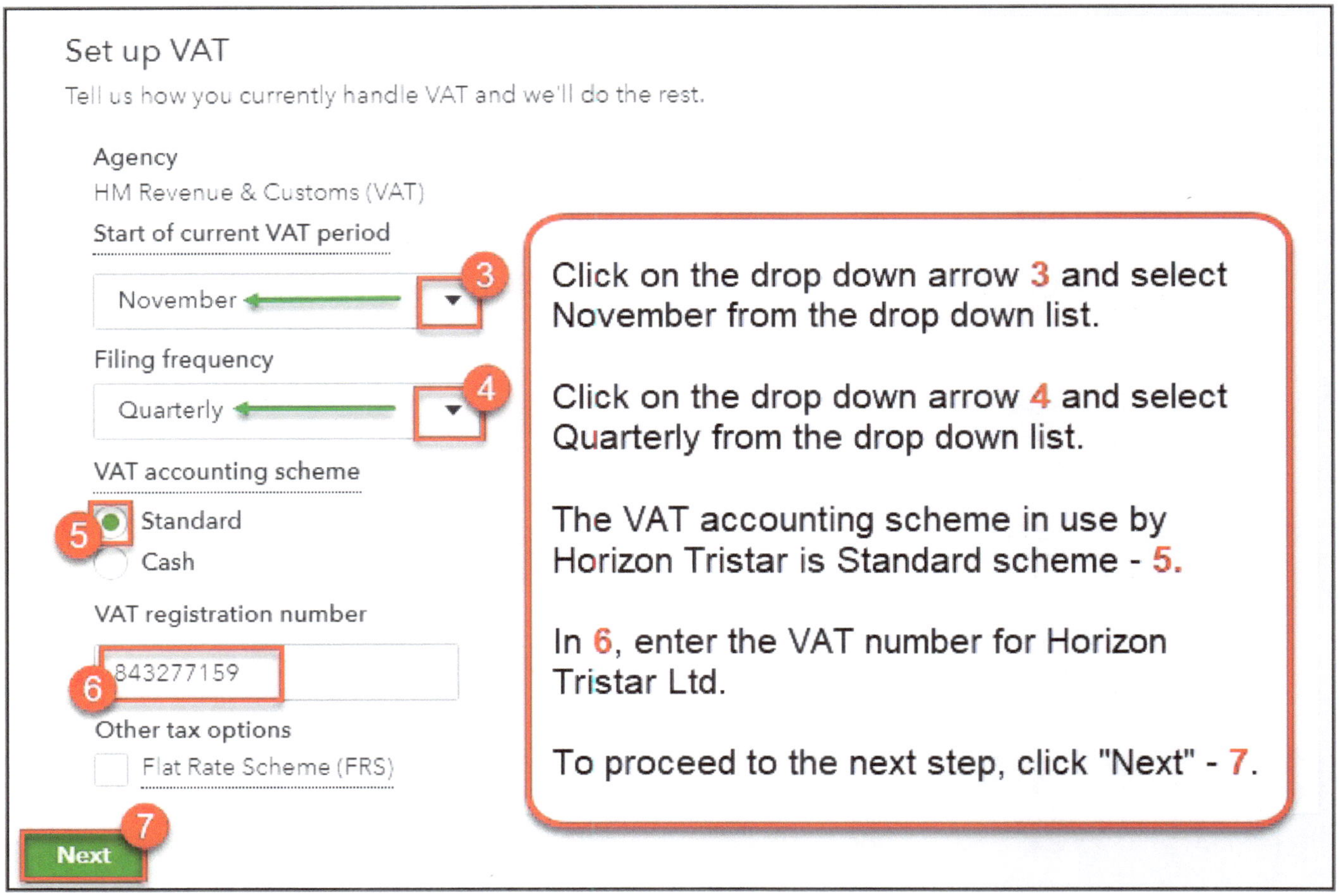

Set up VAT
Tell us how you currently handle VAT and we'll do the rest.
Agency
HM Revenue & Customs (VAT)
Start of current VAT period
November
3
Filing frequency
Quarterly
4
VAT accounting scheme
5
Standard
Cash
VAT registration number
6
843277159
Other tax options
Flat Rate Scheme (FRS)
7
Next
Click on the drop down arrow 3 and select November from the drop down list.
Click on the drop down arrow 4 and select Quarterly from the drop down list.
The VAT accounting scheme in use by Horizon Tristar is Standard scheme - 5.
In 6, enter the VAT number for Horizon Tristar Ltd.
To proceed to the next step, click "Next" - 7.

Fig. 20

Now you can add VAT to your transactions, and record your VAT payments in QuickBooks.
Visit the VAT page whenever you want to view your history, run reports, or track payments.
8
Got it
Click on "Got it" to proceed

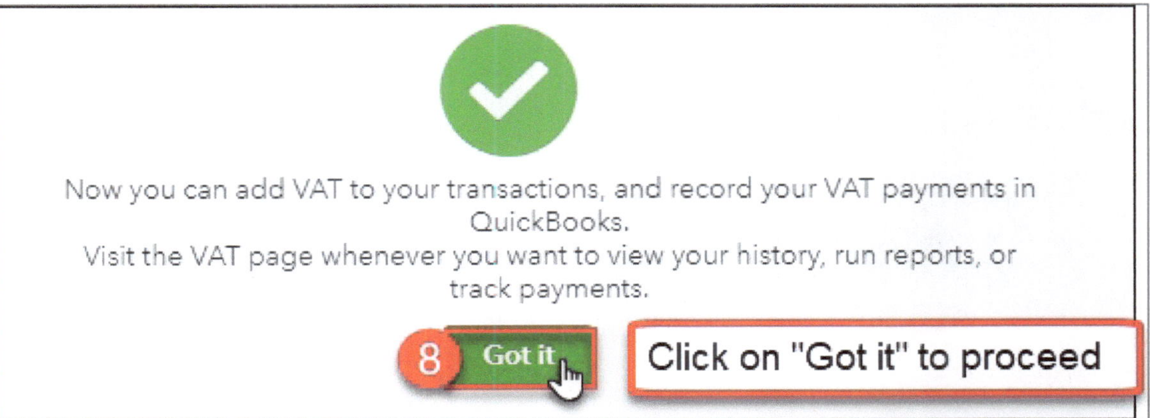

Fig. 21

This space is for notes

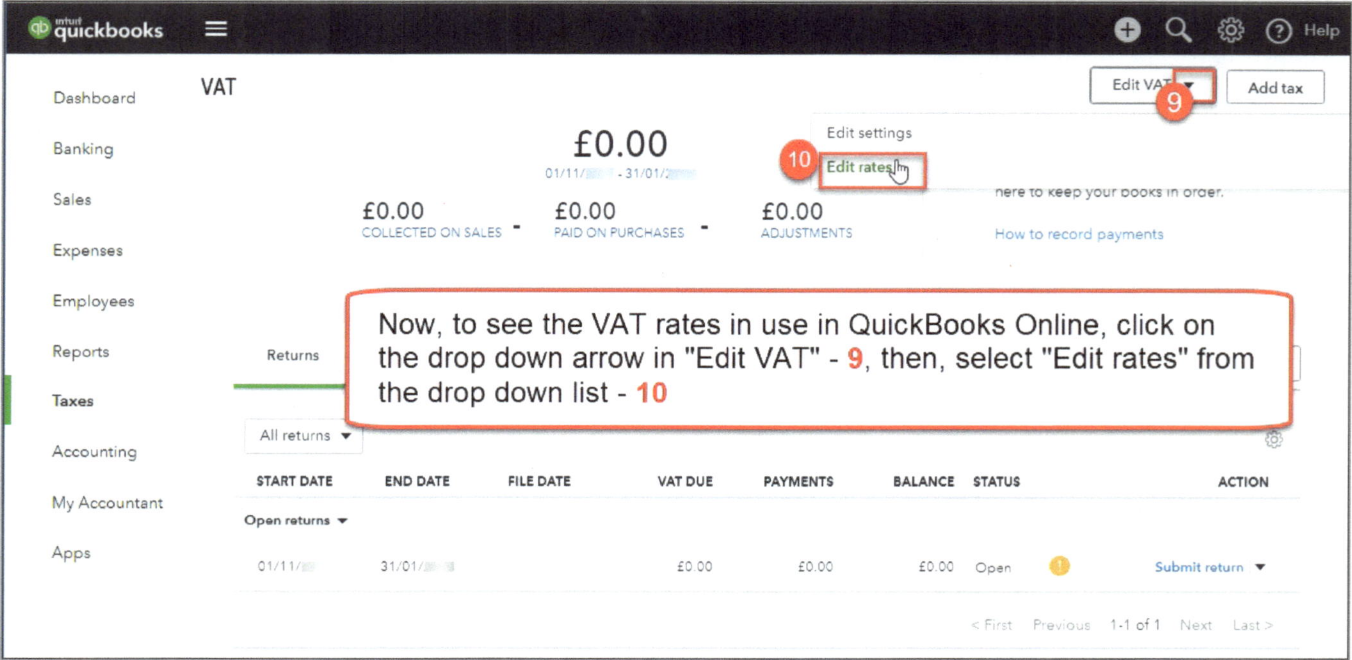

Fig. 22

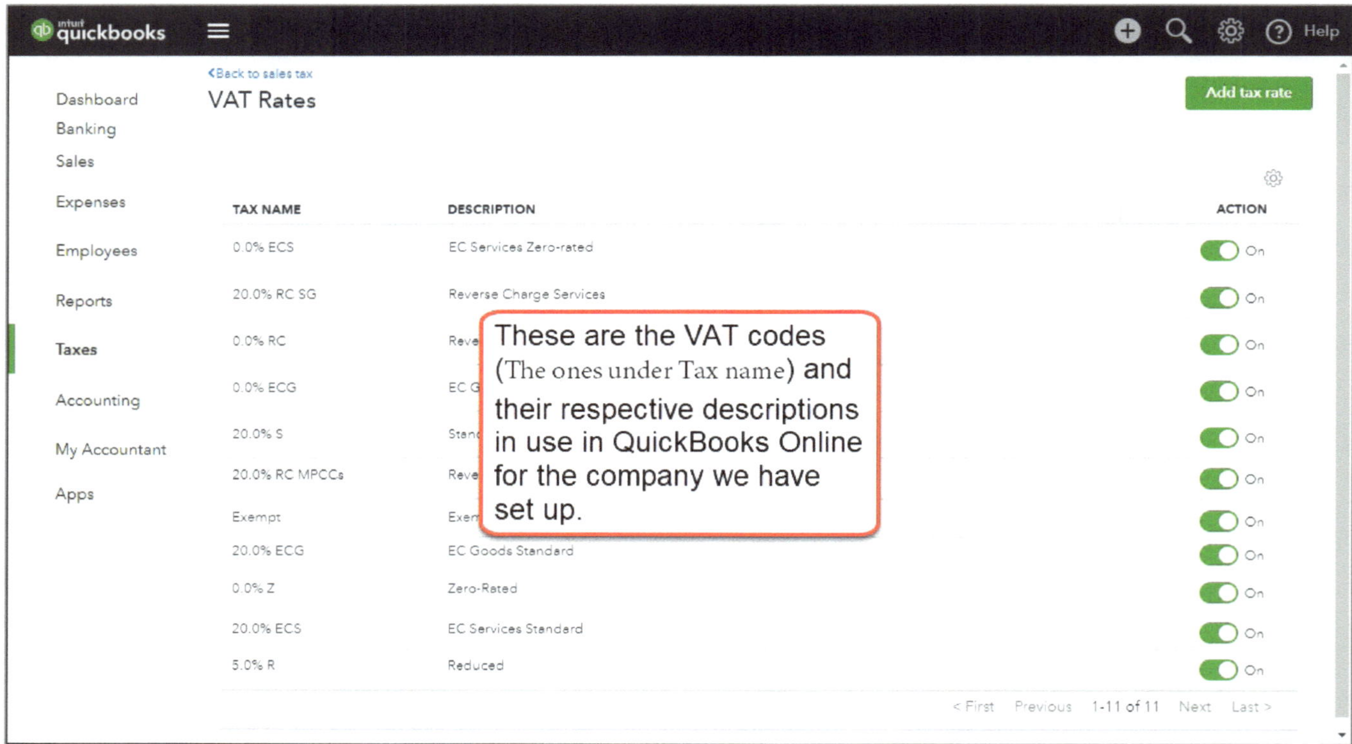

Fig. 23

The VAT setup is now complete. Let's move on to QuickBooks chart of accounts next.

Task 1a(iii). Understanding QuickBooks Online chart of accounts

Chart of Accounts is the complete list of all the company's accounts and balances. In QuickBooks, it represents and organises the company's assets, liabilities, income, and expense.
QuickBooks Online automatically creates your Chart of Accounts based on the type of company/business you choose when creating your company file.

Let's have a look at the chart of accounts for the company we created – Horizon Tristar Ltd.

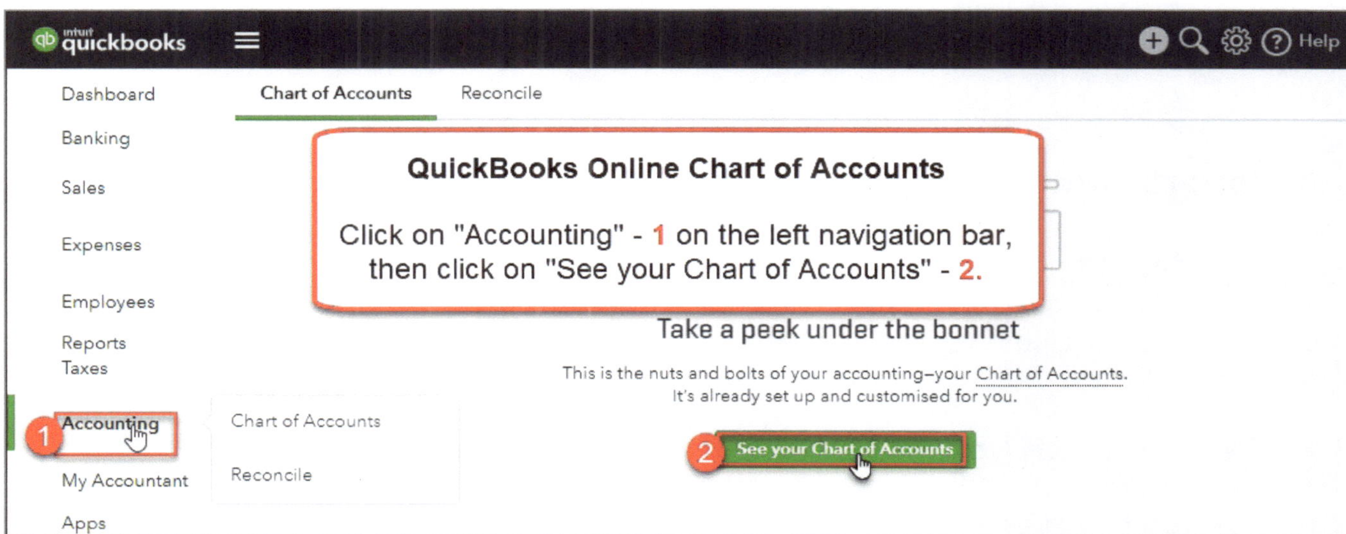

Fig. 24

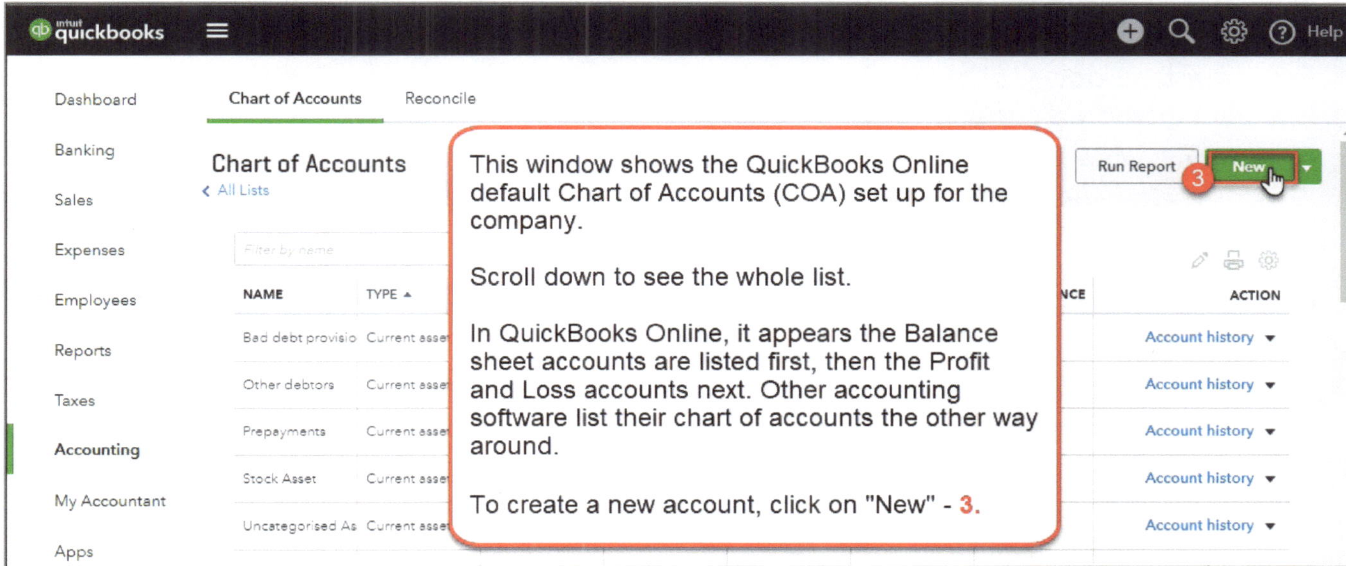

Fig. 25

Here are some new accounts you need to create:

- ✓ The Company Current Bank Account
- ✓ Petty Cash Account
- ✓ The bank Deposit Account
- ✓ Income/Sales account for Office furniture, Office equipment and Consumables

The Company Current Bank Account

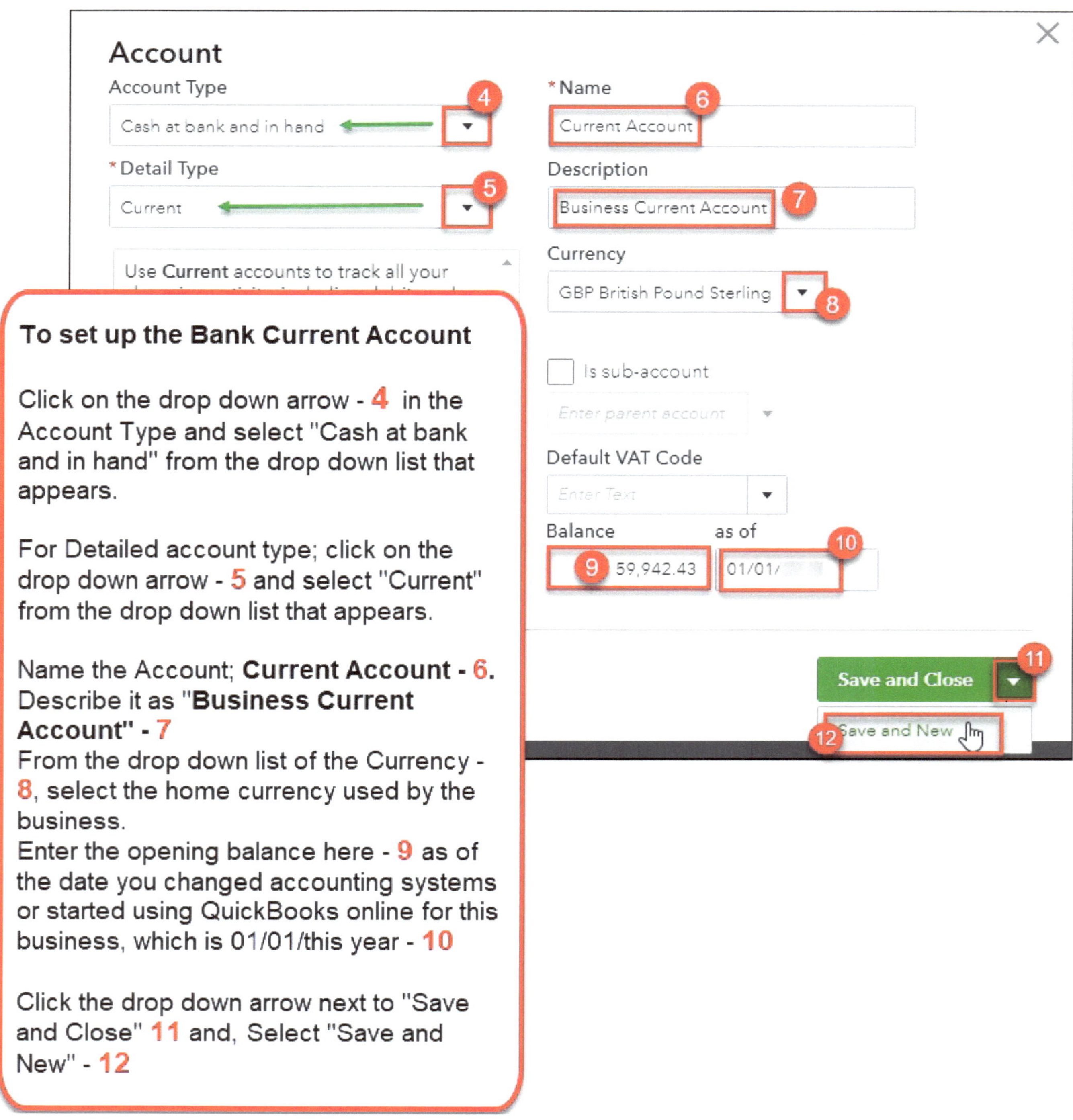

Fig. 26

Next is Petty Cash Account.

Petty Cash Account

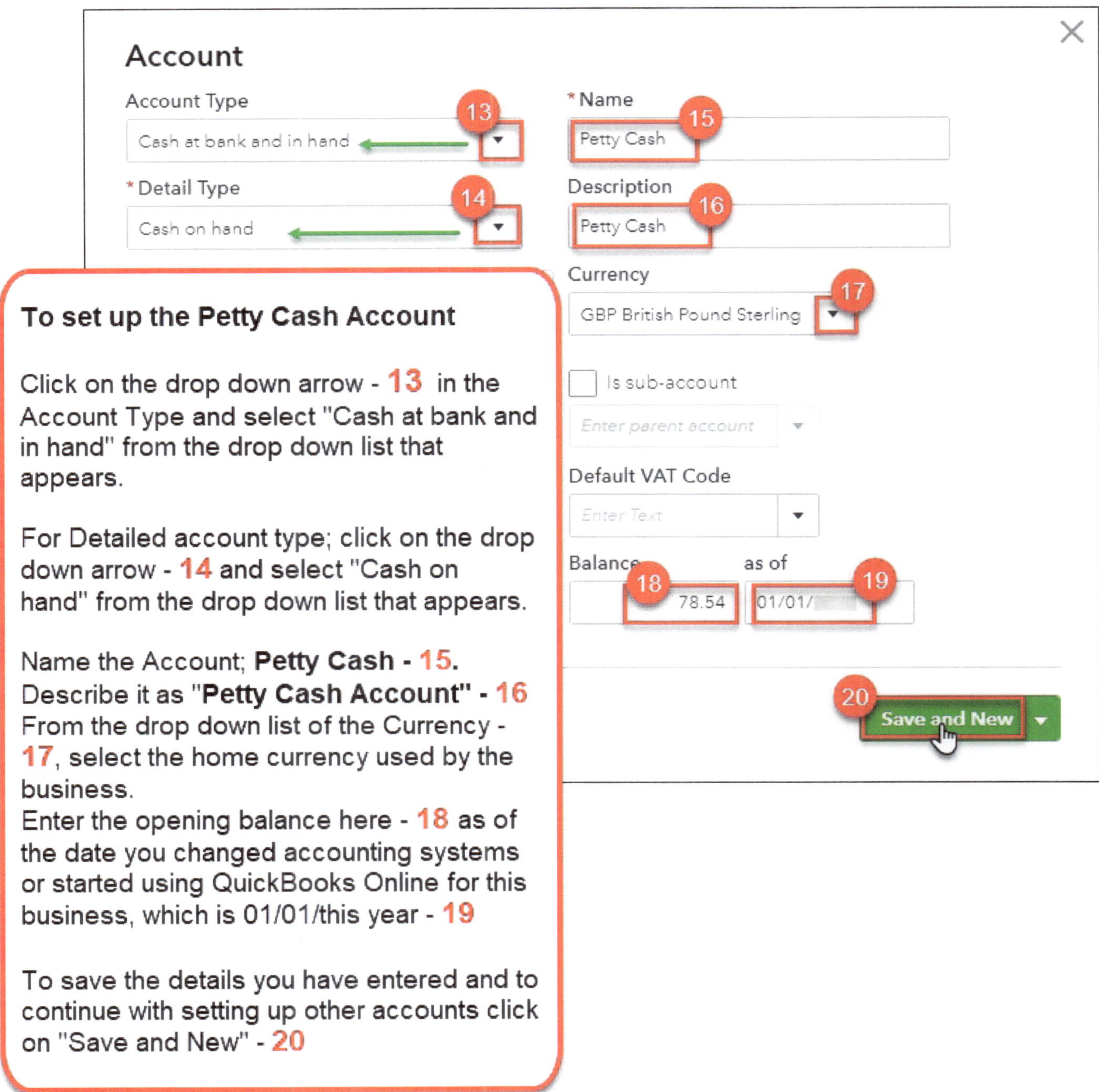

Fig. 27

This space is for notes

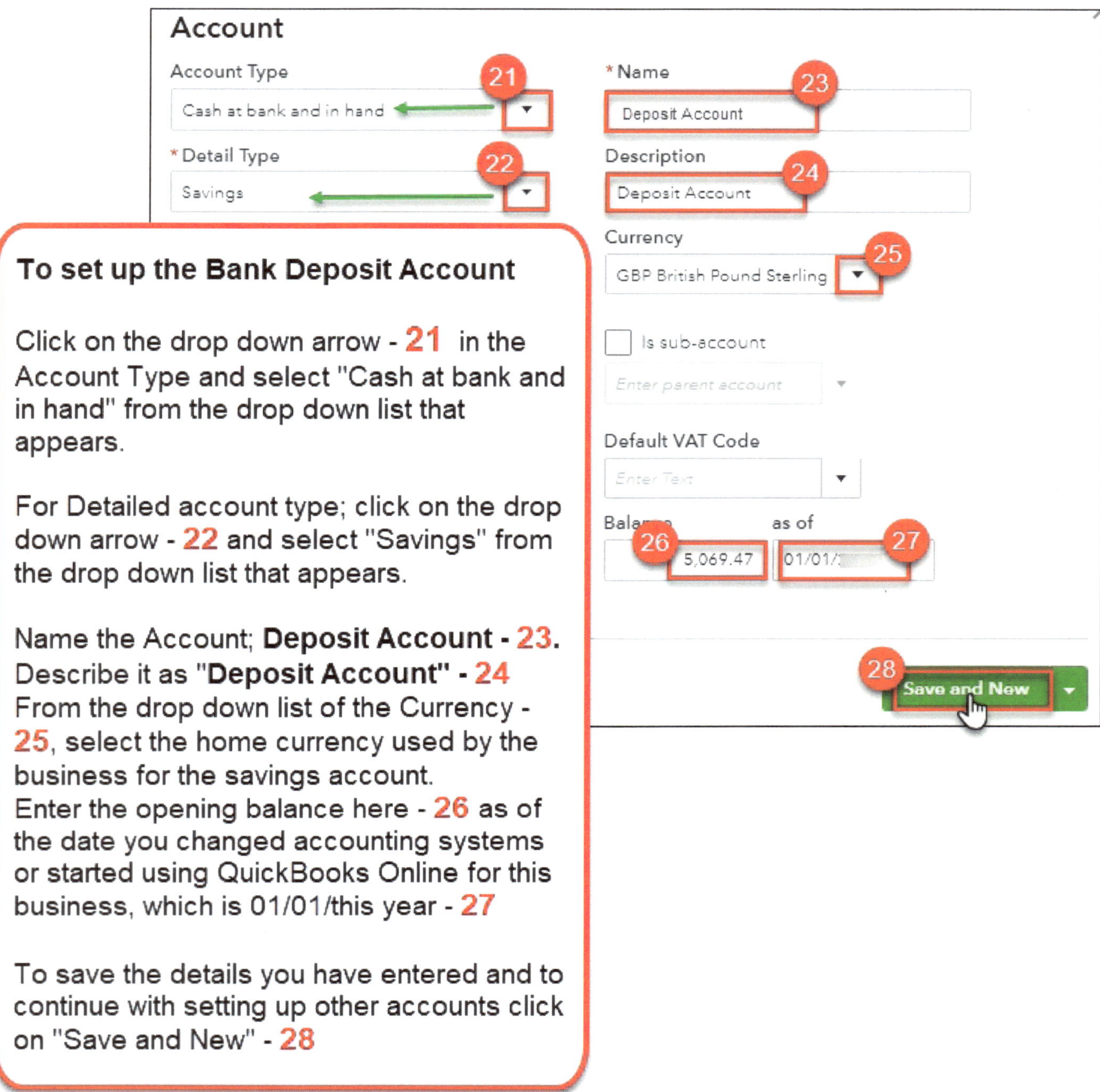

Fig. 28

Current Account, Petty Cash Account and Bank Deposit Account done. If you needed to create a credit card account and Savings account, you would follow the same steps as above making sure you keep Account type as Cash at bank and in hand and changing all the other entries as required.

Let's move on to creating new accounts for income.

This space is for notes

Income Accounts:

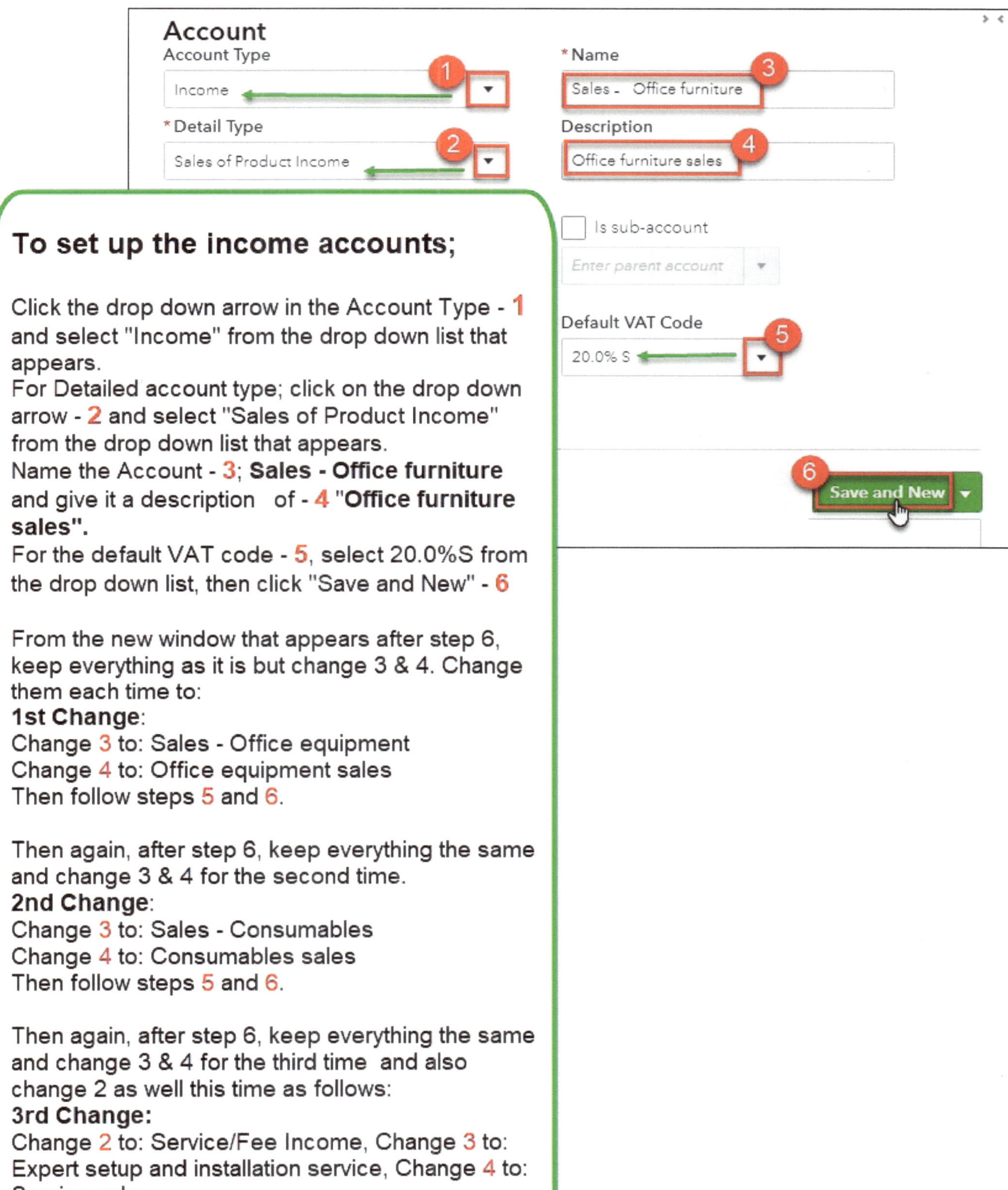

Fig. 29

Task 1b: Setting up Customers & Suppliers

Task 1b(i): Setting up Customers and corresponding opening balances

You can add Customers in QuickBooks online in two ways:

1. Add them directly as shown in the figure below
   or
2. Upload them using a csv template that has the customer details you want to add to QuickBooks Online.

The direct way of adding a Customer to QuickBooks Online is as illustrated in the figure below.

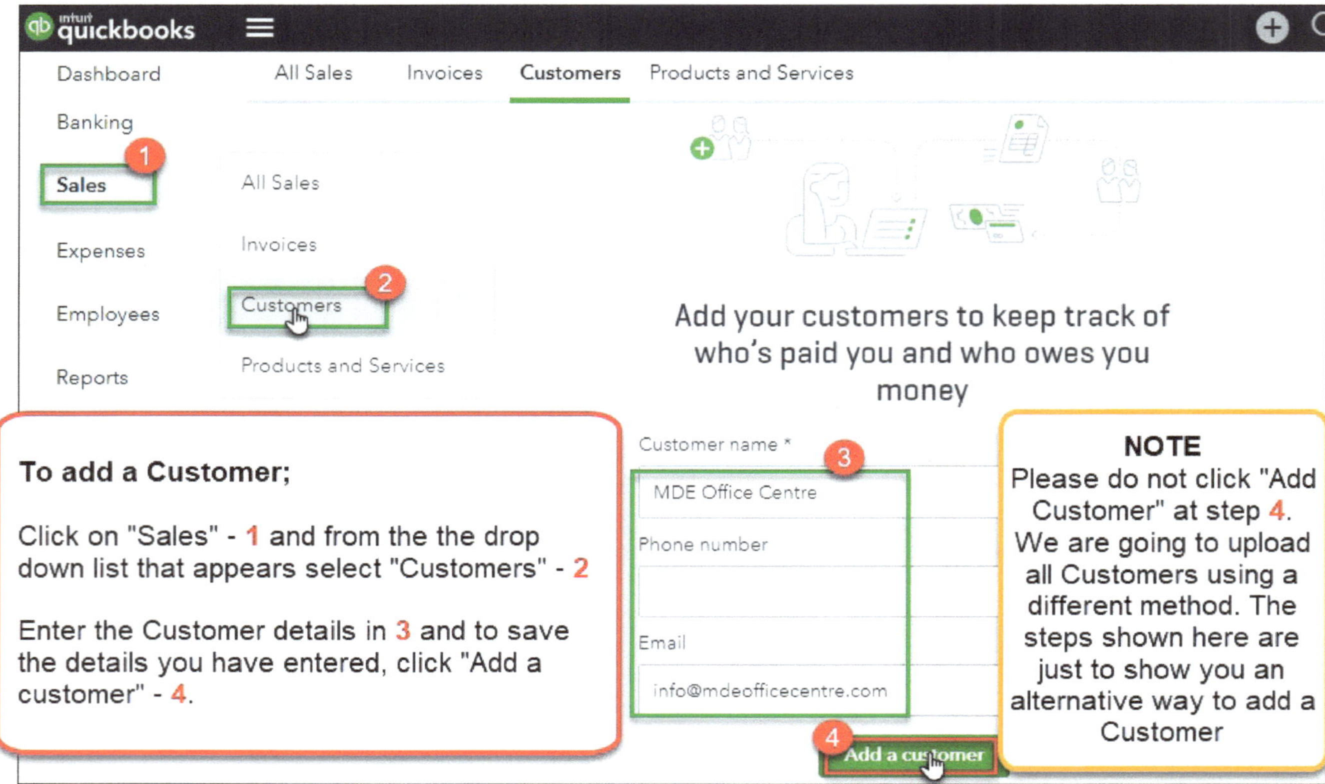

Fig. 30

Let's now look at an alternative way to add a customer to QuickBooks Online – the second option in our tutorial.

The second option is much faster and enables you to add more details about the customer at once. So, we will be using the second method, but I will also show you how to use the first method.

This space is for notes

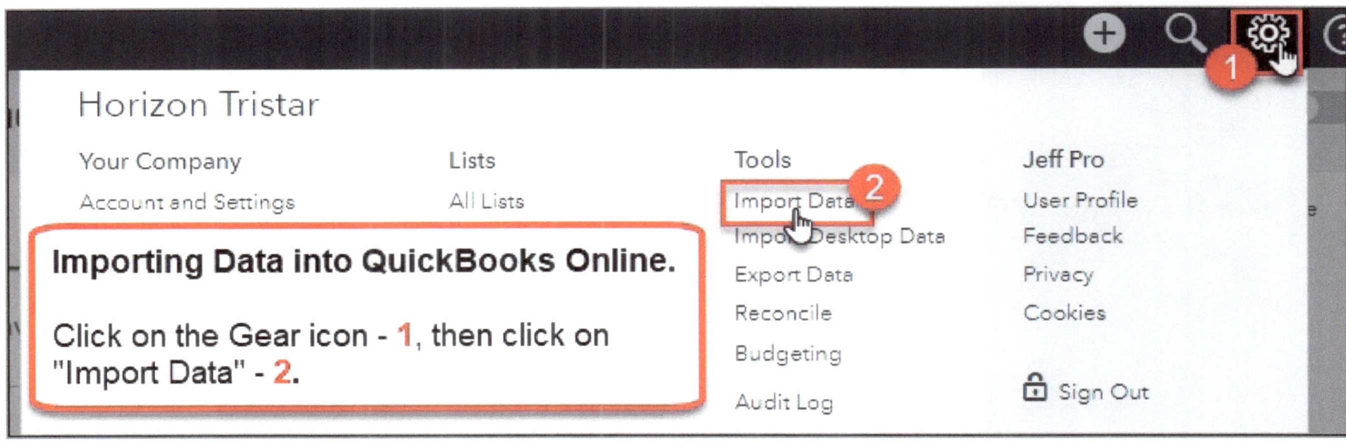

Fig. 31

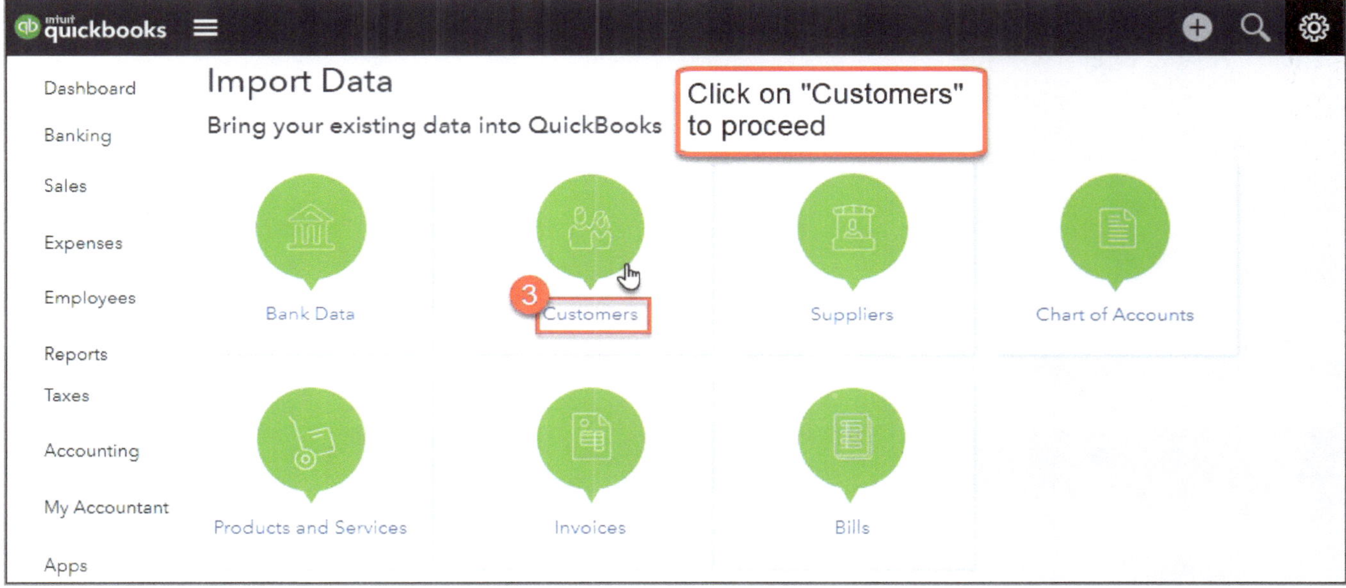

Fig.32

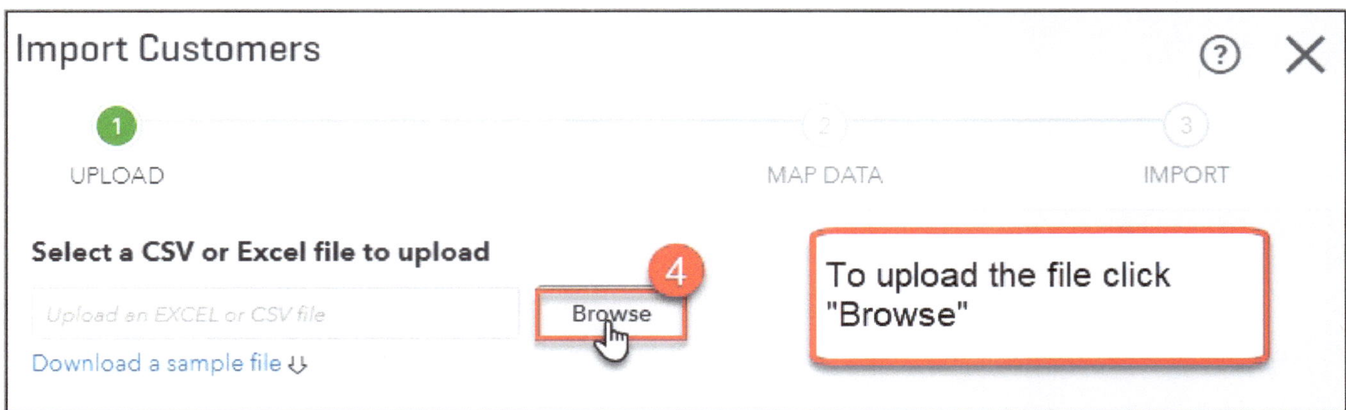

Fig. 33

This PC › Desktop
Search Desktop
Organize
New folder
Desktop
Downloads
Documents
Pictures
Horizon Tristar
Music
This PC
Network
Name
Grammarly
Horizon - QuickBooks_Online_Customer_File
Horizon - QuickBooks_Online_Supplier details_File
Horizon -QuickBooks_Online_products n services_Fi
Kindle Previewer 3
File name: Horizon - QuickBooks_Online_Customer_File
Open
Cancel
To upload the file;
Where is the Customer details file saved on your computer? Select it - 5. In this case the file was saved on the desktop (Yours could be a different location)
Click on the file once you've located it - 6, and then click "Open" - 7

Fig. 34

Import Customers
UPLOAD
MAP DATA
IMPORT
Select a CSV or Excel file to upload
Abacus - QuickBooks_Online_Customer_File.xls
Browse
Download a sample file
Once the file is uploaded, click "Next" to proceed to the next step.
Cancel
Next

Fig. 35

This space is for notes

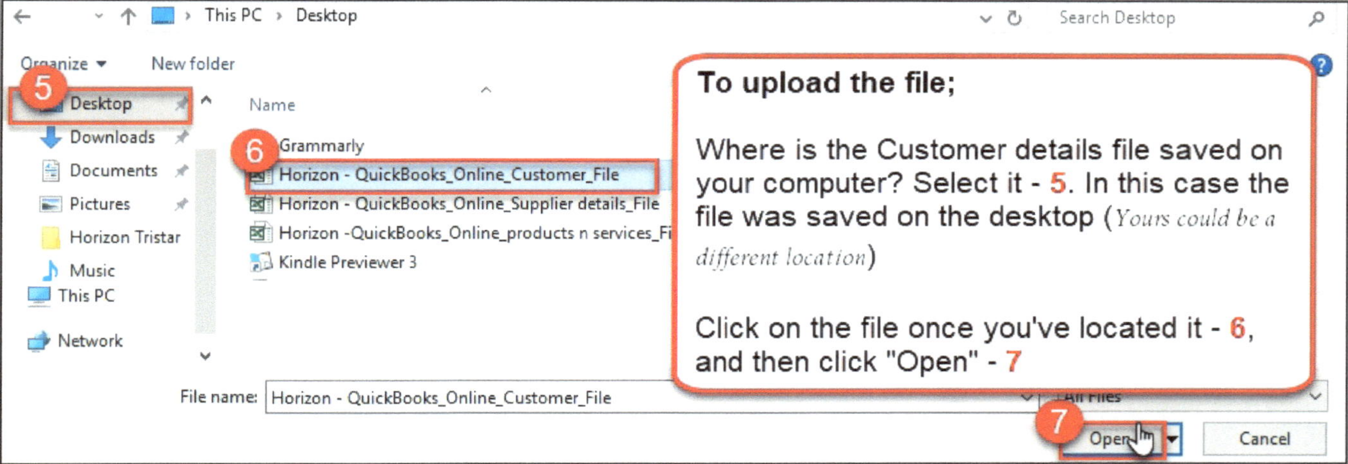

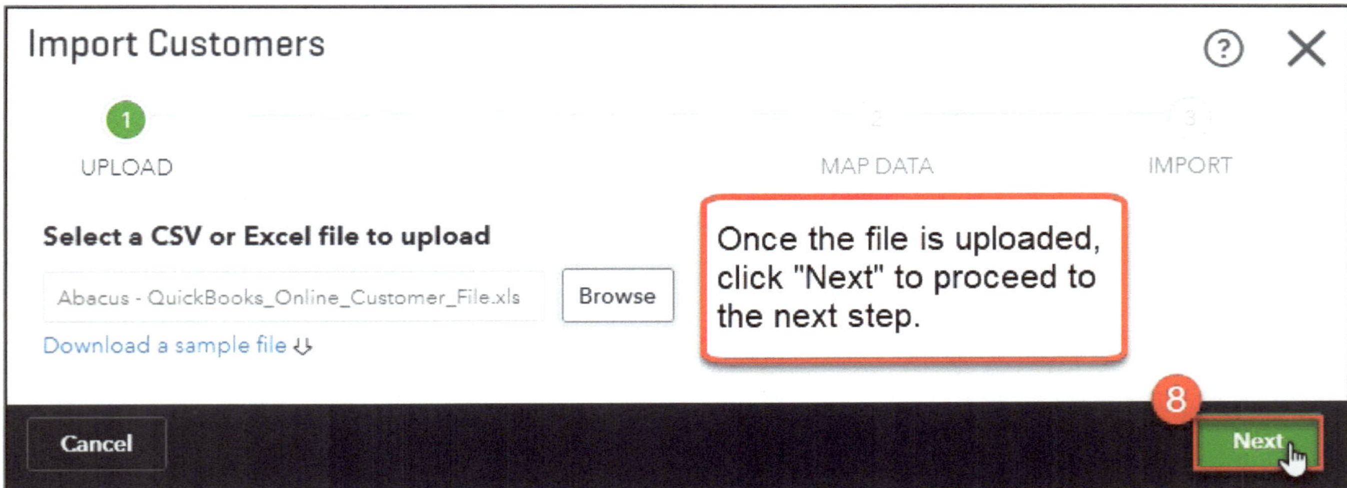

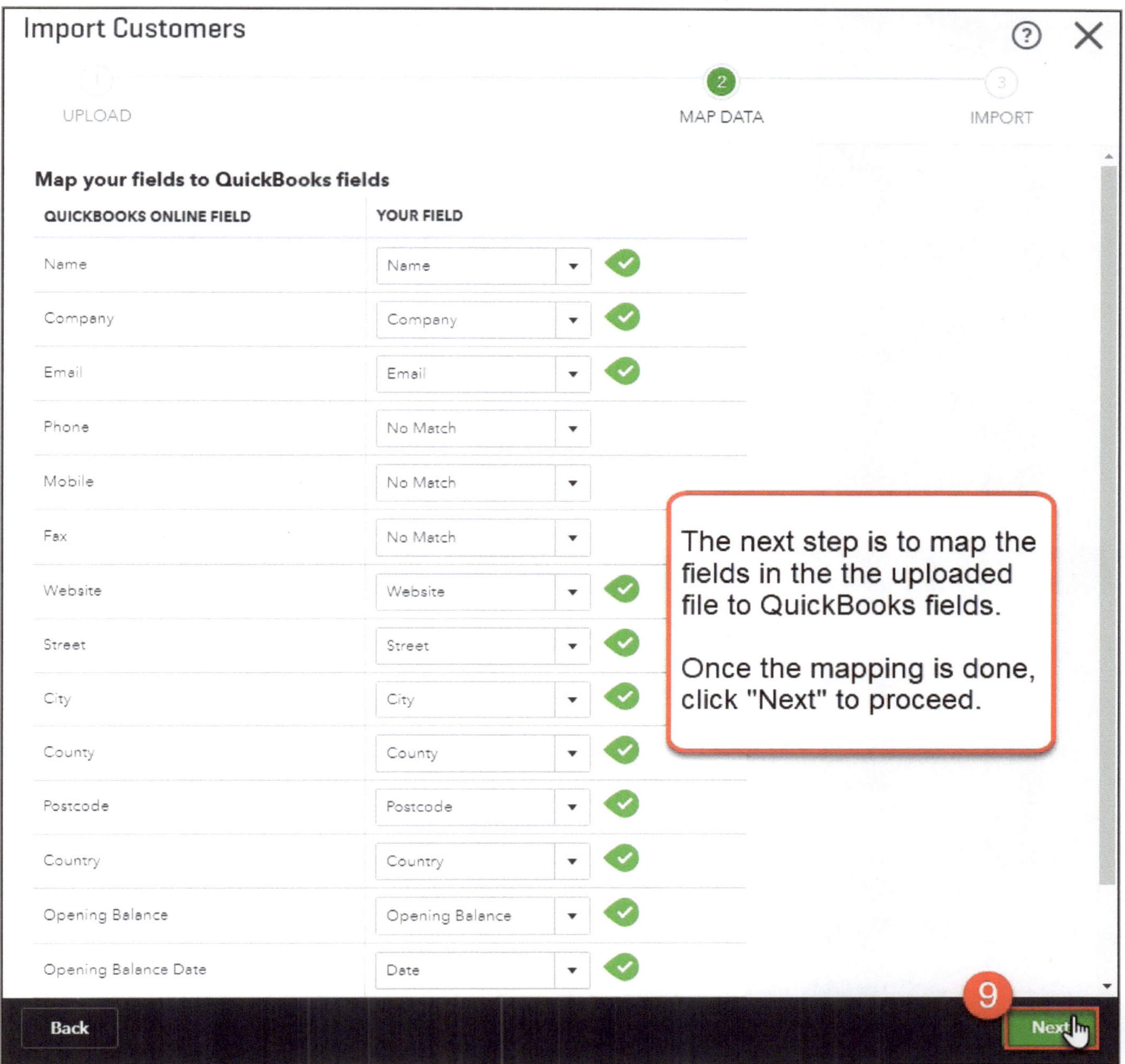

Fig. 36

This space is for notes

Import Customers
UPLOAD
MAP DATA
IMPORT
7 customers are ready to be imported
NAME
COMPANY
EMAIL
WEBSITE
STREET
CITY
COUNTY
POSTCODE
COUNTRY
CURRENCY
10. Write the date in the format: YYYY-MM-DD. In this work experience, that will be:
This year-01-01
11. Click "Import" to complete the customer import process.
Back
Import

Fig. 37

Dashboard
Banking
Sales
Expenses
Employees
Reports
Taxes
Accounting
My Accountant
Import Data
7 of 7 customers successfully imported.
Bring your existing data into QuickBooks
All Sales
Invoices
Customers
Products and Services
To see your new list of imported Customers;
Hover your mouse on "Sales" - 12, then select "Customers" - 13 from the drop down list that appears.
Products and Services
Invoices
Bills

Fig. 38

This space is for notes

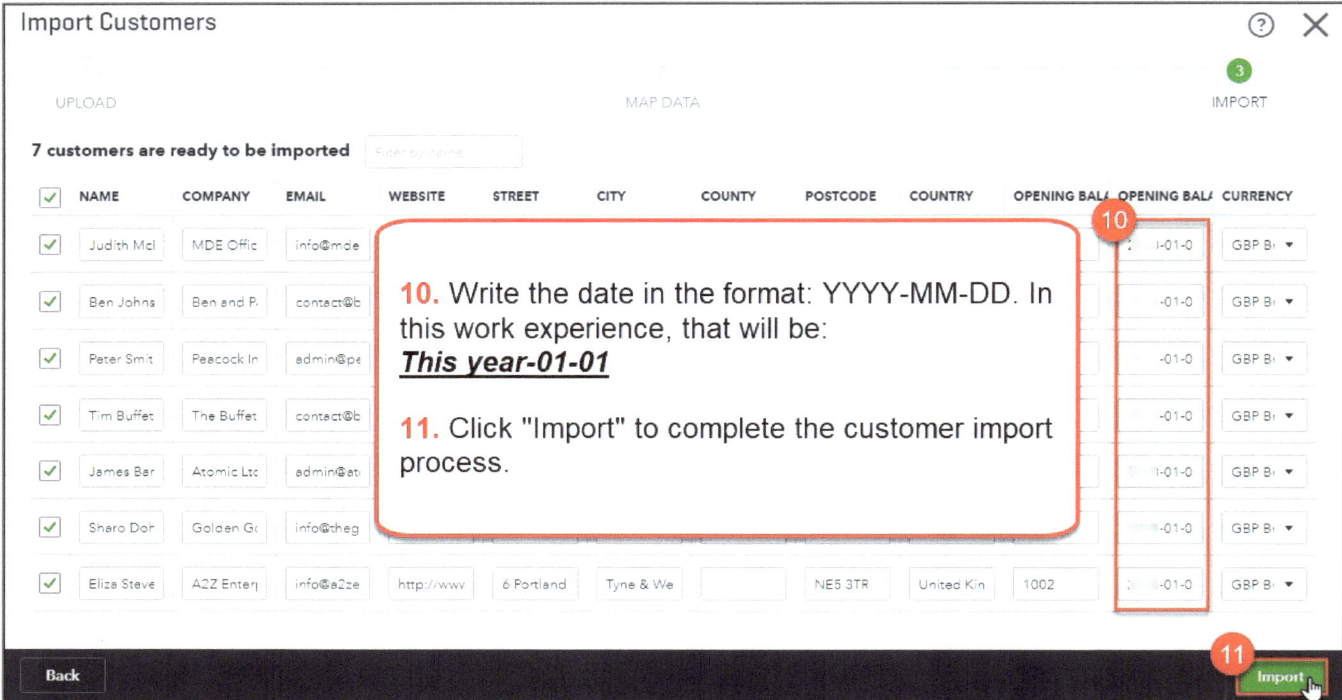

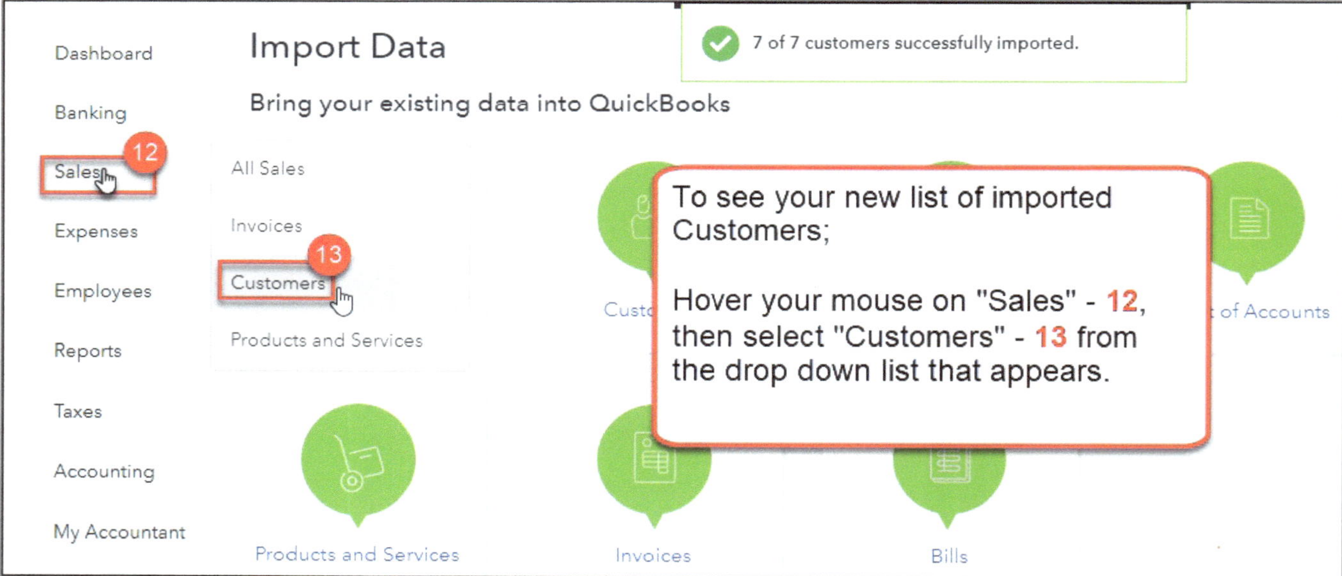

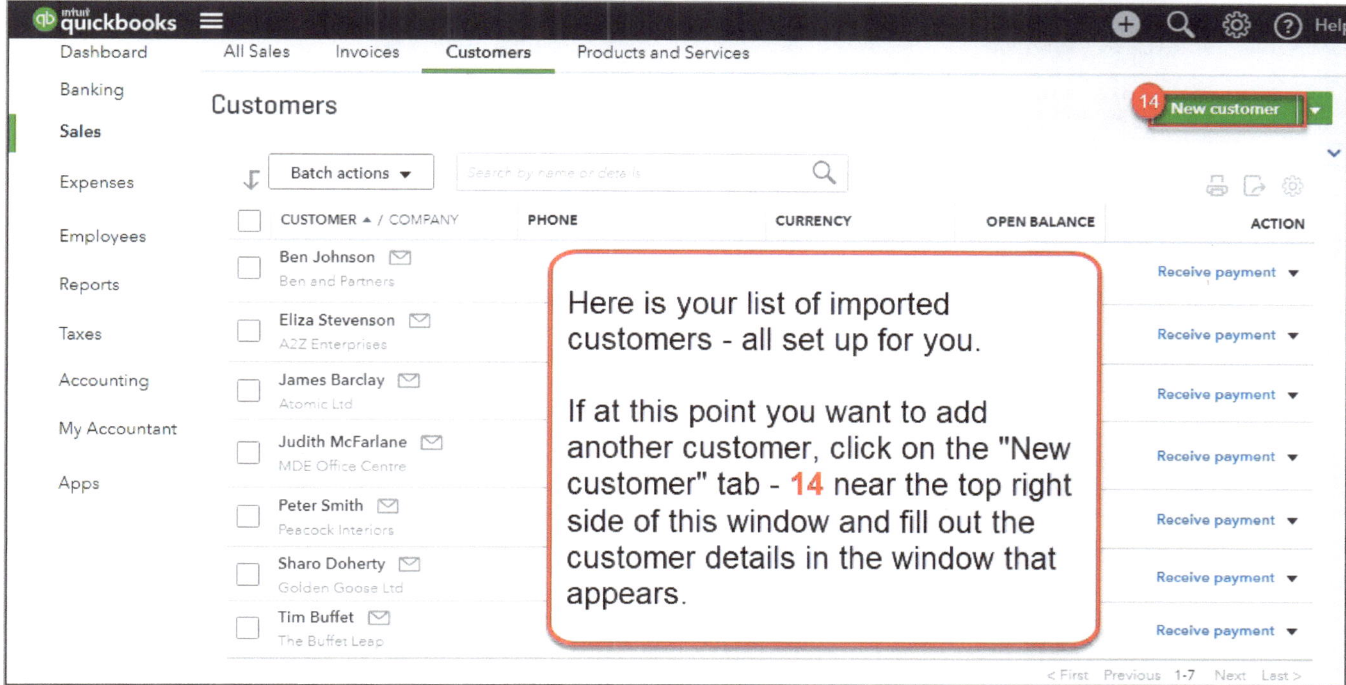

Fig. 39

Please note that when you import Customers to QuickBooks Online the way we have just done, QuickBooks puts the contact persons for each of the Customers you set up as the display names for those respective Customers. It does not pick up the Business names and puts them as display names. So, we will need to edit the Customers details so that the display names reflect the Company/Business name instead of the Customers contact persons name.

Editing Customer details:

The display name for the customers at this point is the Customer contact person. We need to change the display name to the Company name to make it easier later to invoice the customers through the create button.

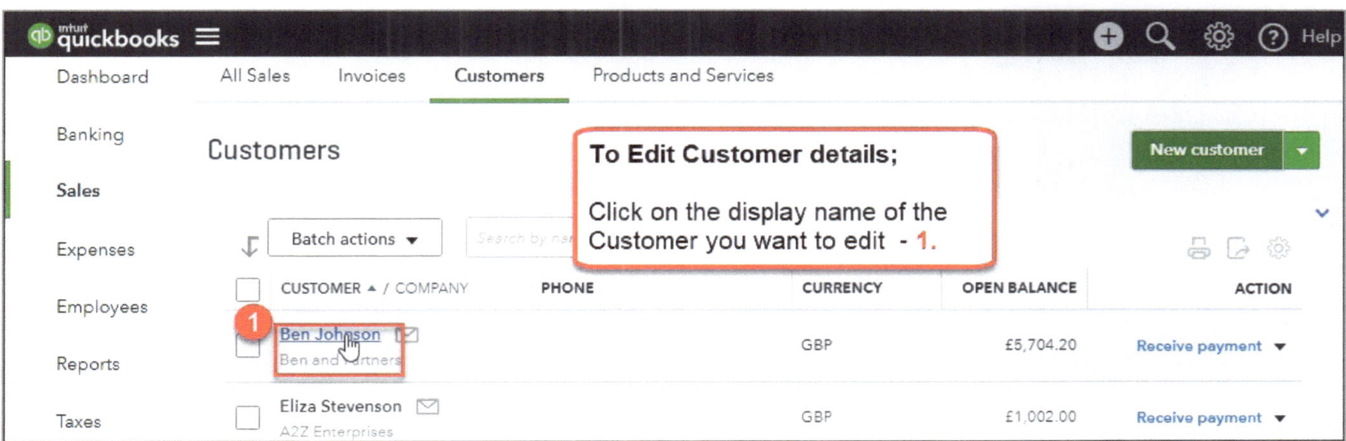

Fig. 40

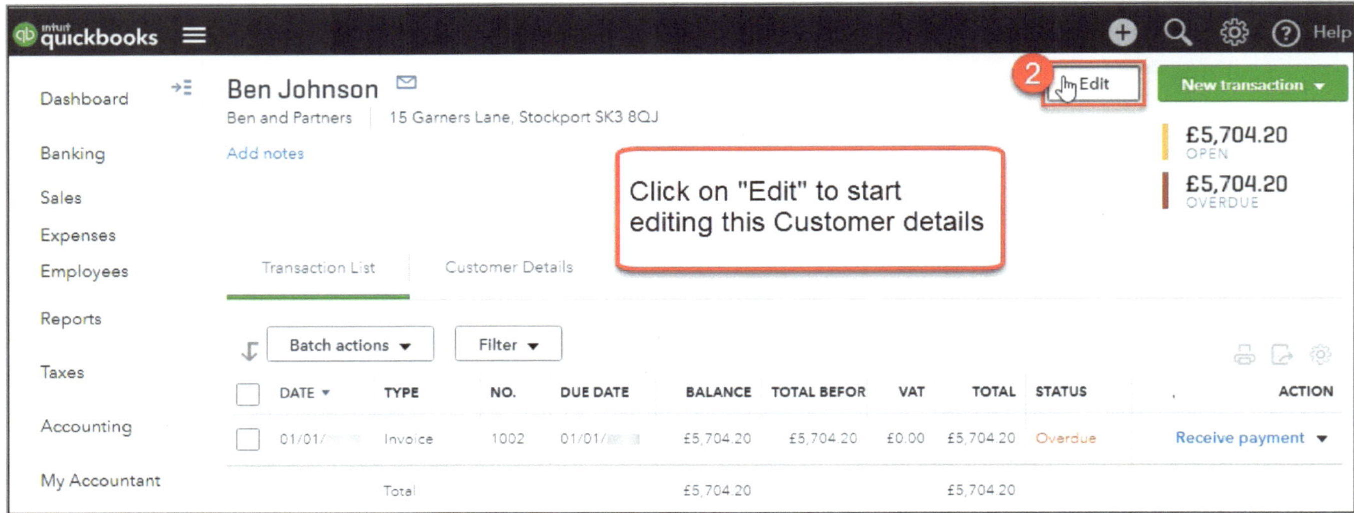

Fig. 41

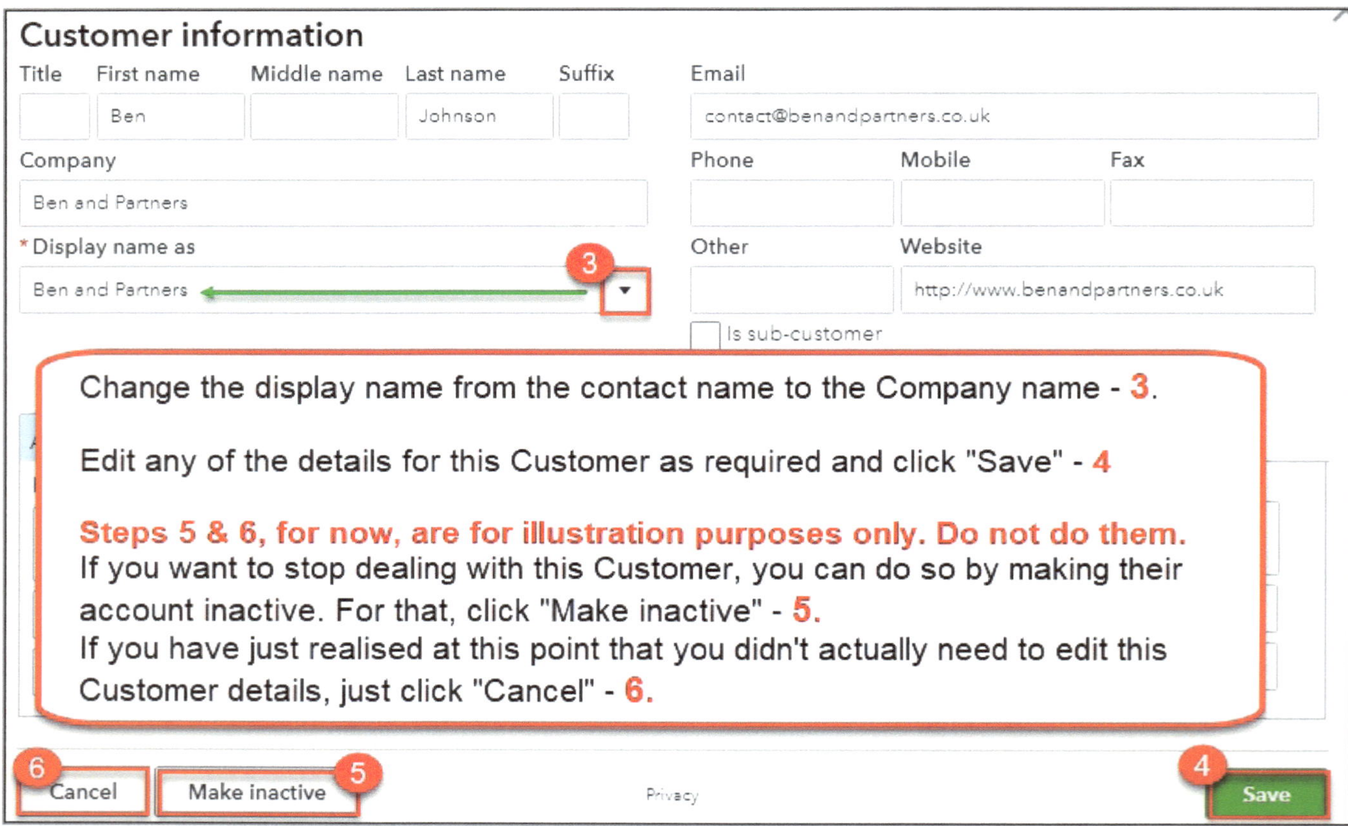

Fig. 42

Please go ahead and edit the display names for the rest of the other Customers. Do not proceed to the next task before editing the display names for all the Customers.

Task 1b(ii): Setting up Suppliers and corresponding opening balances

You can add Suppliers in QuickBooks online in two ways:

i. Add them directly, or,
ii. Upload them using a csv template that has the Suppliers details you want to add to QuickBooks Online.

The direct way of adding a Supplier to QuickBooks Online is as illustrated in the figure below.

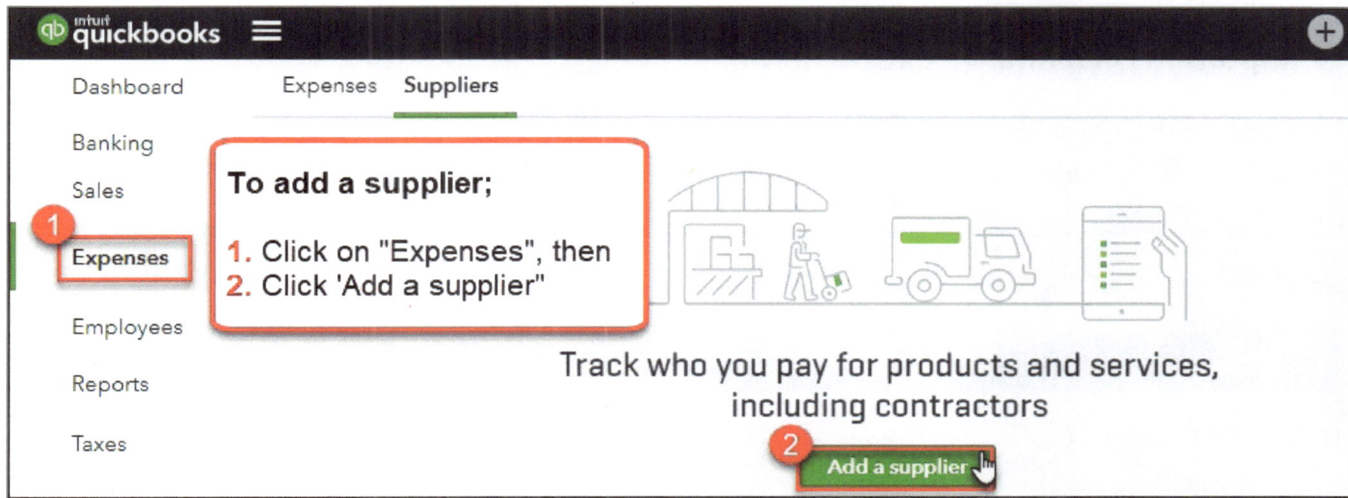

Fig. 43

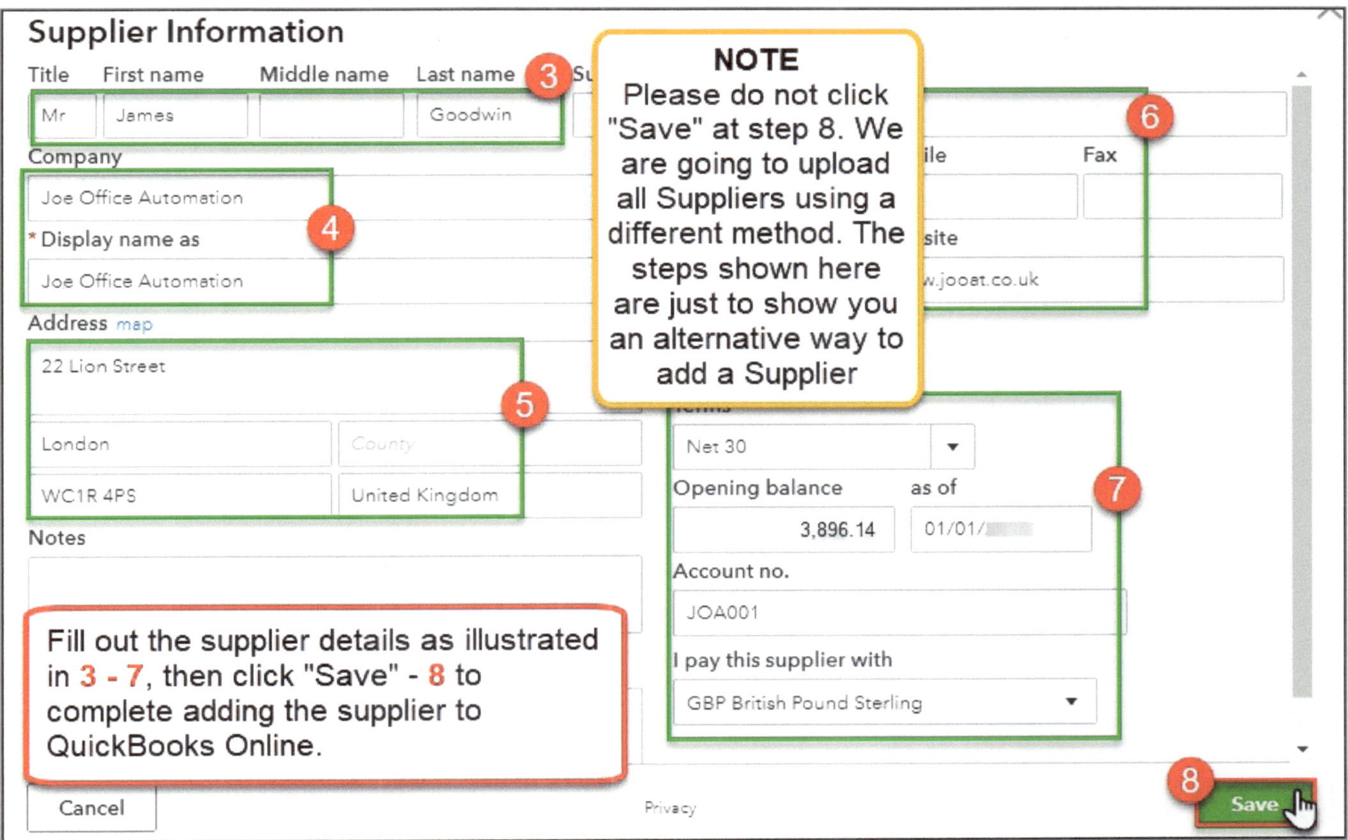

Fig. 44

The second option is much faster and enables you to add more suppliers at once. So, let's do it.

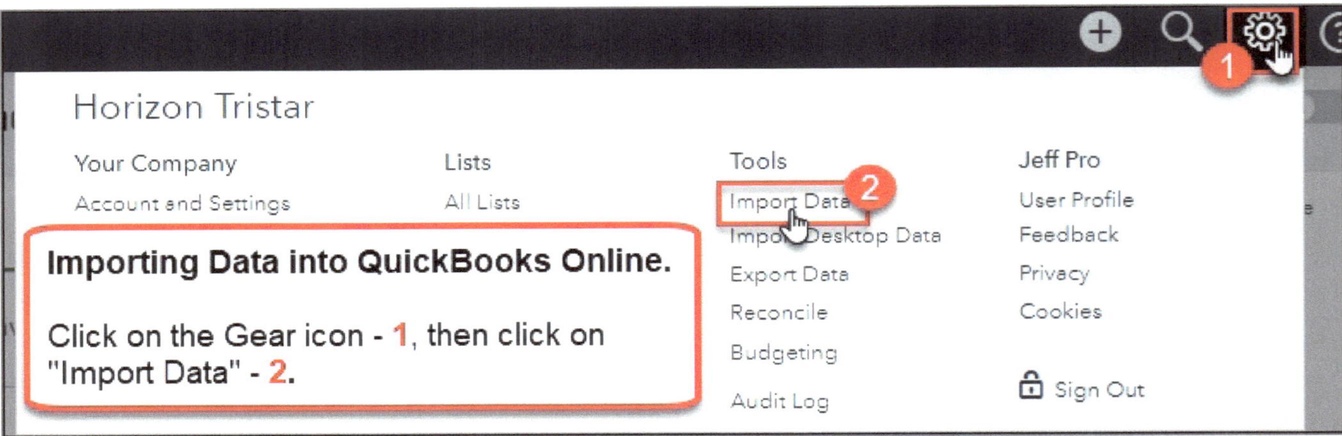

Fig. 45

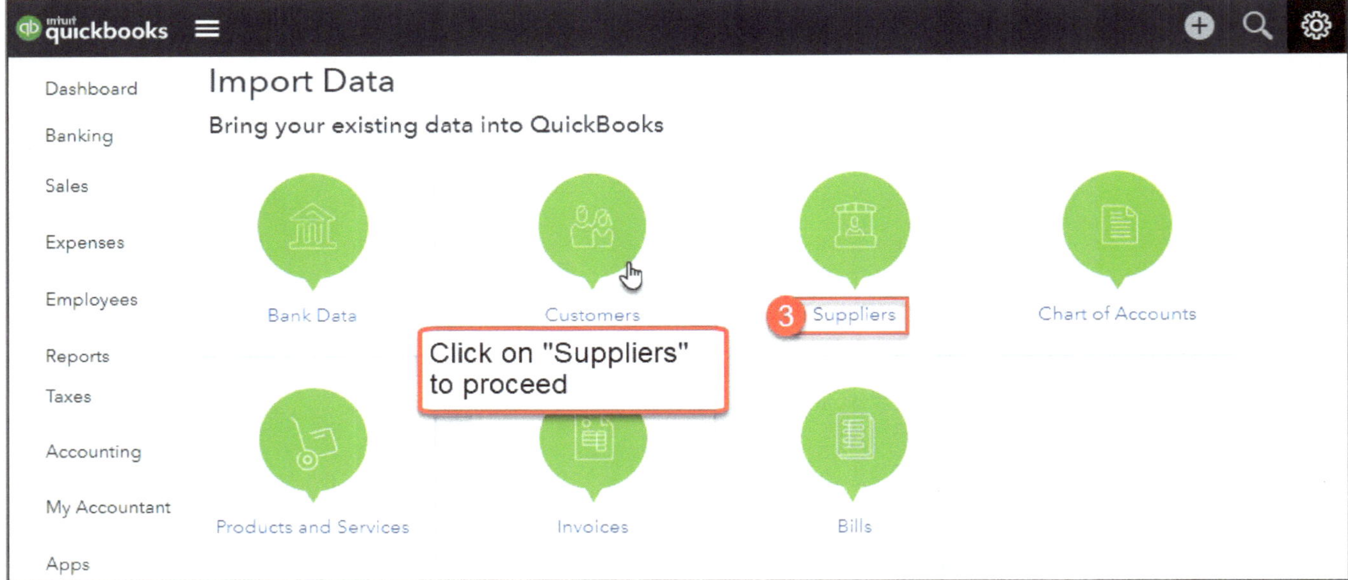

Fig. 46

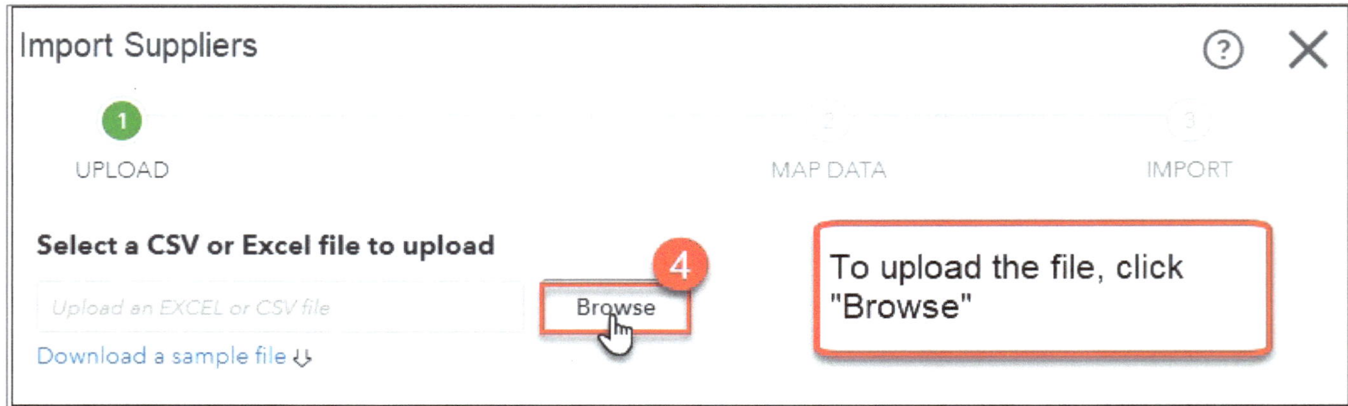

Fig. 47

This PC > Desktop
Search Desktop
Organize
New folder
5
Desktop
Downloads
Documents
Pictures
Horizon Tristar
Music
This PC
Network
Name
Grammarly
Horizon - QuickBooks_Online_Customer_File
6
Horizon - QuickBooks_Online_Supplier details_File
Horizon -QuickBooks_Online_products n services_File
Kindle Previewer 3
File name: Horizon - QuickBooks_Online_Supplier details_File
7
Open
Cancel
To upload the file;
Where is the Supplier details file saved on your computer? Select it - 5. In this case the file was saved on the desktop (Yours could be a different location)
Click on the file once you've located it - 6, and then click "Open" - 7

Fig. 48

Import Suppliers
1
UPLOAD
MAP DATA
IMPORT
Select a CSV or Excel file to upload
Abacus - QuickBooks_Online_Supplier details_File.
Browse
Download a sample file
Once the file is uploaded, click "Next" to proceed to the next step.
Cancel
8
Next

Fig. 49

This space is for notes

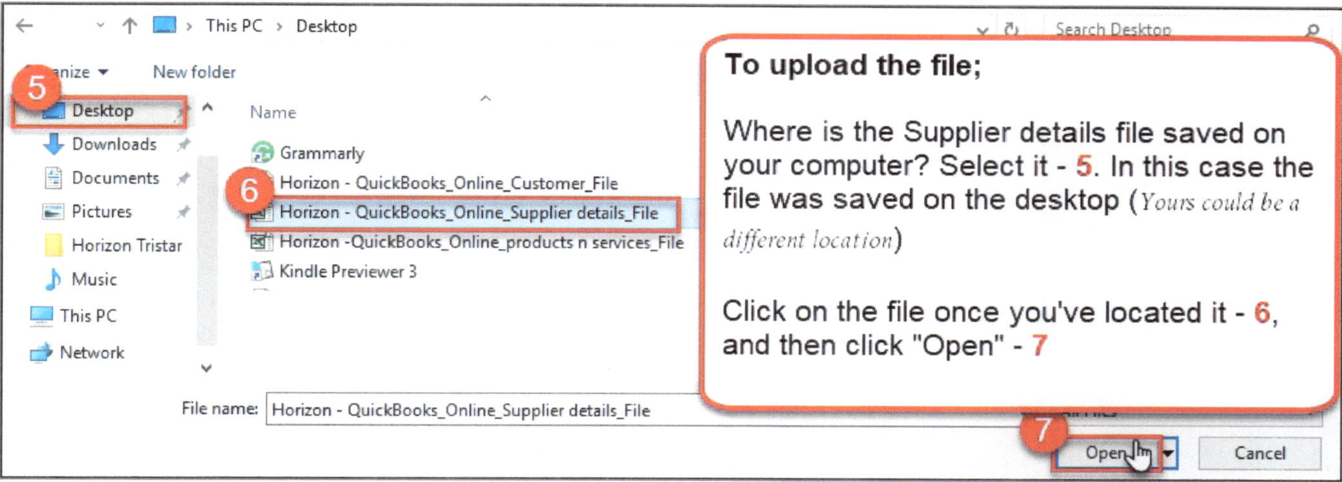

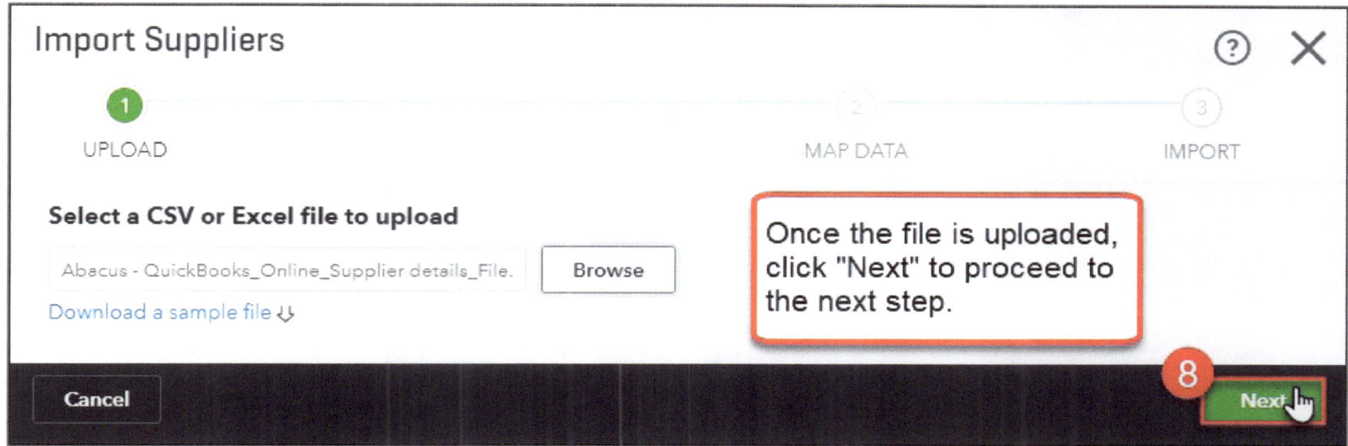

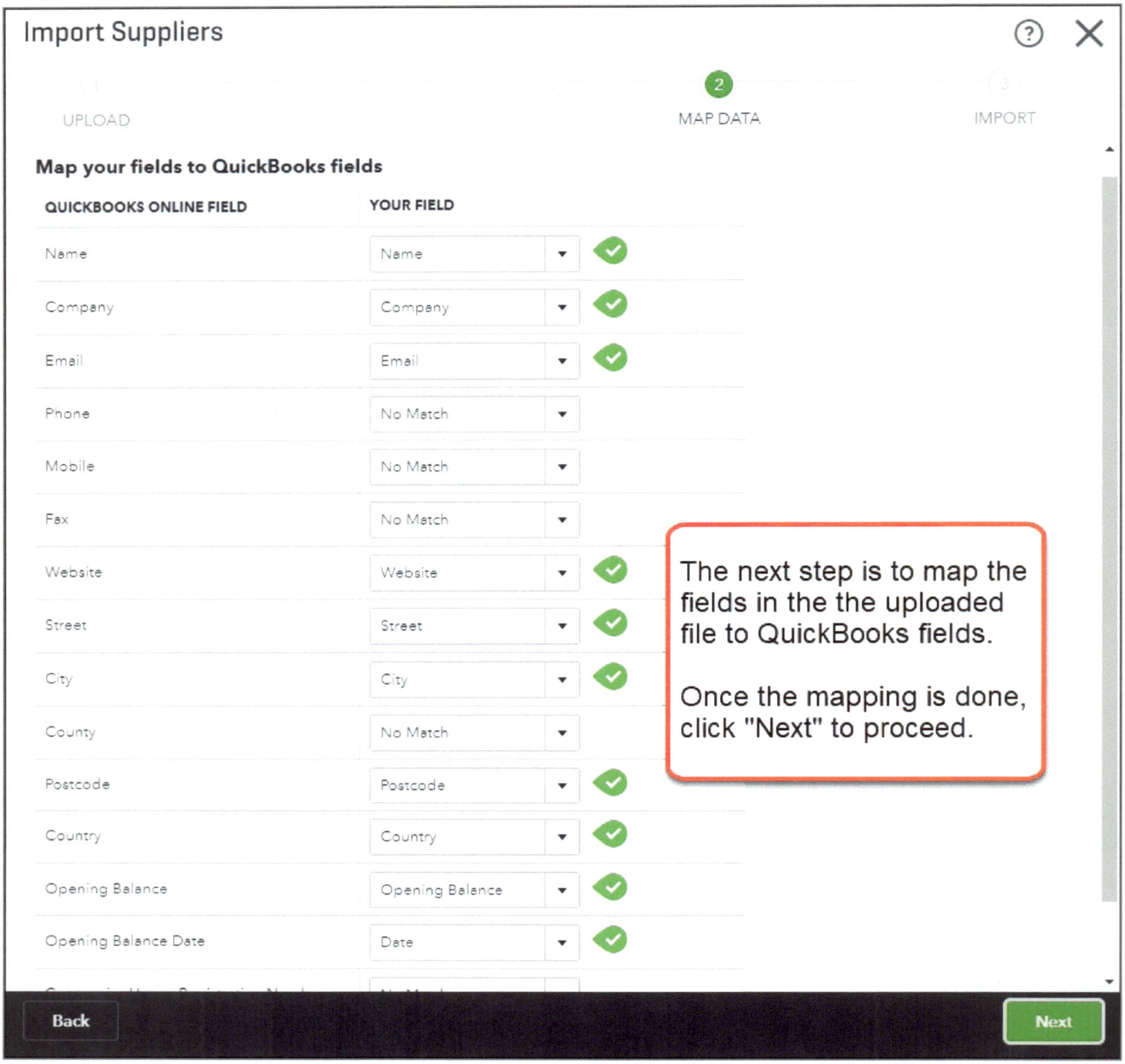
Import Suppliers
UPLOAD
2
MAP DATA
IMPORT
Map your fields to QuickBooks fields
QUICKBOOKS ONLINE FIELD
YOUR FIELD
Name
Name
Company
Company
Email
Email
Phone
No Match
Mobile
No Match
Fax
No Match
Website
Website
Street
Street
City
City
County
No Match
Postcode
Postcode
Country
Country
Opening Balance
Opening Balance
Opening Balance Date
Date
The next step is to map the fields in the the uploaded file to QuickBooks fields.
Once the mapping is done, click "Next" to proceed.
Back
Next

Fig. 50

This space is for your notes

Import Suppliers
UPLOAD
MAP DATA
IMPORT
7 suppliers are ready to be imported
NAME
COMPANY
EMAIL
WEBSITE
STREET
CITY
POSTCODE
COUNTRY
OPENING BALAN
OPENING BALAN
CURRENCY
Write the date in the format: YYYY-MM-DD. In this work experience, that will be: This year-01-01 - 10.
Click "Import" - 11 to complete the Supplier import process
Back
Import

Fig. 51

quickbooks
Dashboard
Banking
Sales
Expenses
Employees
Reports
Taxes
Accounting
My Accountant
Import Data
7 of 7 suppliers successfully imported.
Bring your existing data into QuickBooks
Bank Data
Customers
Suppliers
Products and Services
Invoices
Bills
To see your new list of imported Suppliers, click on "Expenses" - 12.

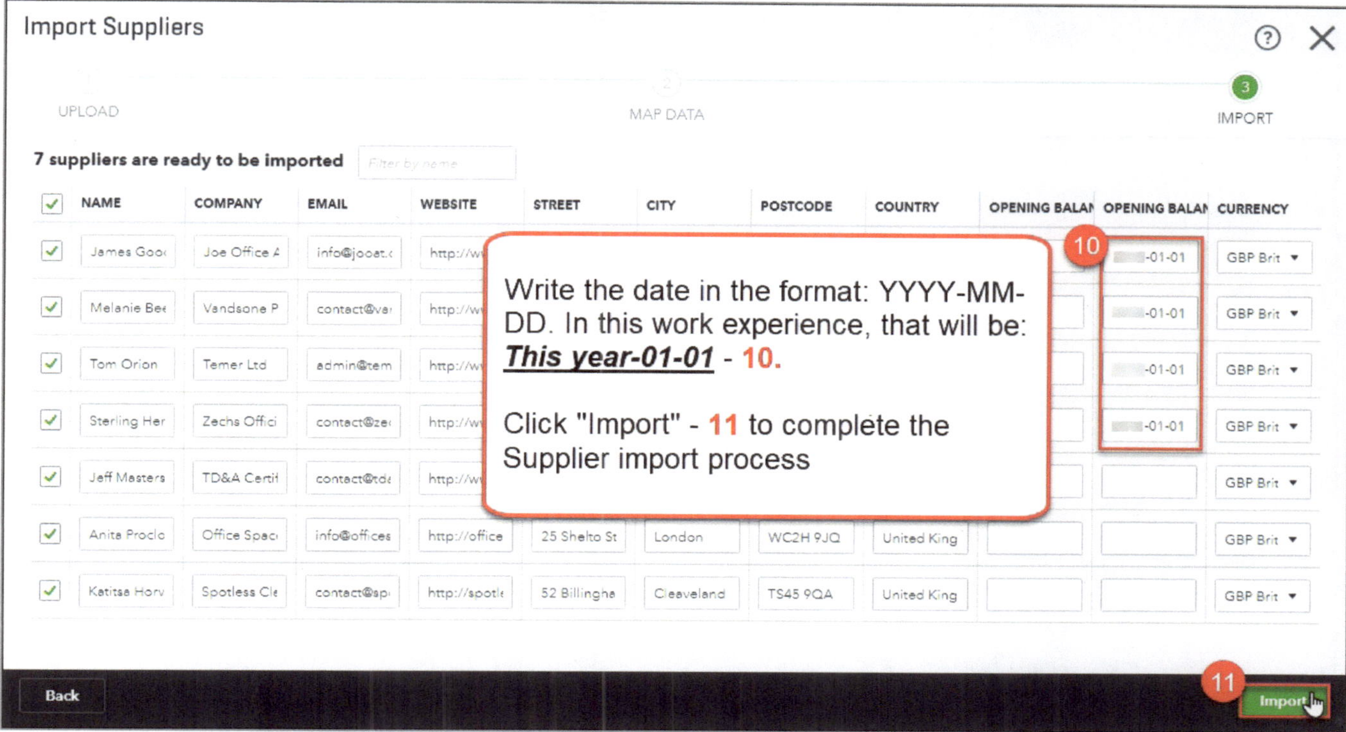

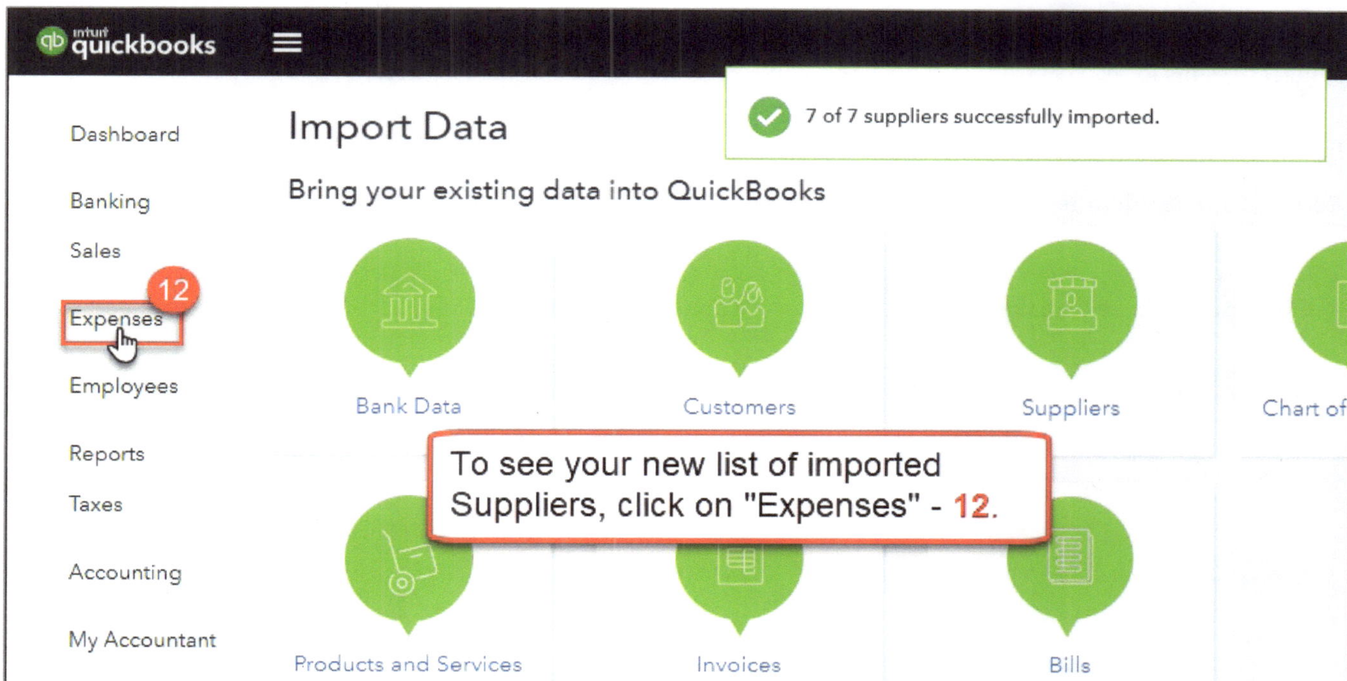

Fig. 52

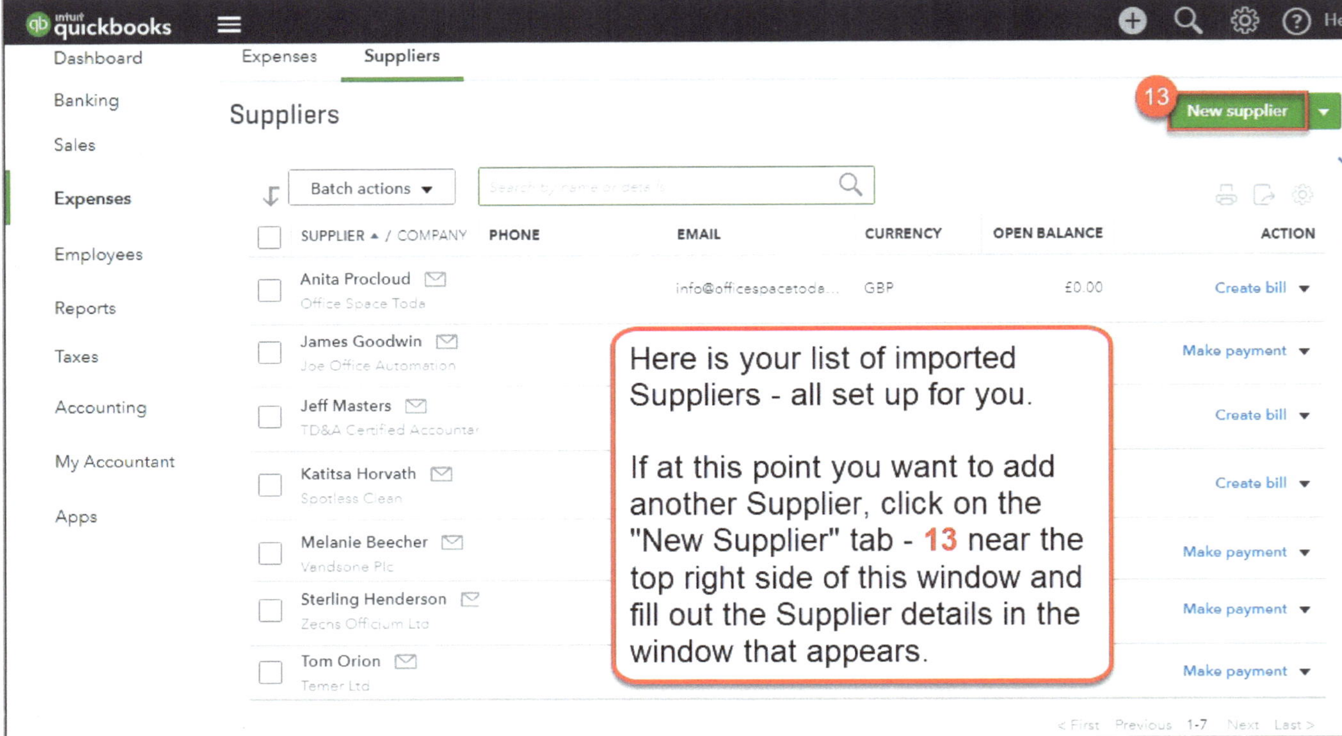

Fig. 53

Please note that when you import Suppliers to QuickBooks Online the way we have just done, QuickBooks puts the contact persons for each of the Suppliers you set up as the display names for those respective Suppliers. It does not pick up the Suppliers business or Company names. So, we will need to edit the supplier details so that the display names reflect the Suppliers Company/Business name instead of the Suppliers contact persons name.

Editing Supplier details:

The display name for the customers at this point is the Supplier contact person. We need to change the display name to the Company name to make it easier later to record invoices/bills from the Suppliers through the create button.

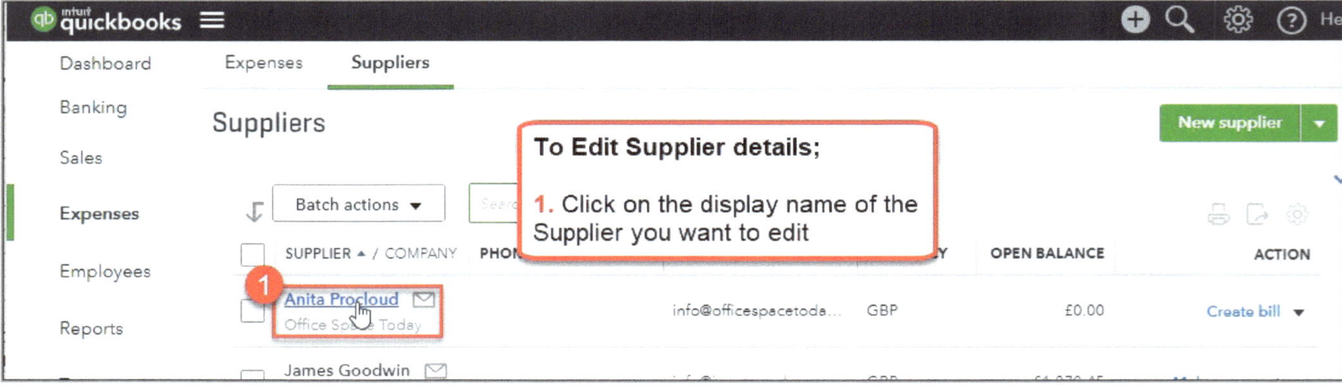

Fig. 54

Fig. 55

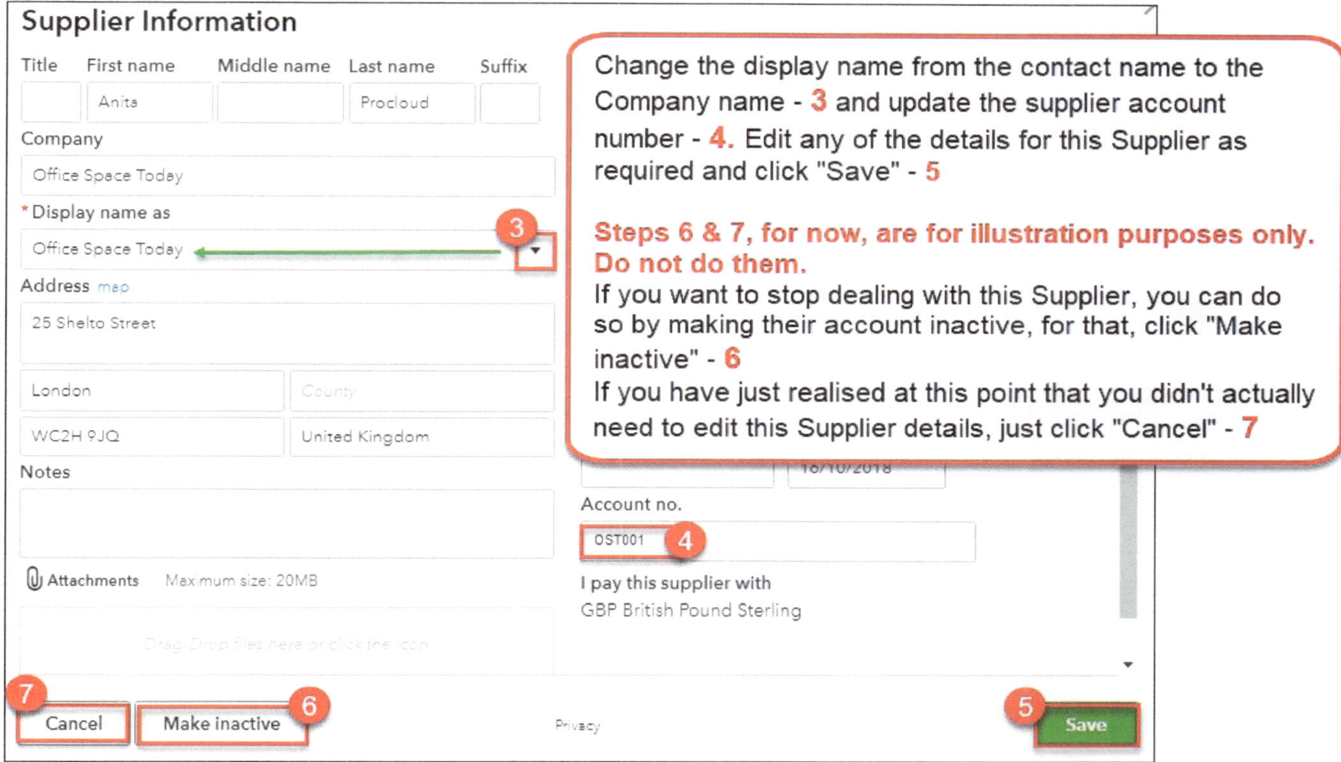

Fig. 56

Please go ahead and edit the display names for the rest of the other Suppliers. Do not proceed to the next task before editing the display names for all the Suppliers.

Task 1c: Setting up products & services

You can get to add a product or service in QuickBooks Online in two ways;

You can do so by clicking the Gear icon, then selecting products and services, then clicking on “Add a product or service” - see below

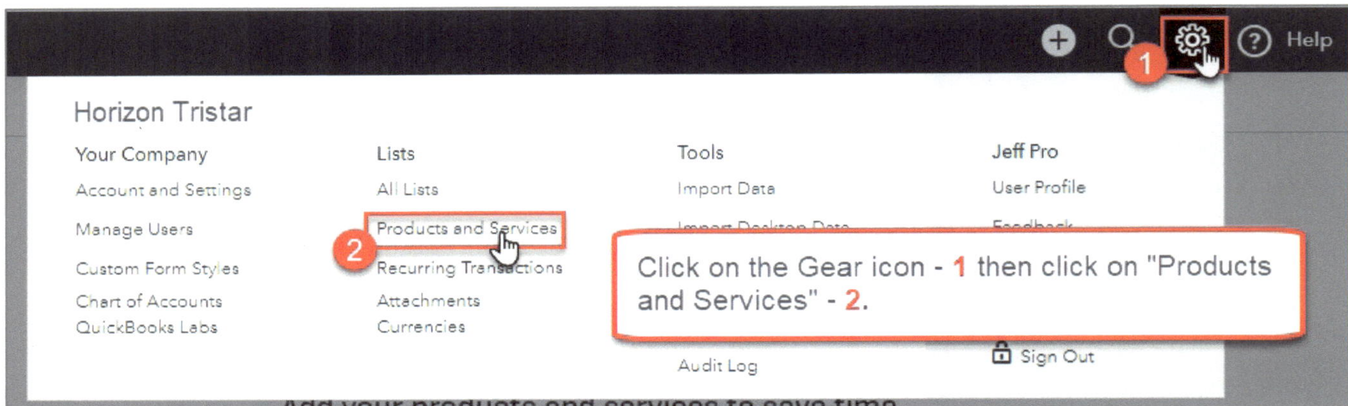

Fig. 57

Or,

You can also get to add a product or service by clicking on Sales, Products and Services, then click on “Add a product or service – see below.

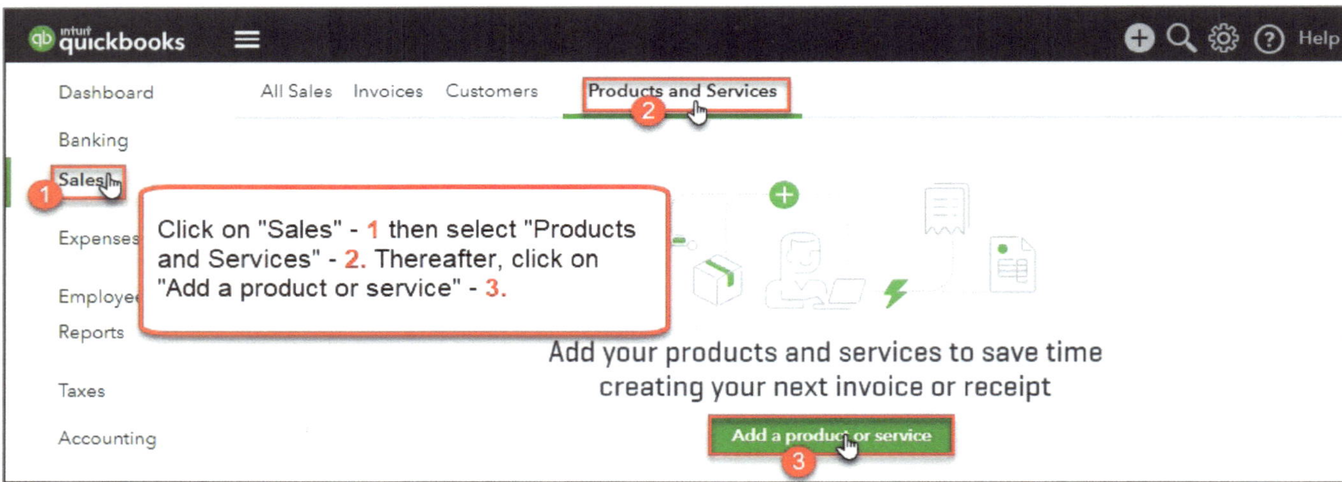

Fig. 58

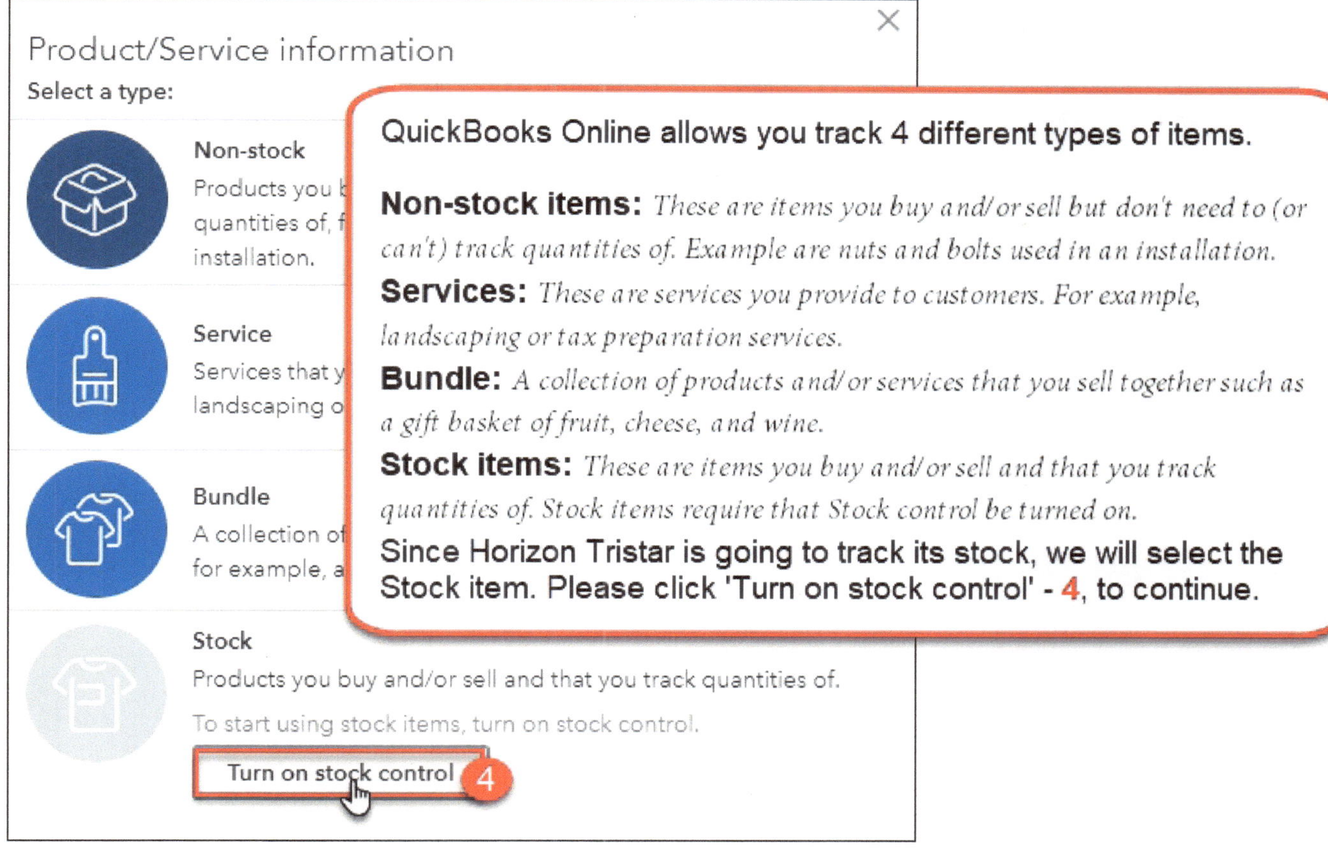

Fig. 59

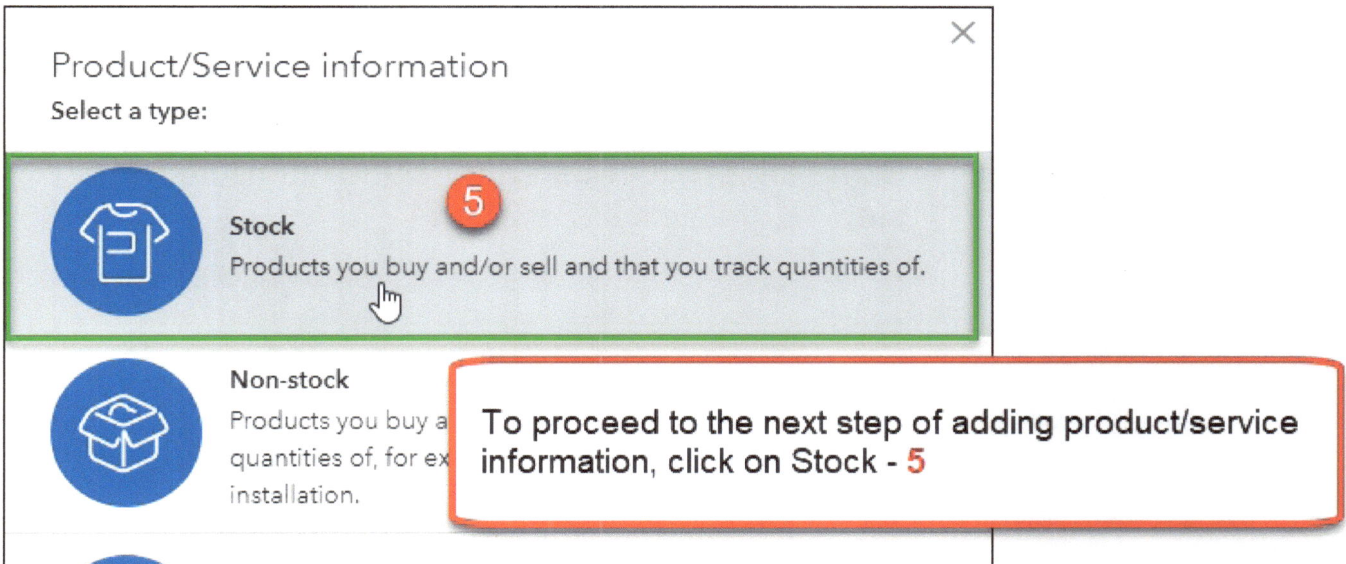

Fig. 60

This space is for notes

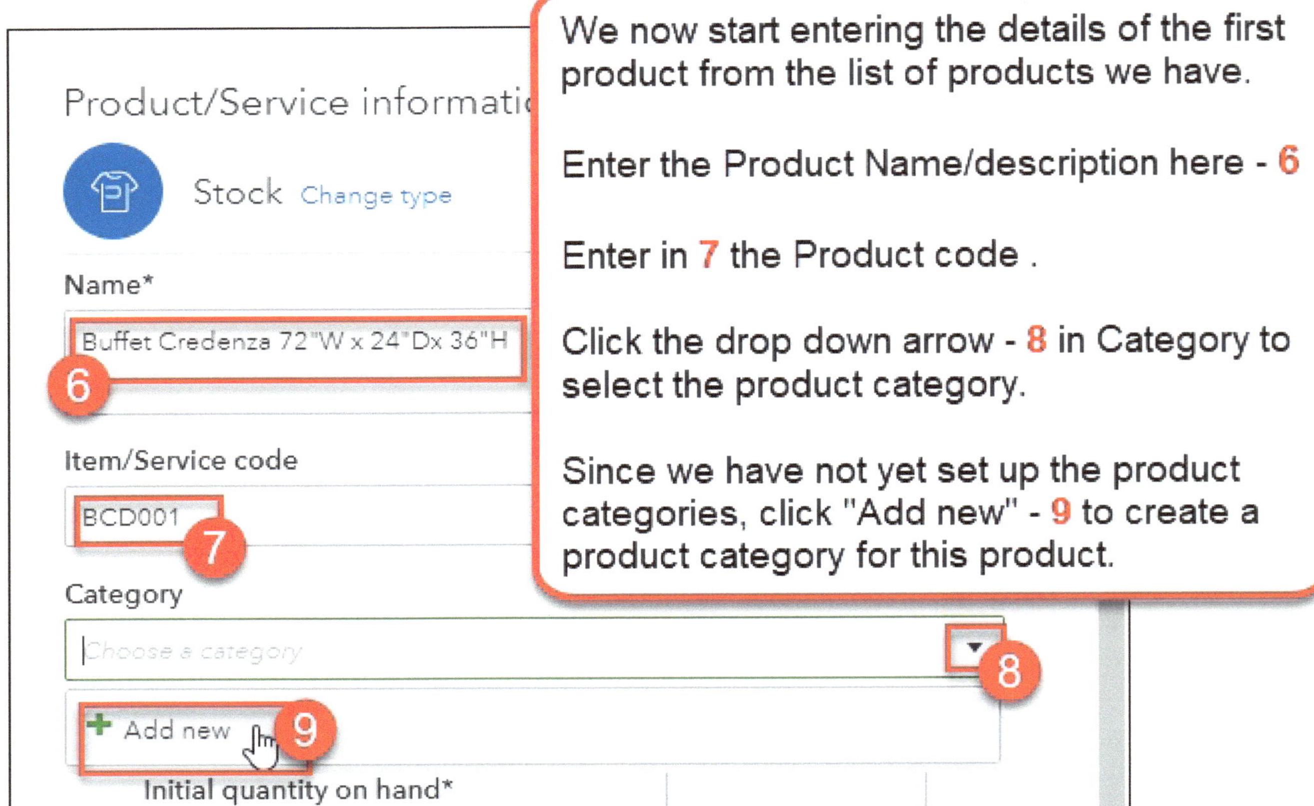

Fig. 61

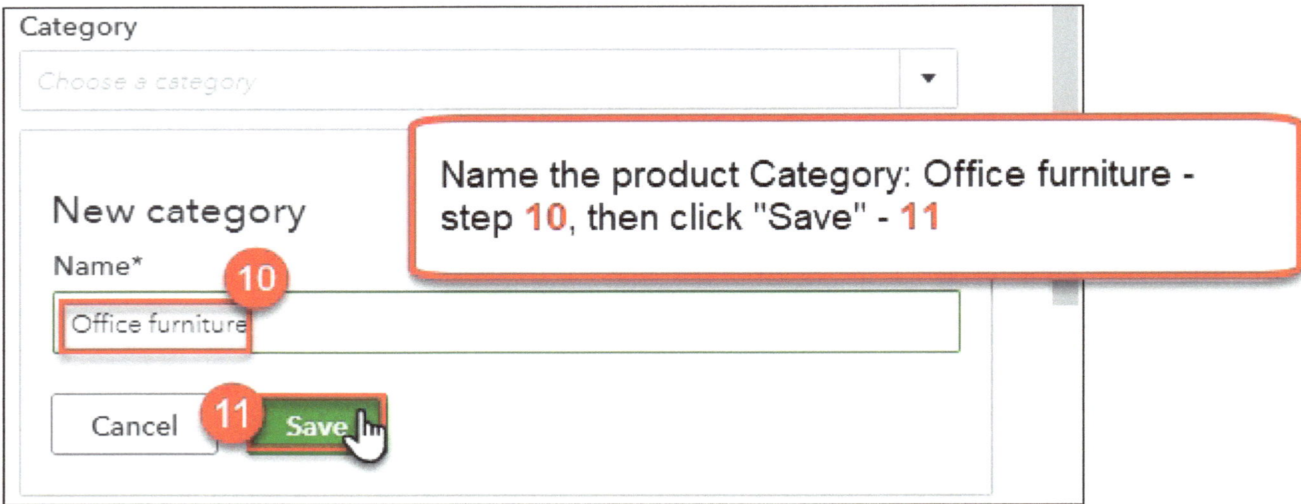

Fig. 62

This space is for notes

12
Initial quantity on hand*
5
As of date*
What's the as of date?
01/01/
Low stock alert
What's the low stock alert?
3
Stock asset account
13
Stock Asset
Sales information
Office furniture sales - Buffet Credenza
Sales price/rate
15
778
Income account
14
Sales - Office furniture
Tax
20.0% S
Fill out the details as shown in 12 -15 and scroll down

Fig. 63

Purchasing information
16
Office furniture purchase - COS
Follow steps 16 to 22 to complete adding the product to QuickBooks Online
Cost
17
520
Expense account
18
Cost of sales
Inclusive of purchase tax
Purchase tax
19
20.0% S
Preferred Supplier
20
Vandsone Plc
NOTE
Please do not click "Save and new" at step 22. We are going to upload all products and service details using a different method. The steps shown here are just to show you an alternative way to add a product to QuickBooks Online
22
Save and new
21
Save and close

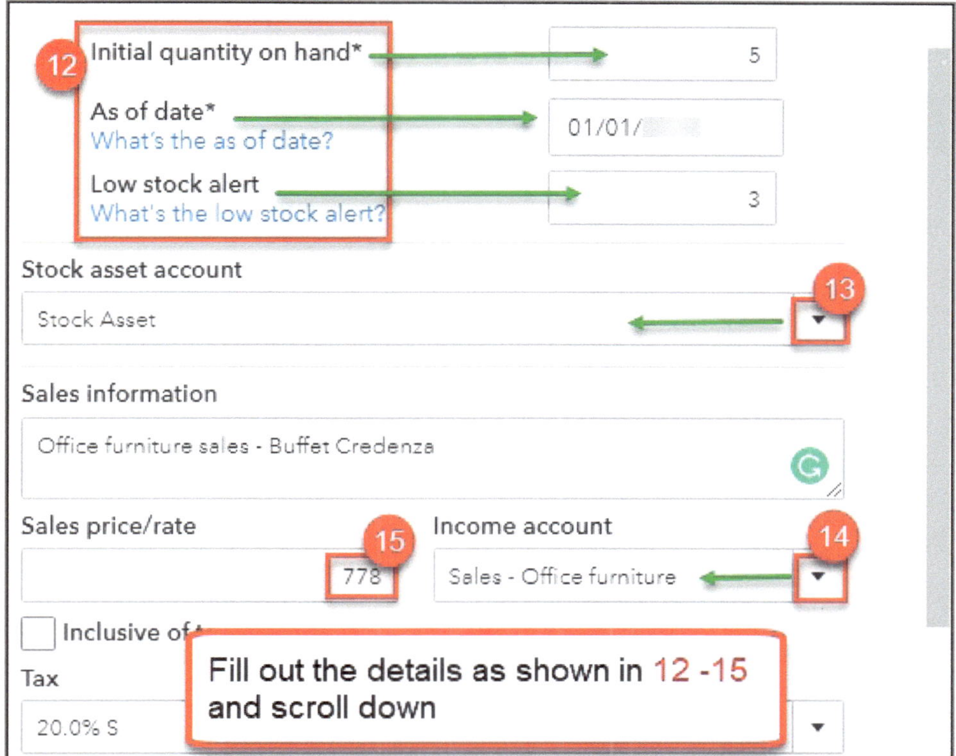

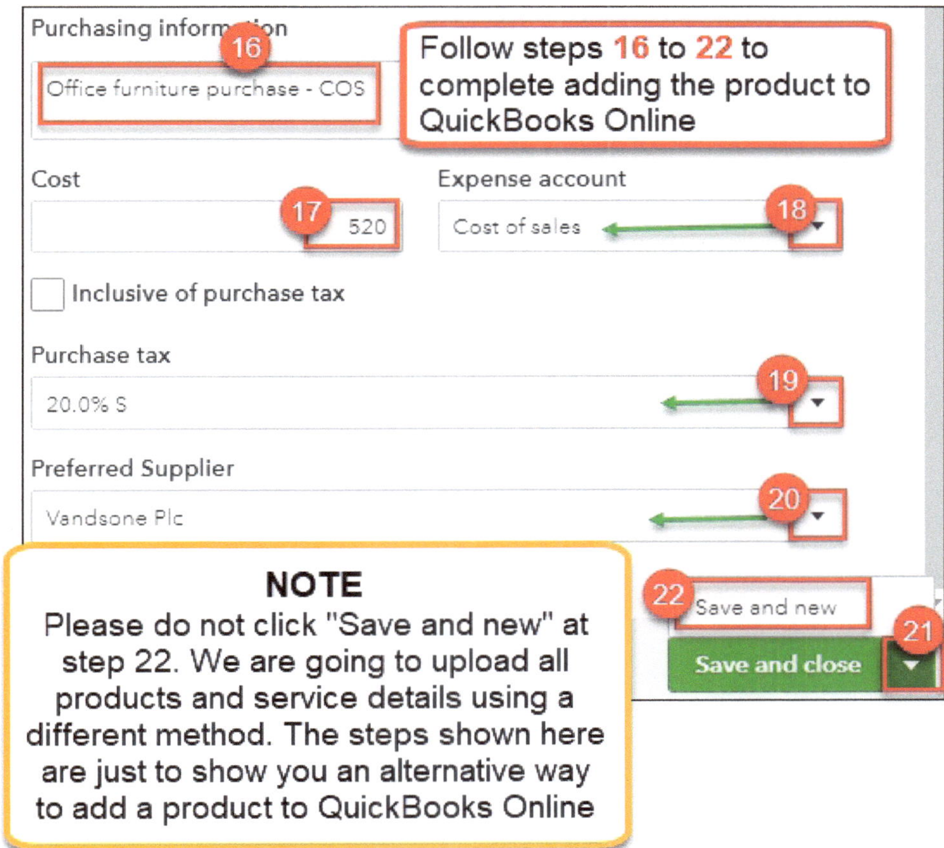

Fig. 64

The alternative way to add products and services to QuickBooks Online is by uploading a CSV or excel file that has all the products and services already added. Let me show you how to do it.

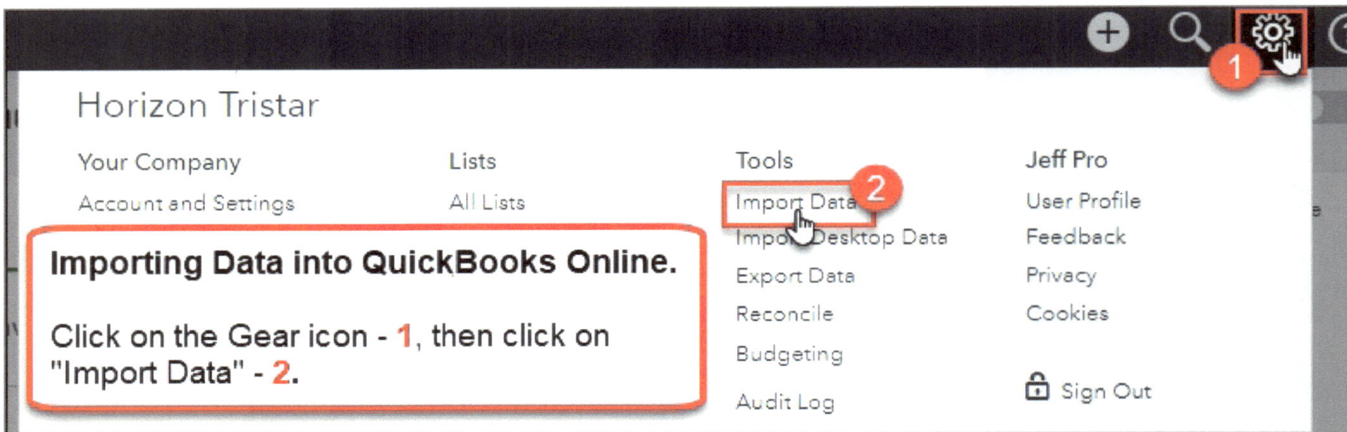

Fig. 65

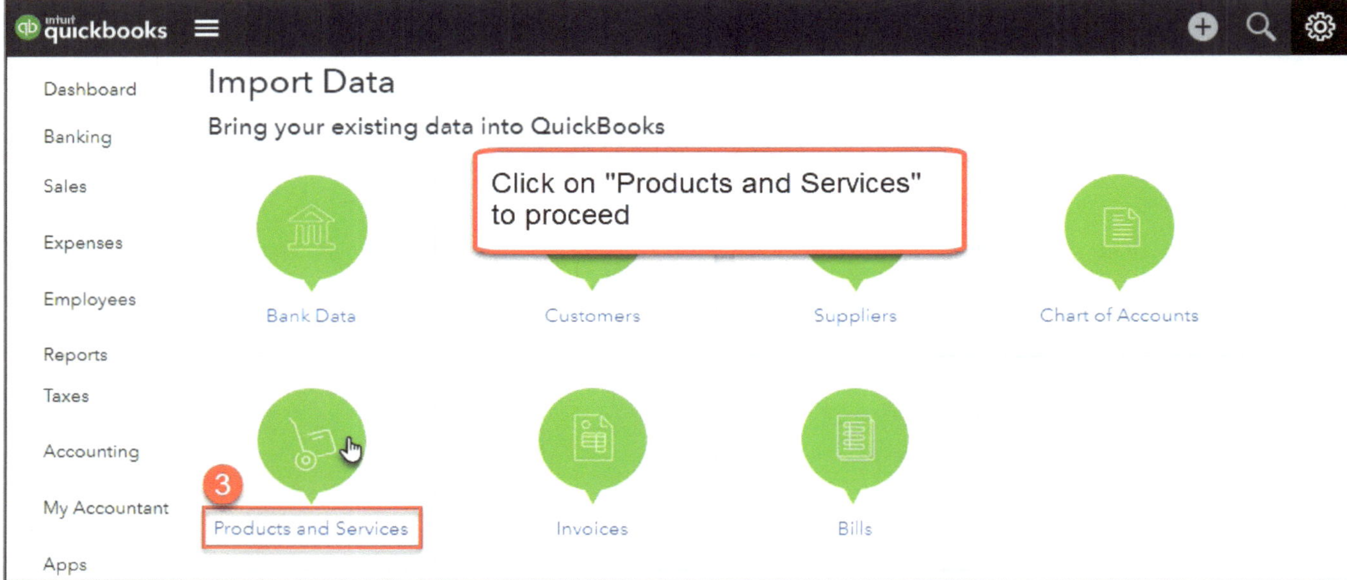

Fig. 66

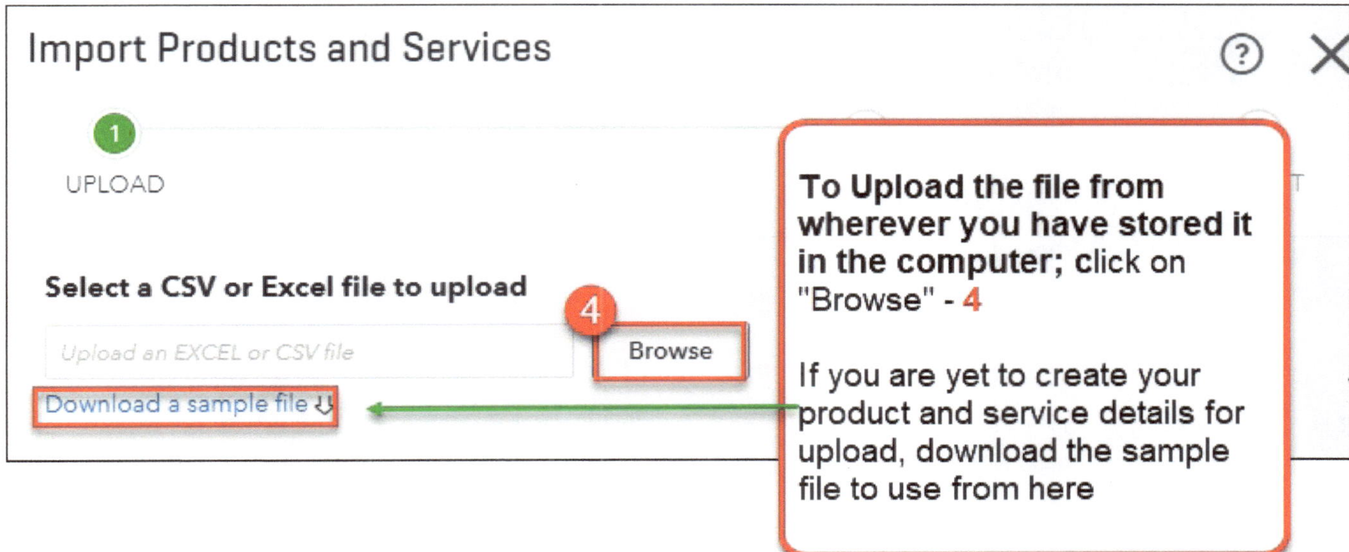

Fig. 67

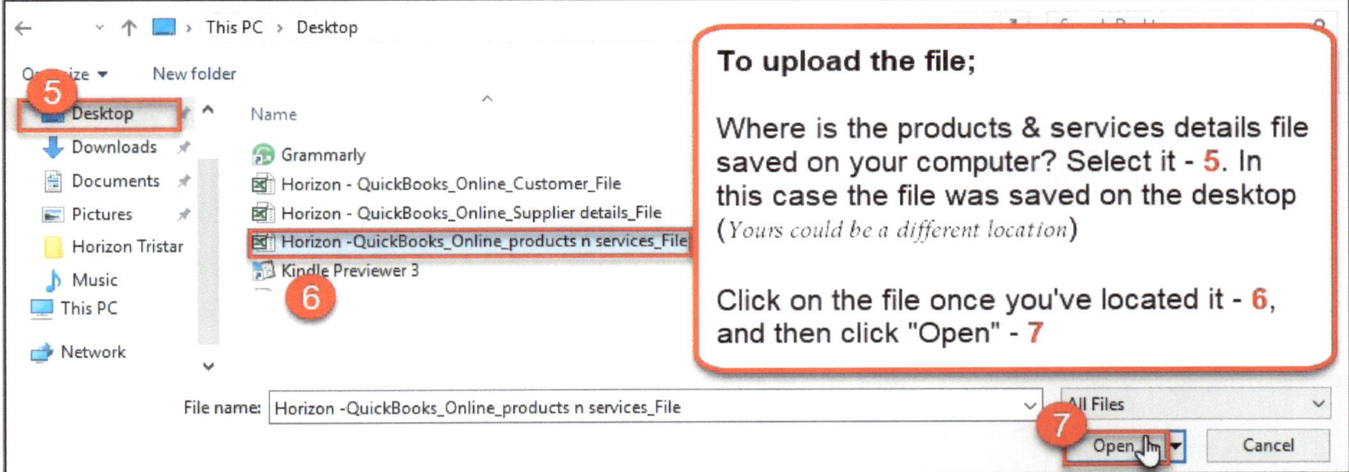

Fig. 68

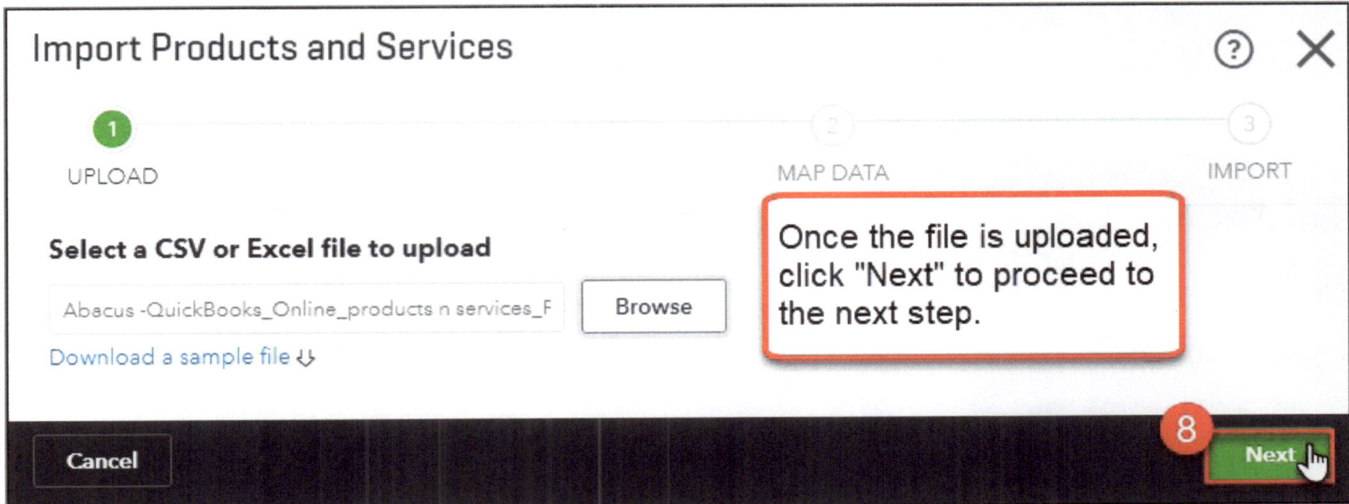

Fig. 69

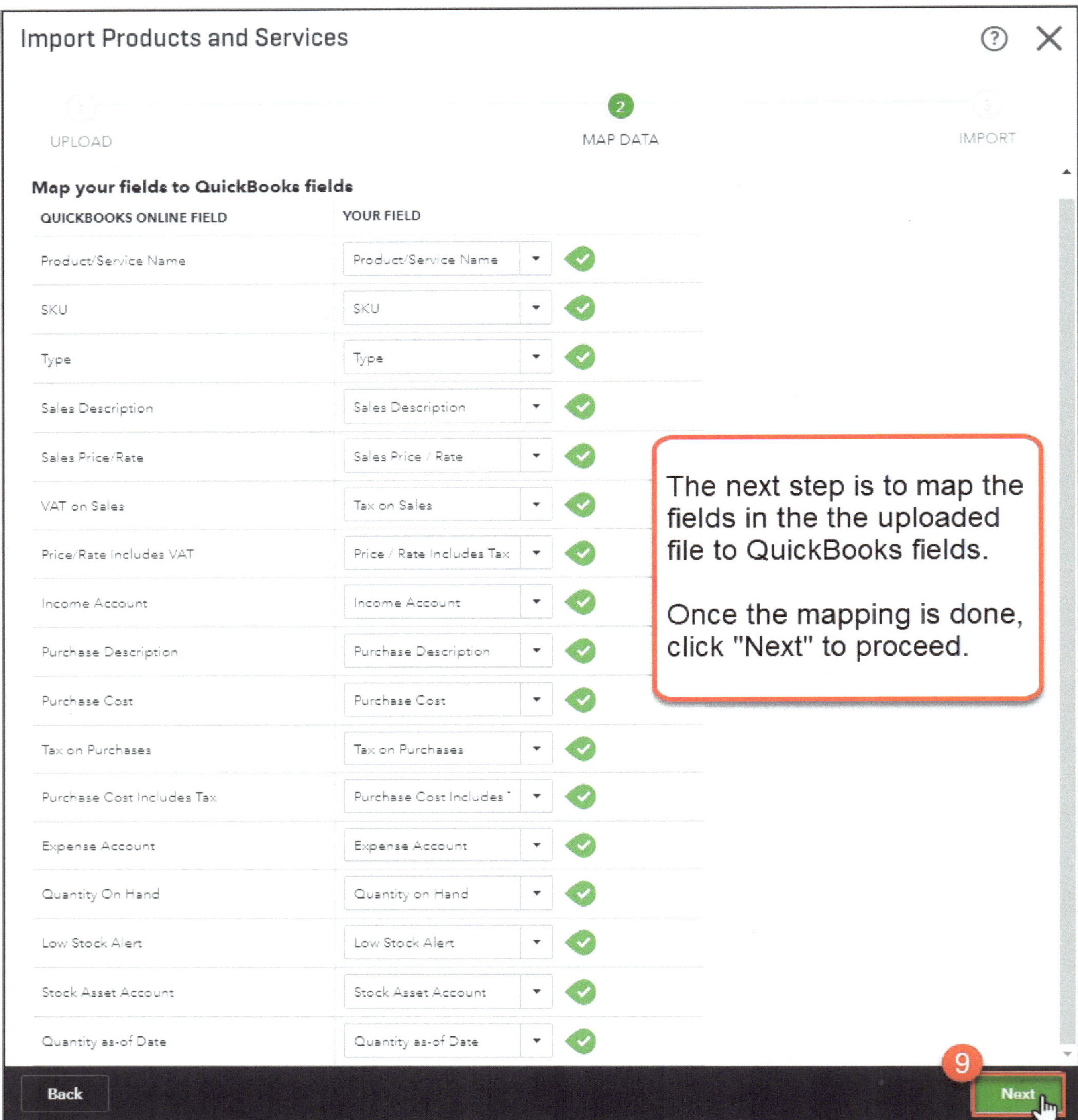

Fig. 70

This space is for notes

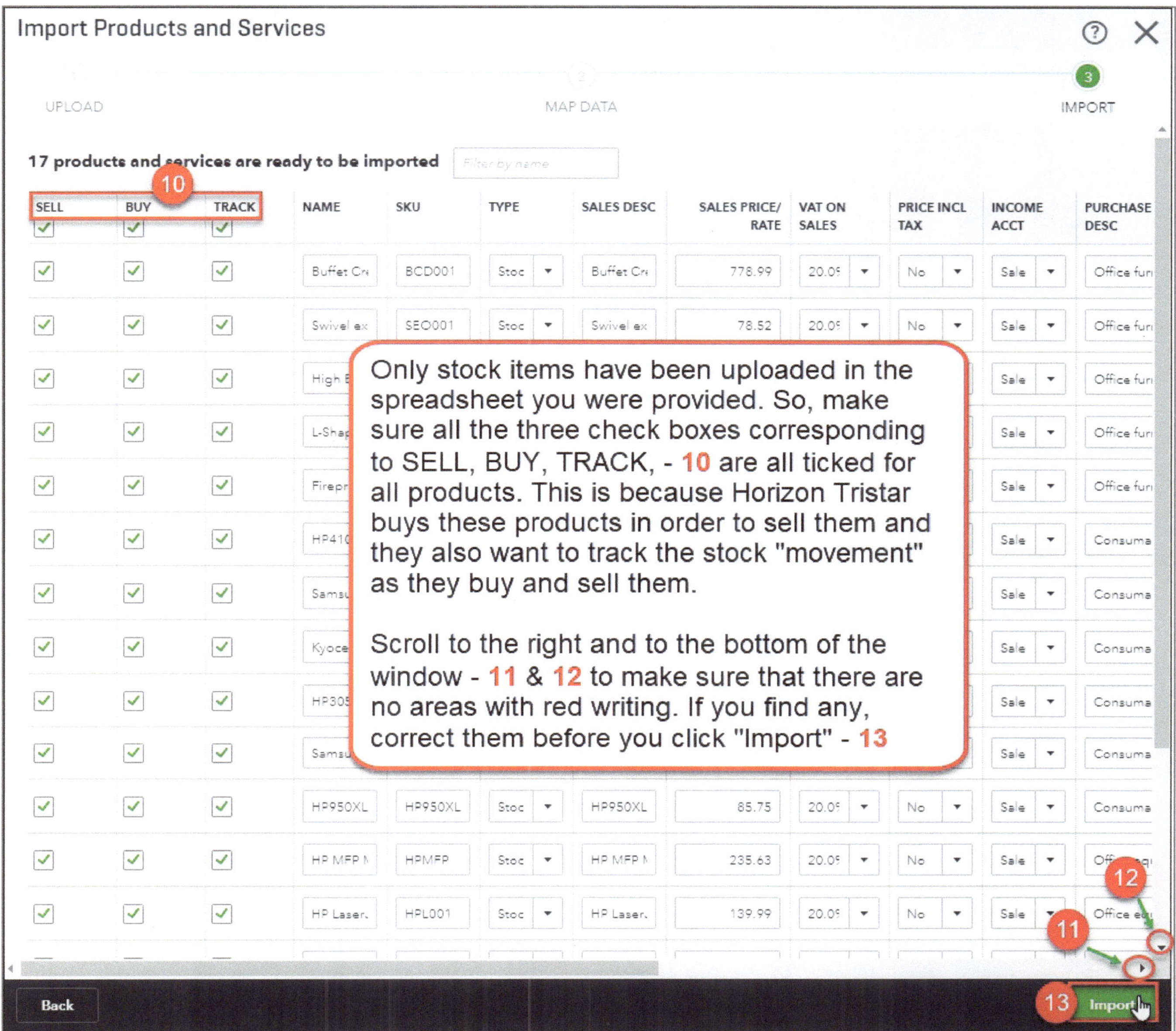

Fig. 71

This space is for notes

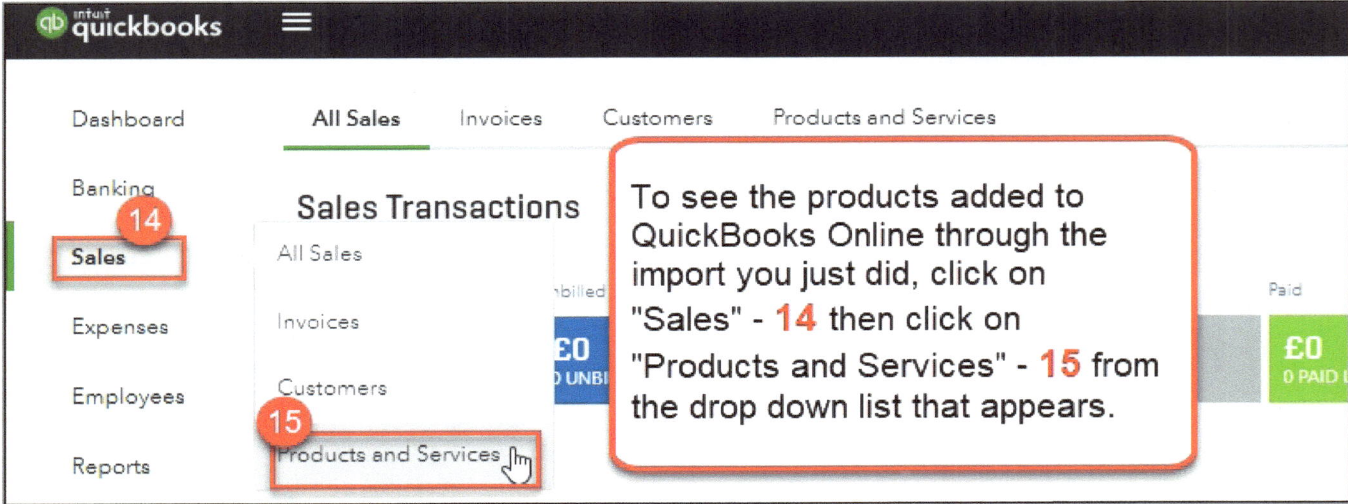

quickbooks
Dashboard
Banking
Sales
Expenses
Employees
Reports
All Sales
Invoices
Customers
Products and Services
Sales Transactions
All Sales
Invoices
Customers
Products and Services
14
15
To see the products added to QuickBooks Online through the import you just did, click on "Sales" - 14 then click on "Products and Services" - 15 from the drop down list that appears.
Paid
£0
0 PAID

Fig. 72

quickbooks
Help
Dashboard
Banking
Sales
Expenses
Employees
Reports
Taxes
Accounting
My Accountant
Apps
All Sales
Invoices
Customers
Products and Services
Products and Services
All Lists
More
New
16
17
18
19
Manage categories
Run report
4
LOW STOCK
0
OUT OF STOCK
NAME
ACTION
Edit
All the products imported will be listed here.
If you want to import many more products at once, click on the drop down arrow marked - 16 and select "Import" (you don't need to this now)
If you want to add just one product or service, click on "New" - 17 (you don't need to this now)
Here is what you need to do.
There are three categories of products that Abacus Enterprises has - Office furniture, Office equipment and Consumables. You need to add those categories to the products and services details. To do so, click on the drop down arrow next to "More" - 18 and select "Manage categories" - 19

Fig. 73

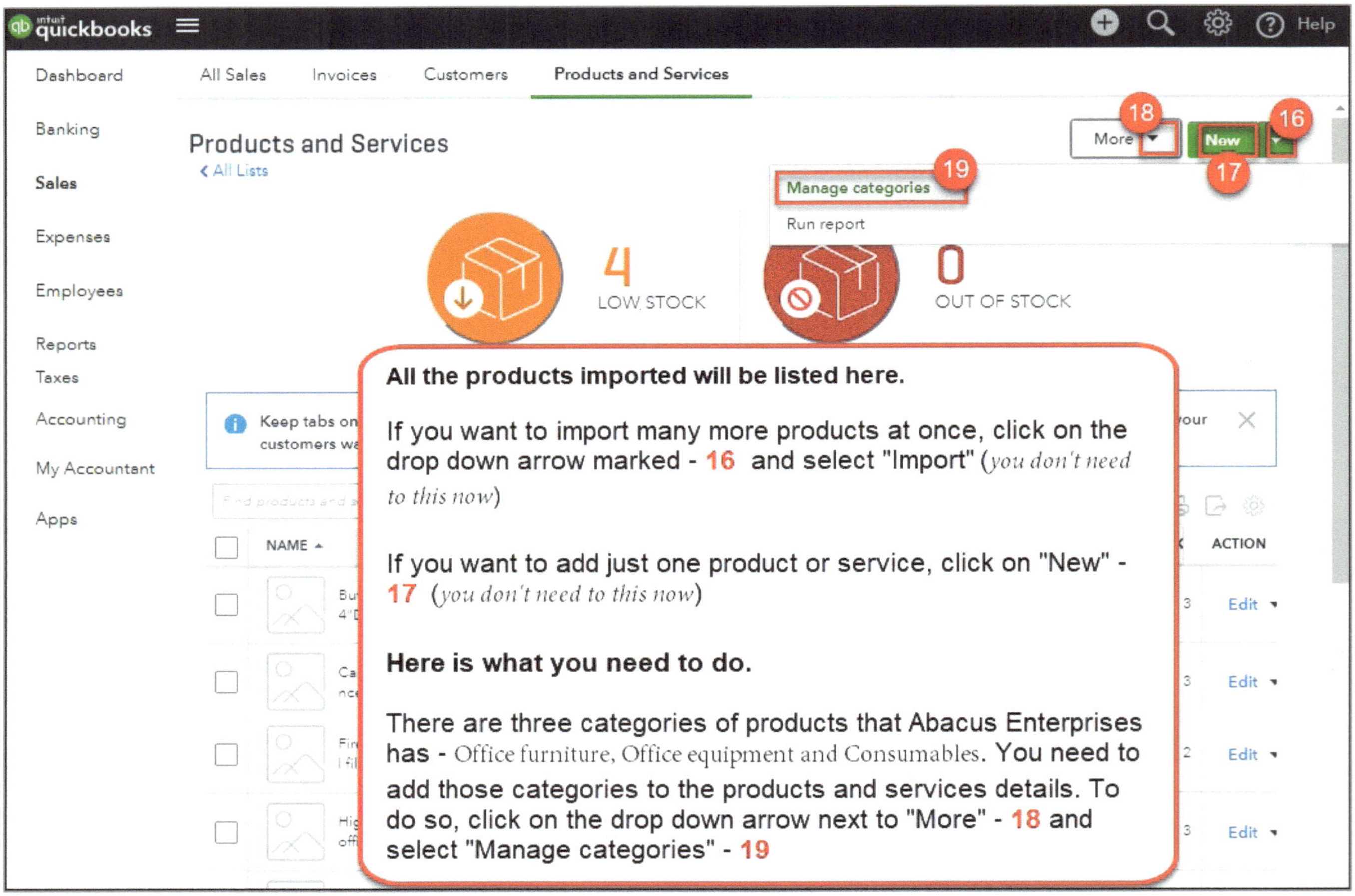

Fig. 74

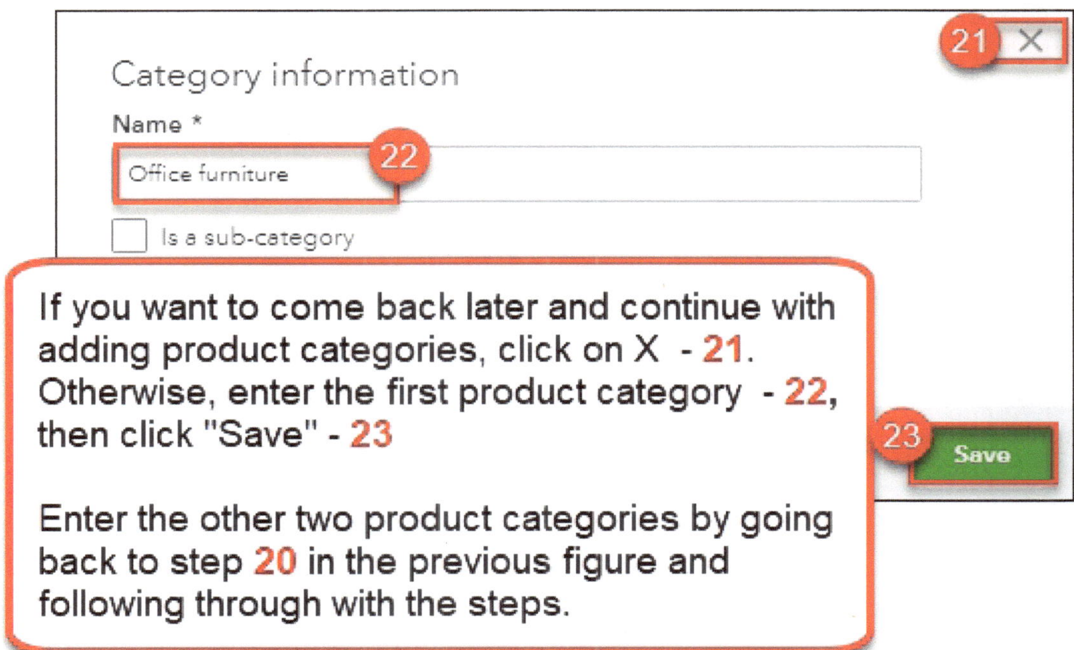

Fig. 75

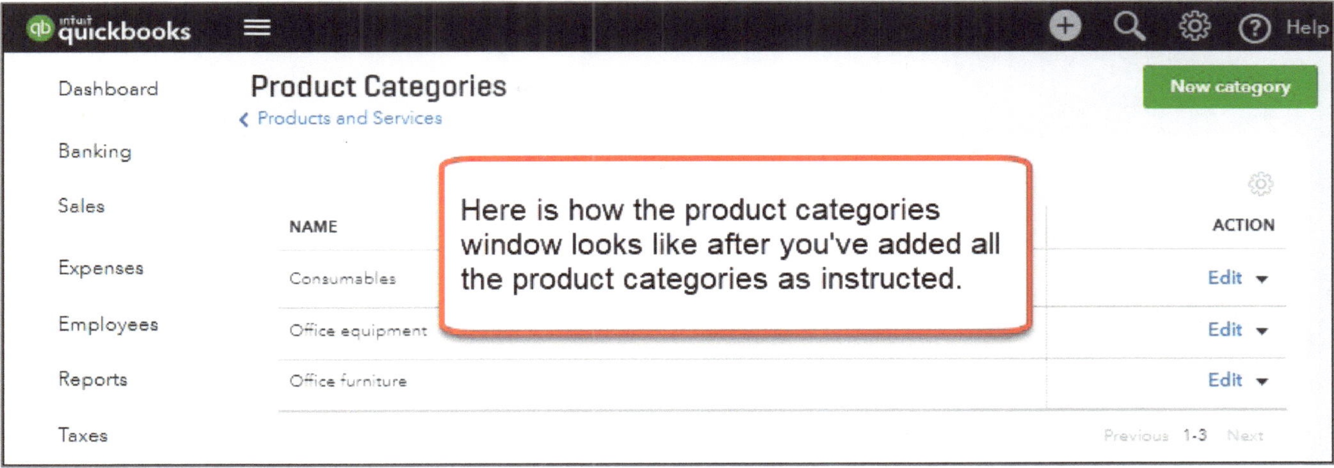

Fig. 76

Task 1d: Setting up the fixed assets register

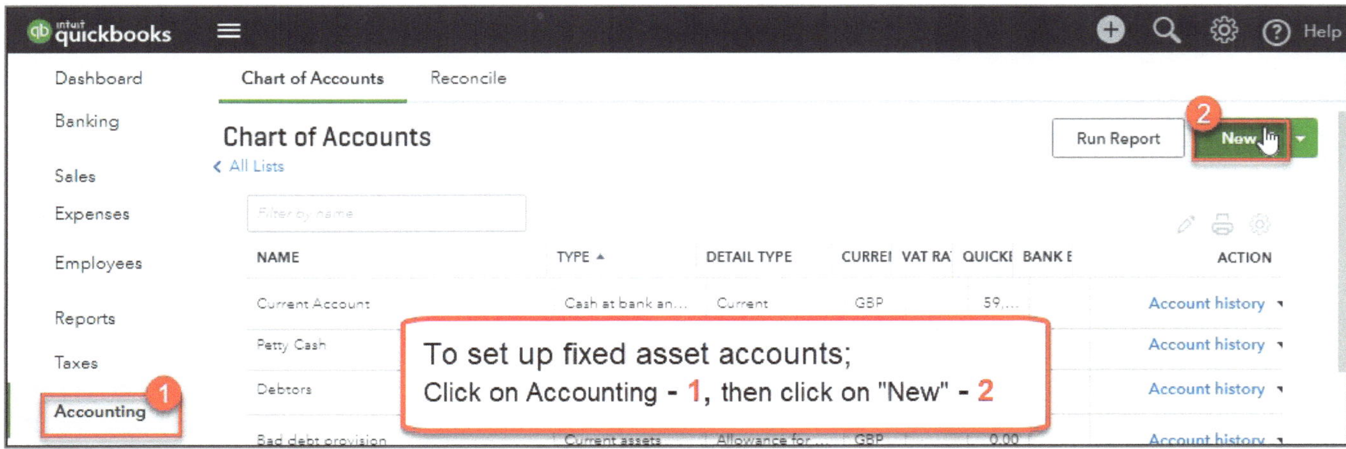

Fig. 77

Using the list of the Fixed assets you have been given, here is how to set up the fixed asset accounts for them. I will do the first one with you; then you can carry on with the rest.

Fixed assets are any assets that cannot be easily converted to cash. They are typically tangible, physical things that have an economic life of longer than a year. These include buildings, vehicles, furniture and office equipment. Fixed assets normally don't include intangible things like royalties and brand names.

Fixed assets are also known as non-current and long-term assets. They may also be referred to as property, plant and equipment. They are assets intended to be used within the business, not sold or converted to cash.

This space is for notes

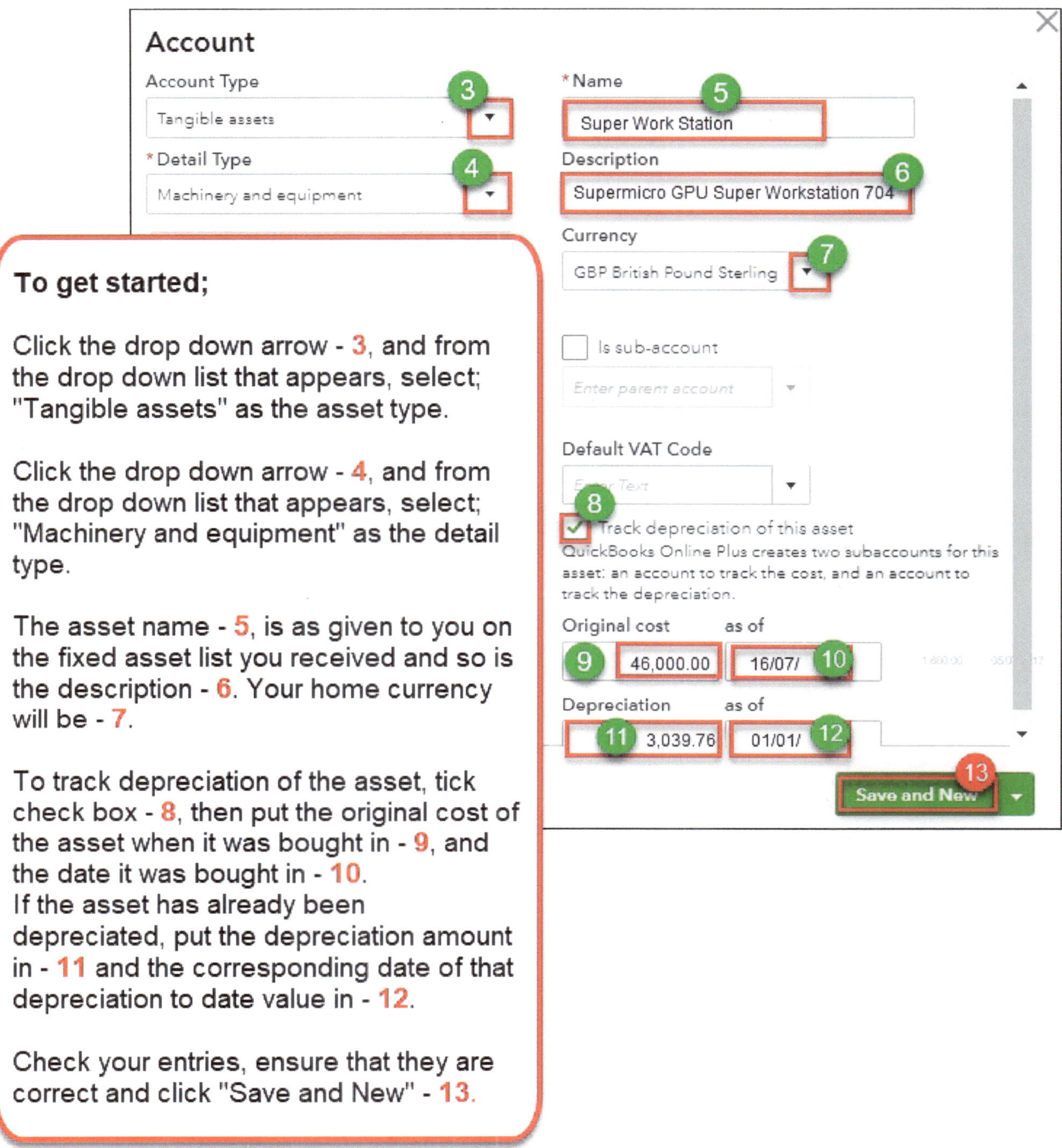

Fig. 78

This space is for notes

Task 1e: Setting up opening balances from the Trial balance

Overview of this task

The opening balance is the balance that is brought forward from the end of one accounting period to the beginning of a new accounting period or from one accounting system to a new accounting system.

The funds in a company's/business accounts at the start of a new financial period are called the opening balances. The opening balance is the first entry in a company's accounts, either when they are first starting up or at the start of a new financial year or when changing accounting systems.

In the case of a new company, the opening balances usually are just two: one is the cash on hand, and the other is the capital contributed by the company's founders or loan from investors.

Opening balances are entered into the accounting system using the double entry accounting principles.
The best way to gather your opening balances is to prepare an opening trial balance. This is done by listing all your nominal accounts and the value (balance) on each account.

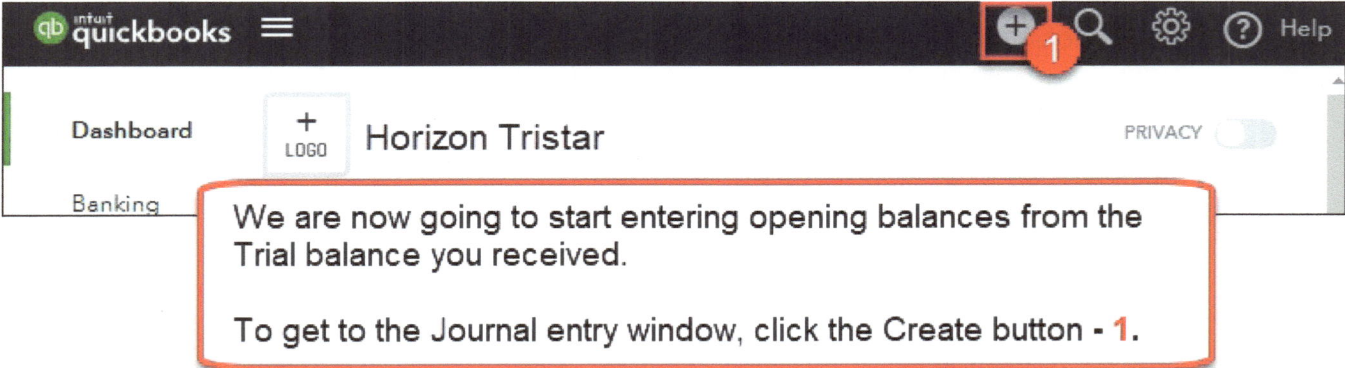

Fig. 79

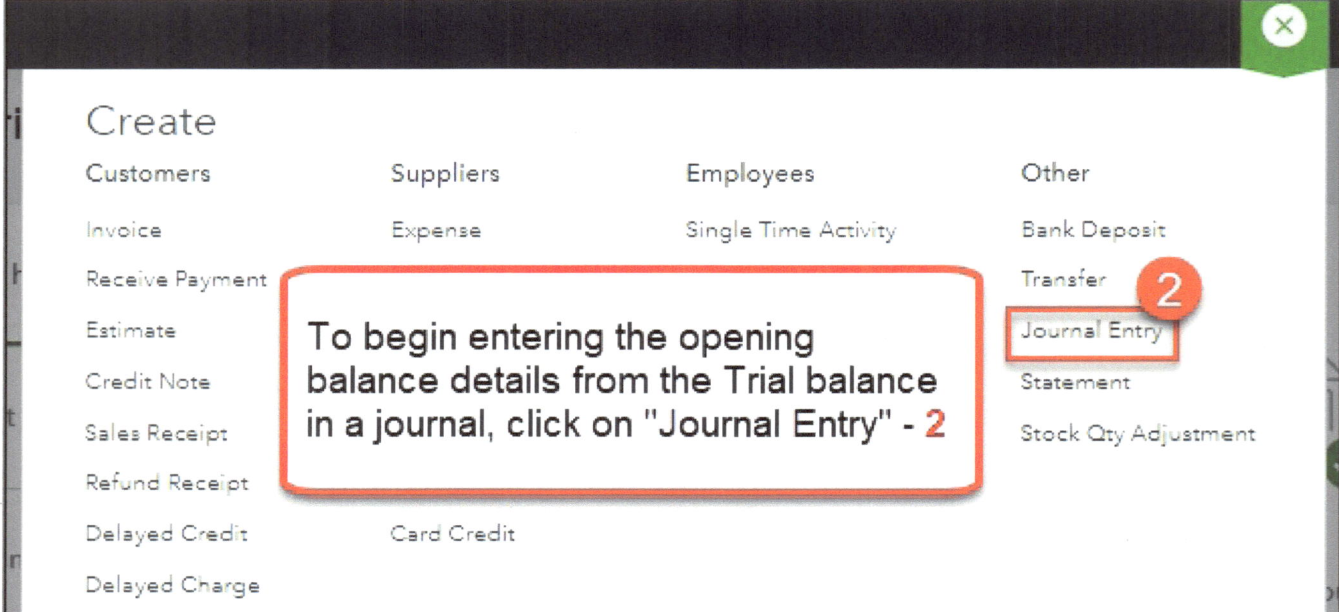

Fig. 80

In the set-up steps earlier on did record opening balances for the items in the trial balance up until Creditors Control Account, we will continue from Sales tax Control Account (Credit balance of 22,182.53 in the Trial balance) and then enter the rest of the balances as shown in the Trial balance.

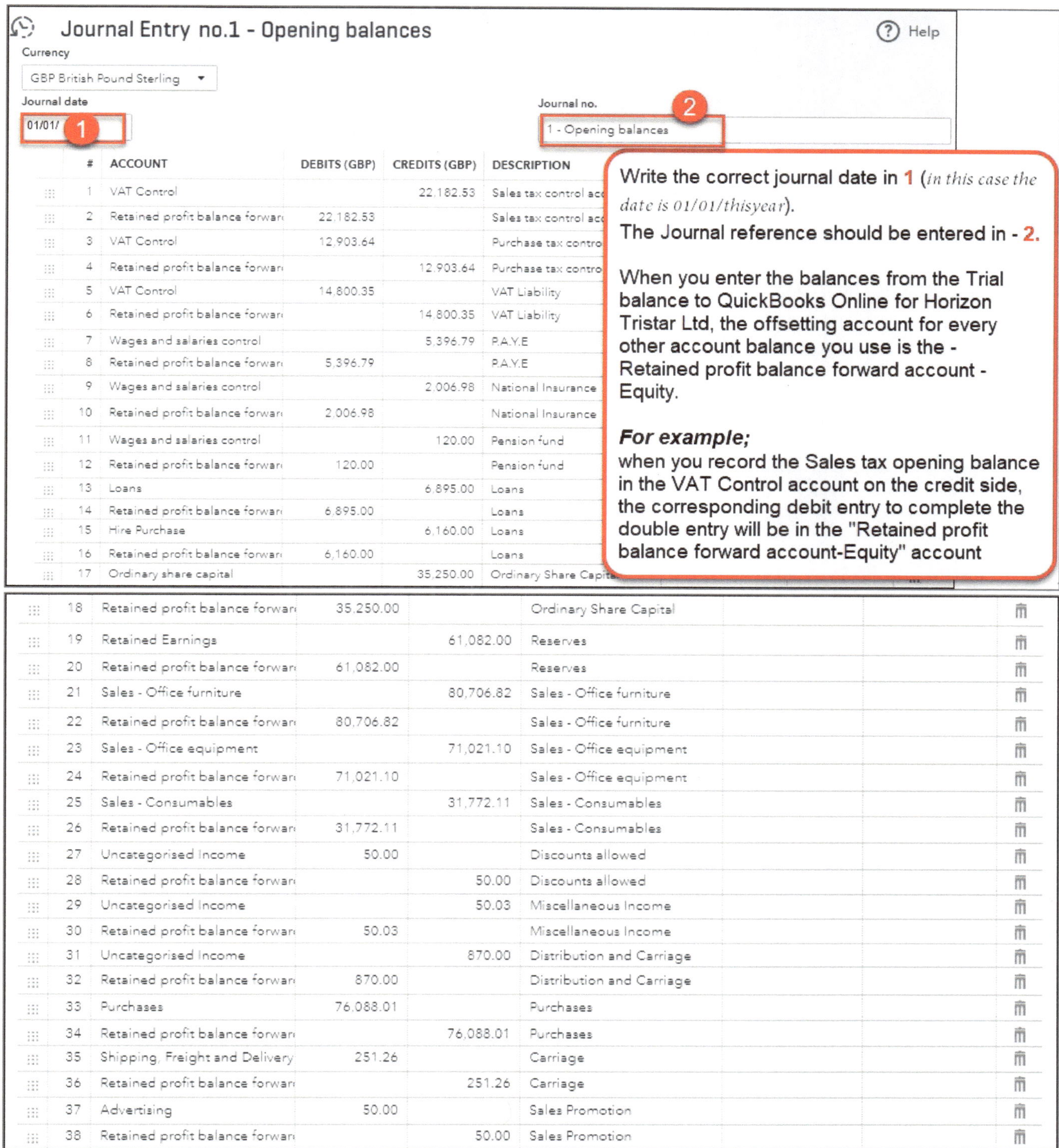

#	ACCOUNT	DEBITS (GBP)	CREDITS (GBP)	DESCRIPTION
1	VAT Control		22,182.53	Sales tax control acc
2	Retained profit balance forwar	22,182.53		Sales tax control acc
3	VAT Control	12,903.64		Purchase tax contro
4	Retained profit balance forwar		12,903.64	Purchase tax contro
5	VAT Control	14,800.35		VAT Liability
6	Retained profit balance forwar		14,800.35	VAT Liability
7	Wages and salaries control		5,396.79	P.A.Y.E
8	Retained profit balance forwar	5,396.79		P.A.Y.E
9	Wages and salaries control		2,006.98	National Insurance
10	Retained profit balance forwar	2,006.98		National Insurance
11	Wages and salaries control		120.00	Pension fund
12	Retained profit balance forwar	120.00		Pension fund
13	Loans		6,895.00	Loans
14	Retained profit balance forwar	6,895.00		Loans
15	Hire Purchase		6,160.00	Loans
16	Retained profit balance forwar	6,160.00		Loans
17	Ordinary share capital		35,250.00	Ordinary Share Capit
18	Retained profit balance forwar	35,250.00		Ordinary Share Capital
19	Retained Earnings		61,082.00	Reserves
20	Retained profit balance forwar	61,082.00		Reserves
21	Sales - Office furniture		80,706.82	Sales - Office furniture
22	Retained profit balance forwar	80,706.82		Sales - Office furniture
23	Sales - Office equipment		71,021.10	Sales - Office equipment
24	Retained profit balance forwar	71,021.10		Sales - Office equipment
25	Sales - Consumables		31,772.11	Sales - Consumables
26	Retained profit balance forwar	31,772.11		Sales - Consumables
27	Uncategorised Income	50.00		Discounts allowed
28	Retained profit balance forwar		50.00	Discounts allowed
29	Uncategorised Income		50.03	Miscellaneous Income
30	Retained profit balance forwar	50.03		Miscellaneous Income
31	Uncategorised Income		870.00	Distribution and Carriage
32	Retained profit balance forwar	870.00		Distribution and Carriage
33	Purchases	76,088.01		Purchases
34	Retained profit balance forwar		76,088.01	Purchases
35	Shipping, Freight and Delivery	251.26		Carriage
36	Retained profit balance forwar		251.26	Carriage
37	Advertising	50.00		Sales Promotion
38	Retained profit balance forwar		50.00	Sales Promotion

⁝⁝⁝	39	Advertising	465.00		Advertising	
⁝⁝⁝	40	Retained profit balance forwar		465.00	Advertising	
⁝⁝⁝	41	Advertising	115.00		Gifts and Samples	
⁝⁝⁝	42	Retained profit balance forwar		115.00	Gifts and Samples	
⁝⁝⁝	43	Advertising	1,050.00		P.R. (Literature & Brochures)	
⁝⁝⁝	44	Retained profit balance forwar		1,050.00	P.R. (Literature & Brochures)	
⁝⁝⁝	45	Gross Wages	32,472.11		Gross wages	
⁝⁝⁝	46	Retained profit balance forwar		32,472.11	Gross wages	
⁝⁝⁝	47	Employer s NI contributions	3,327.24		Employers NI	
⁝⁝⁝	48	Retained profit balance forwar		3,327.24	Employers NI	
⁝⁝⁝	49	SSP	107.60		Statutory Sick Pay reclaimed	
⁝⁝⁝	50	Retained profit balance forwar		107.60	Statutory Sick Pay reclaimed	
⁝⁝⁝	51	SMP	255.00		Statutory Maternity Pay	
⁝⁝⁝	52	Retained profit balance forwar		255.00	Statutory Maternity Pay	
⁝⁝⁝	53	Rent	12,720.00		Rent	
⁝⁝⁝	54	Retained profit balance forwar		12,720.00	Rent	
⁝⁝⁝	55	Light and heat	1,052.00		Electricity	
⁝⁝⁝	56	Retained profit balance forwar		1,052.00	Electricity	
⁝⁝⁝	57	Motor running expenses	620.95		Fuel and Oil	
⁝⁝⁝	58	Retained profit balance forwar		620.95	Fuel and Oil	

⁝⁝⁝	59	Motor running expenses	492.15		Repairs & Servicing	
⁝⁝⁝	60	Retained profit balance forwar		492.15	Repairs & Servicing	
⁝⁝⁝	61	Motor running expenses	67.50		Miscellaneous Motor Expen	
⁝⁝⁝	62	Retained profit balance forwar		67.50	Miscellaneous Motor Expen	
⁝⁝⁝	63	Motor running expenses	90.27		Scale Charges	
⁝⁝⁝	64	Retained profit balance forwar		90.27	Scale Charges	
⁝⁝⁝	65	Travelling expenses	201.00		Travelling Expenses	
⁝⁝⁝	66	Retained profit balance forwar		201.00	Travelling Expenses	
⁝⁝⁝	67	Travelling expenses	150.00		Car hire	
⁝⁝⁝	68	Retained profit balance forwar		150.00	Car hire	
⁝⁝⁝	69	Travelling expenses	720.00		Hotels	
⁝⁝⁝	70	Retained profit balance forwar		720.00	Hotels	
⁝⁝⁝	71	Entertaining	149.50		U.K. Etertainment	
⁝⁝⁝	72	Retained profit balance forwar		149.50	U.K. Etertainment	
⁝⁝⁝	73	Printing, postage and stationer	54.10		Printing	
⁝⁝⁝	74	Retained profit balance forwar		54.10	Printing	
⁝⁝⁝	75	Printing, postage and stationer	102.50		Postage and Carriage	
⁝⁝⁝	76	Retained profit balance forwar		102.50	Postage and Carriage	
⁝⁝⁝	77	Telephone	178.72		Telephone	
⁝⁝⁝	78	Retained profit balance forwar		178.72	Telephone	

Fig. 81

This space is for notes

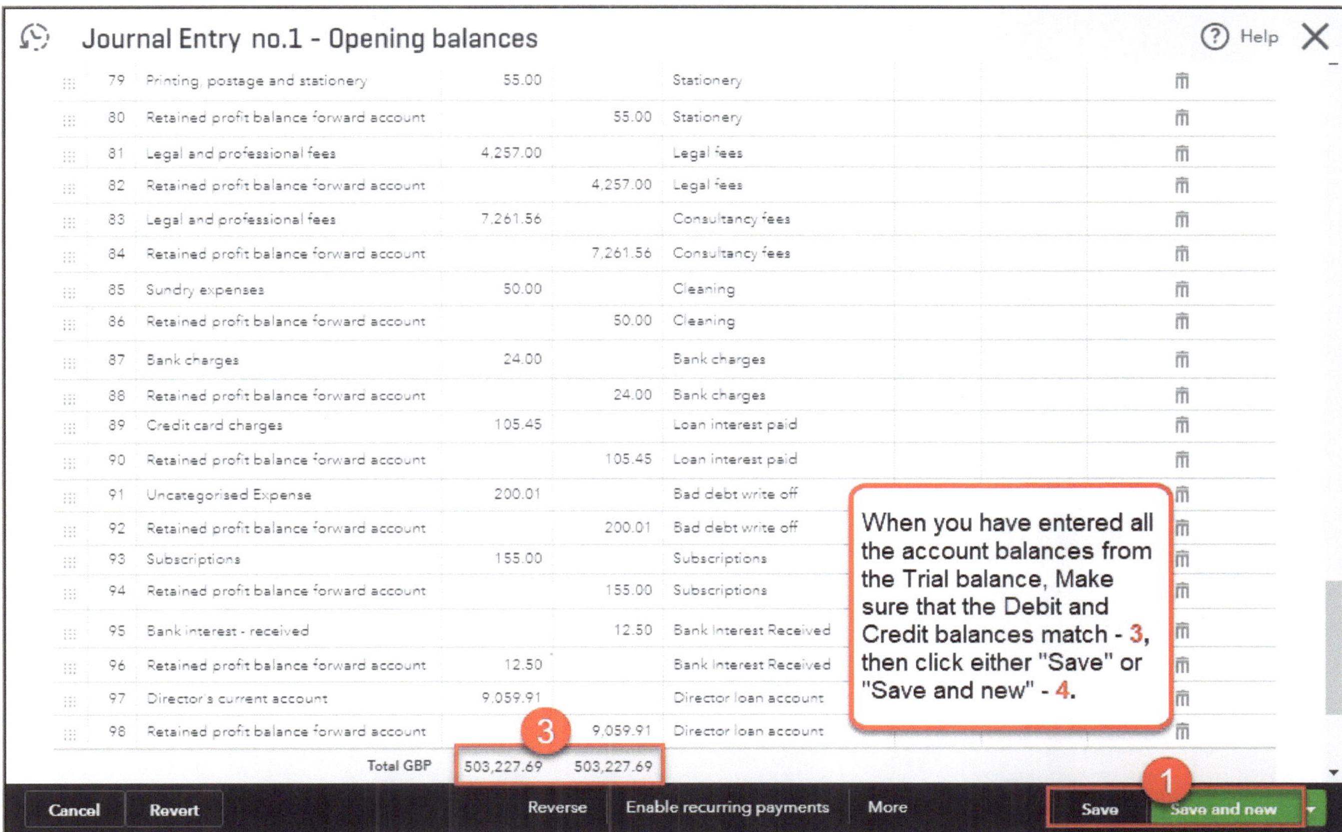

Fig. 82

This space is for notes

What is Opening balance

The opening balance is the balance that is brought forward from the end of one accounting period to the beginning of a new accounting period or from one accounting system to a new accounting system.

TASK 2: HOW TO DO BUDGETING IN QUICKBOOKS ONLINE

In the context of business management, the purpose of budgeting includes the following three aspects:

- A forecast of income and expenditure (and thereby profitability)
- A tool for decision making
- A means to monitor business performance

A carefully constructed budget allows a business to continually track where they are financially. This allows for strategic, long-term planning for everything from current operating costs to potential expansion. Knowing where the budget stands opens up the ability to hire new staffers, invest in new product lines and set earning goals in line with the organisations' corporate financial objectives.

Let's get going with producing Horizon Tristar's budget.

To create, access, edit, or delete budgets in QuickBooks Online, you must have Administrator Access Rights (All Access Rights).

Your budget will start with the first month of the fiscal year you have set up in QuickBooks Online (For Horizon Tristar Ltd it is November of last year). Therefore, you should check that the Fiscal Year setting is accurate before continuing with the Budget set up process.

Here is what you need to do to check Fiscal Year settings:

1. Select the **Gear icon** at the top, then choose **Account and Settings** (or **Company Settings**).
2. Select **Advanced.**
3. Check if the first month of fiscal year is ***November***. If not, select the pencil icon in the Accounting section and set it to November last year.
4. Select **Save.**

With that done, let's proceed.

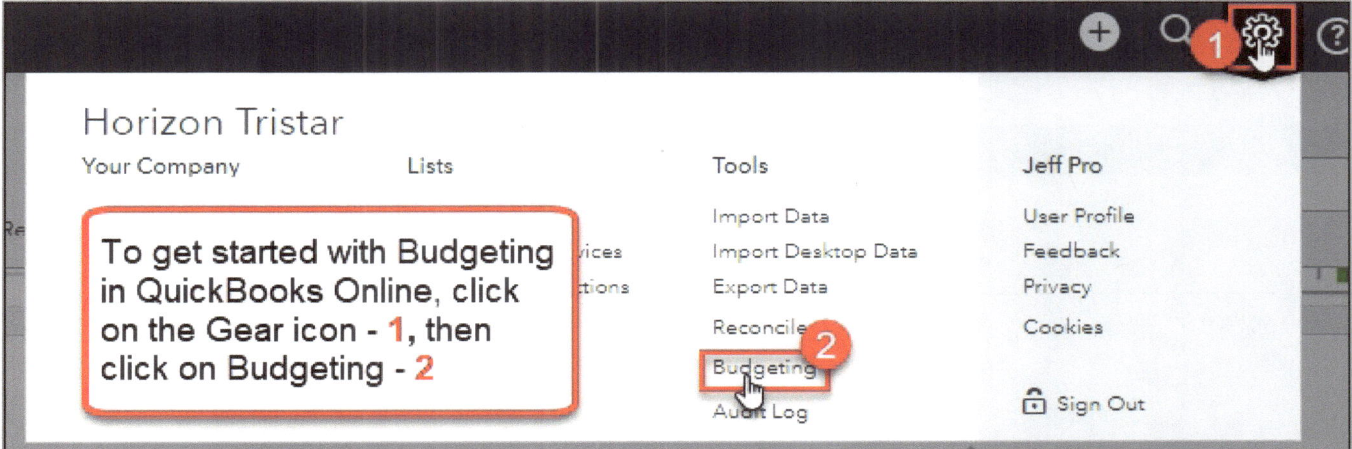

Fig. 83

quickbooks
Help
Dashboard
Banking
Sales
Expenses
Employees
Reports
Taxes
Accounting
My Accountant
Apps
Budgets
To add your first budget for Horizon Tristar Ltd, click "Add budget" - 3.
Add your first budget
Budgets make growing your business easier. Just pre-fill with your data, add your targets, and start towards your goal.
3
Add budget

Fig. 84

New Budget
Name *
4
January - March Budget
Financial Year
FY (Nov - Oct)
5
Interval
Monthly
6
Pre-fill data?
No
7
Subdivide by
Don't subdivide
8
ACCOUNTS
NOV
DEC
JAN
FEB
MAR
APR
MAY
JUN
JUL
AUG
SEP
OCT
TOTAL
INCOME
Billable Expense Income
Expert set up & Installation ser...
Sales
Sales - Consumables
Sales - Office equipment
Sales - Office furniture
Sales of Product Income
Uncategorised Income
Total Income
0.00
0.00
0.00
OTHER INCOME
Bank interest - received
Other finance income
Give the new budget a name e.g. "January - March (this year) budget" - 4.
Select the financial year from the drop down arrow:
FY[this year] (Nov [last year]- Oct [this year]) - 5
From the drop down list from in 6, select "Monthly" as the interval.
Select "No" in 7 so as not to pre-fill the data (We are doing zero based budgeting)
Select "Don't subdivide" in the drop down arrow 8
Next

Fig. 85

This space is for notes

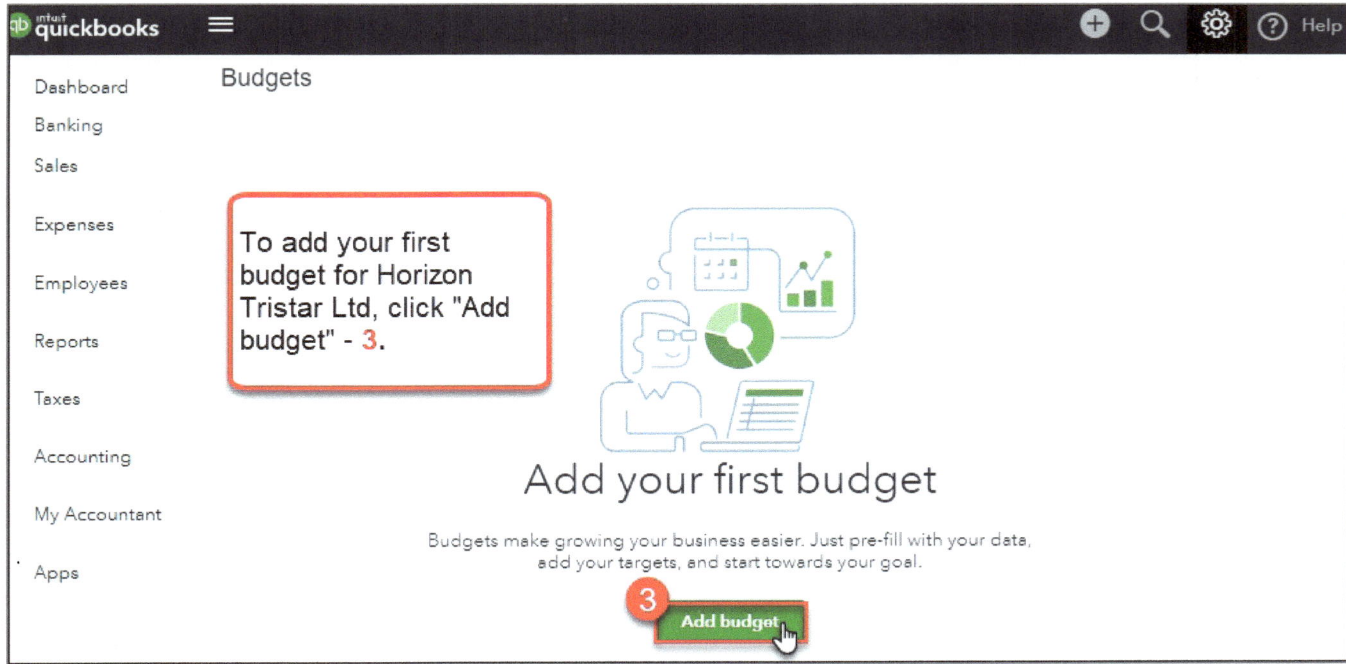

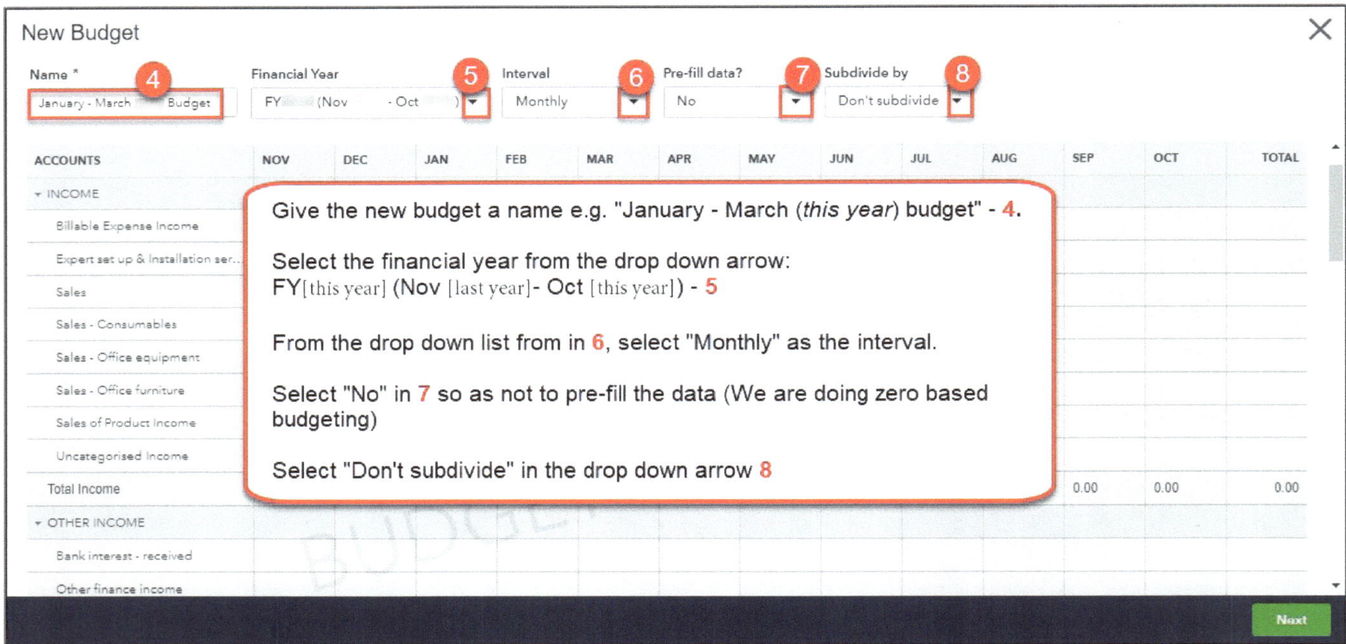

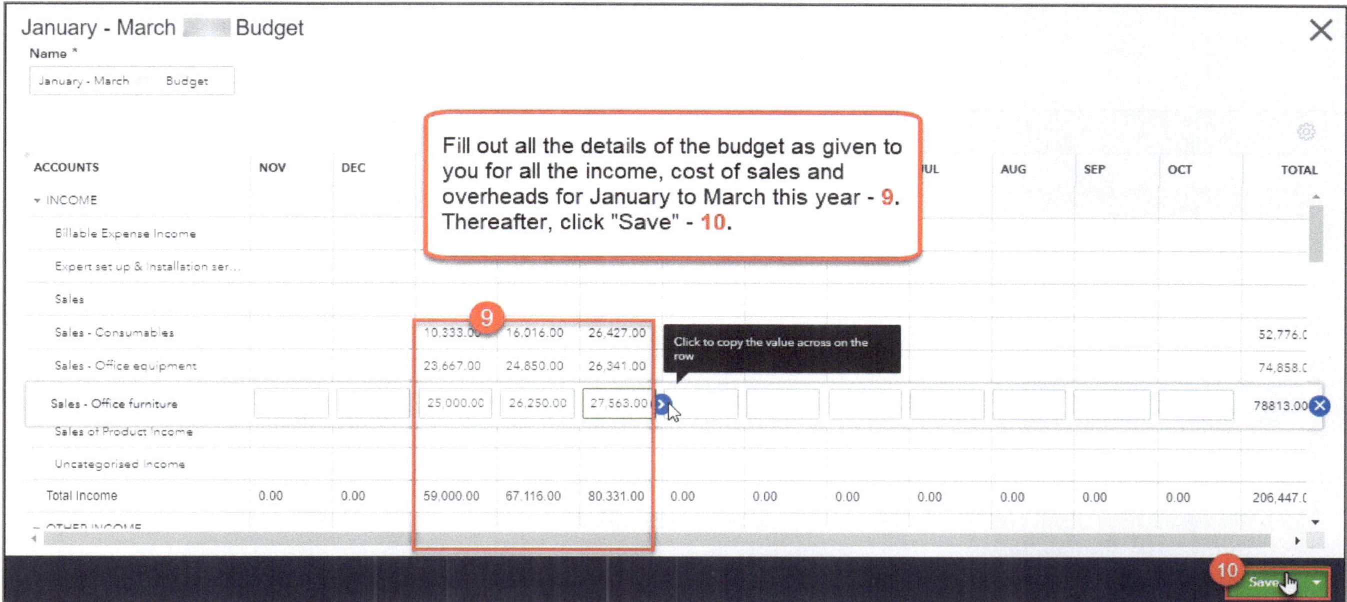

Fig. 86

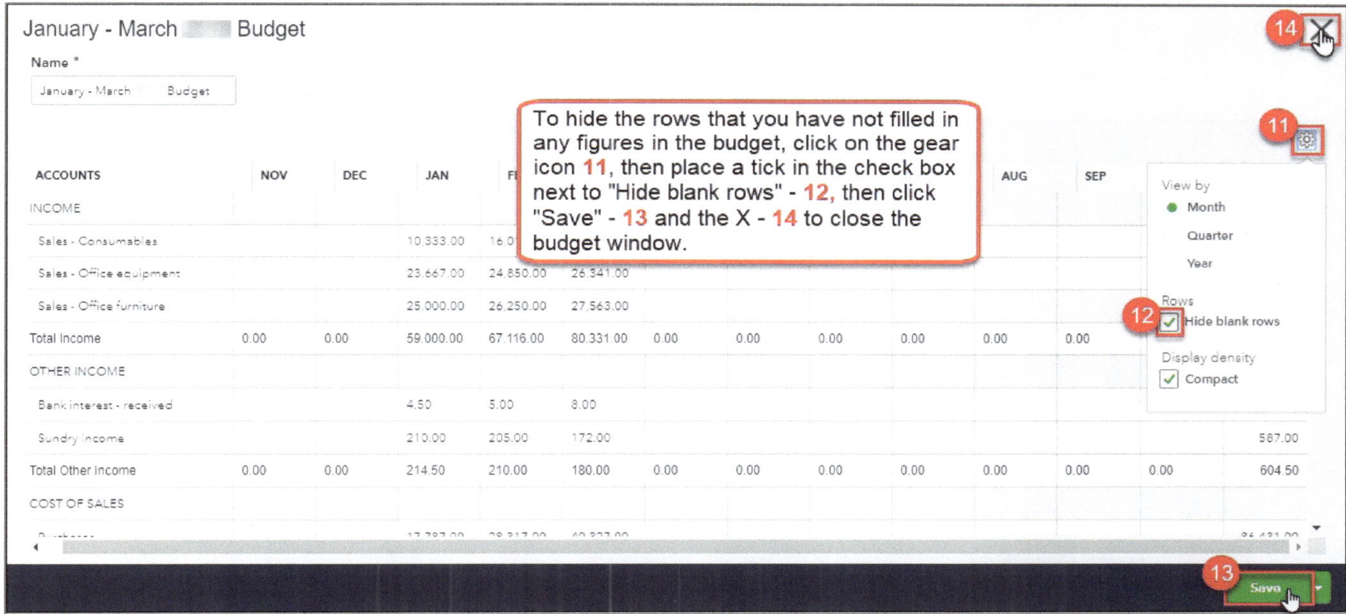

Fig. 87

This space is for notes

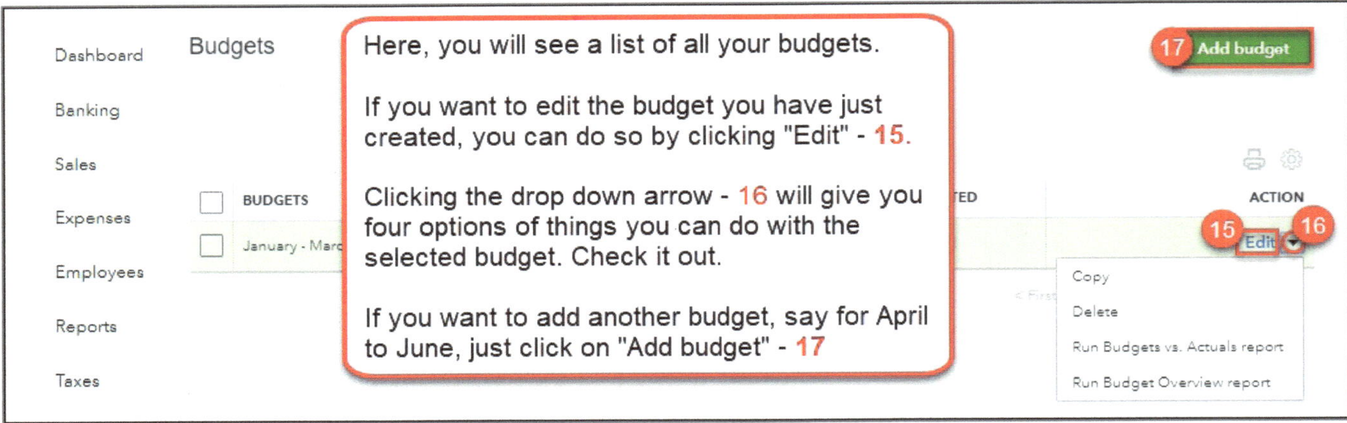

Fig. 88

That's it, you have managed to set up Horizon Tristar's budget for January to March this year. You will have the opportunity in March to compare the budget figures you have just entered to the actual figures that will reflect the actual performance of the business and with that, do some variance analysis.

We will now move on to the next task – Doing Accounts payable tasks.

Notes

"The essential ingredient necessary for winning with money in the long run is self-control and generosity"
Sterling Libs

TASK 3: DOING THE ACCOUNTS RECEIVABLE TASKS

A brief over overview of the Accounts Receivable process – the key steps

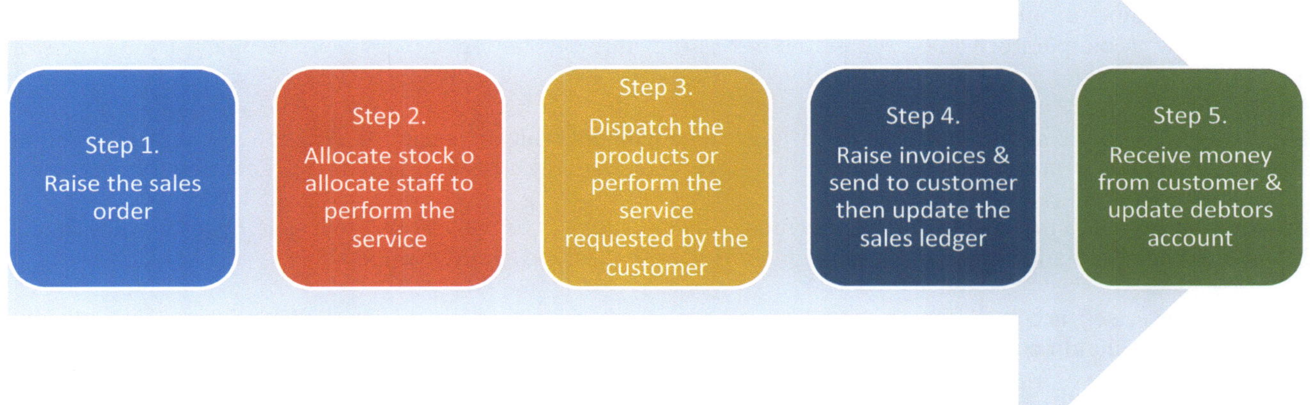

Fig. 88

You see, when a business is involved in selling its products or services, it can do so by selling on credit (this results in what is called Receivables) or selling in cash (this results in what is called technically called in accounting receipts) or you can sell in both ways (and most businesses do it both ways).

Accounting for the sales made on credit is carried out in a series of tasks/procedures called the Accounts receivable process as illustrated in figure 2.

What does 'on credit' mean? Well, it means when you sell a service or item to a customer and are not paid immediately - you are extending credit to them.

So, the accounts receivable process does not apply to sales where you are paid immediately. Sales, where you are paid promptly, are called cash sales or receipts, and their accounting process is a bit different and quite straightforward.

Now, let's look at the **Accounts receivable process** – as illustrated in figure 2 above and understand the steps involved in the process in a bit more detail.

Step 1. Send quotation for your goods/service(s) to the customer

What's a quotation/quote? Well, a quotation or quote in accounting is a formal document which explains a business's pricing for a product or service and gives the customer a precise cost for the product/service.

When a customer asks you for a quote, it means they're seriously considering doing business with you. All your sales and marketing efforts have paid off! You've shown that your service has value, and you're one step away from closing the deal.

Quotations usually are given to customers by sales staff, but the quotation stage is a significant and integral part of the accounts receivable process/function because once accepted by the customer, it has legal status in many countries. So, you usually can't charge more (raise an invoice for a different value - higher) for the product/work than you've quoted.

Step 2: Receive & process customer orders

Once the customer is happy with the quotation, they usually send an order – purchase order (ask for a written one, not verbal and make a note of the purchase order number from the customer) for the goods/services your company has quoted for them.

Your task then is to process that purchase order from the customer by raising a sales order.

A sales order is an internal document of your company, your company itself generates it.

Your sales order should record the customer's originating purchase order which is an external document. Rather than using the customer's purchase order document, an internal sales order form allows the internal audit control of completeness to be monitored as a sequential sales order number can be used by your company for its sales order documents.

The customer's Purchase Order (PO) is the originating document which triggers the creation of the sales order, and a sales order, being an internal document, can, therefore, contain many customer purchase orders under it.

If your business is in a manufacturing environment, a sales order can be converted into a work order to show that work is about to begin to manufacture, build or engineer the products the customer wants.

Many computerised accounting software systems now have the function of sales order processing built in, and hopefully, these should not be a tough task for you.

Step 3&4: Deliver the goods/services to the customer and raise the invoice

Having converted the order from the customer to accounts receivable, you will have to deliver the goods or perform the service(s) as per the request from the customer.

Bear in mind that the invoice you raise for the product or service delivered to your customer is a legal, financial document of which you have to keep records by law.

Therefore, when raising a Sales Invoice, the following should be noted:

- Your business name and address details should be in the invoice

- A unique invoice reference/number that will relate to this invoice only.
- A date for the invoice (which will generally be the date on which the invoice is created/raised)
- The prices and goods/service described in the invoice should be those agreed with the customer (via the quotation step discussed above)
- Invoices should be sent out as soon as possible following the supply of goods/services and no later than "X" number of days after the supply (These depends on what your company policy is)

- Additions and calculations in the invoice should always be checked before invoices are dispatched to customers.
- A total amount for the invoice.

- The payment terms for the invoice (i.e., how long the customer has to pay)
- If you are a registered Limited company, you must include Your Company Number and your full registered company address on the invoice.

Addressing a sales invoice

Correctly addressing invoices is crucial. If an error is made, it may be impossible to collect the outstanding debt from the customer.

The following steps should be taken:

- ✓ Find out who exactly will be making the payment from the customer's side.
- ✓ Invoices should be addressed as follows:

for the attention of:

ABC PLC/LTD

Company's full address

- ✓ Customer Purchase Order Number - so they know which purchase order the invoice relates to if they are using an order management system.
- ✓ Details on how to pay, including bank account details for BACs/ online payments.
- ✓ If you are VAT registered you must also include: The amount of VAT on each line of the invoice and the VAT rate charged OR the total amount of VAT charged on the invoice, and the rate, if VAT applies to all items on the invoice and don't forget to include your VAT number on the invoice.

Step 5: Maintaining invoices & payments

This is the core of your accounts receivable procedures. There is no point in selling to customers on credit and failing to collect the outstanding amounts later.

Here are the steps to follow from the time you give the customer their invoice:-

If you are using a Manual Receivables System (MRS)

a. Print a copy of the invoices and place it into your *Receivables file in sequential order - either by date or invoice number.
b. Make a cover page on which to list the unpaid invoices. Draw up columns to display i) the date, ii) the customer name, iii) the invoice number, iv) the amount, v) paid date. Keep this cover page in the front of the folder.
a. When payment is received, either by cash, cheque or internet banking, write the date it was paid into the 'paid date' column of the Receivables cover page. You can also make a note (hand-written or stamped) of the date paid on the invoice itself.
b. Remove the invoice from the Receivables file and place it into a *Sales Invoice file (an archive for all the paid invoices).

*You could instead have one folder with two sections i) Unpaid Invoices, ii) Paid Invoices, this is just one method. You can change it to suit your requirements, and indeed, design a whole different system, as long as what you do helps you keep a handle on those unpaid invoices.

If you are using Computerised Bookkeeping System (CBS)

If you are using bookkeeping software that has a receivables option, it is easy to check what is due, because when you run a receivables report it will only list the invoices that have not been paid - as long as all the payments received have been entered into the program!

Therefore, you do not need to keep a separate receivables folder. You can just place all invoices directly into the Sales

Invoices folder because you will use the bookkeeping program for the accounts receivable procedures.

Customer/Debtor credit notes

On the other hand, if a customer returns goods to you for full or partial credit, you should issue the customer with a credit note. The amount shown on the credit note should be equal to the amount of error or overcharge identified. All credit notes are to be raised by the Accounts Receivable team.

Invoices raised to correct an undercharge should refer to the original invoice number.

Task 3a: How to raise sales orders, sales invoices and sales credit notes

As seen from the first step in the Accounts Receivable overview, a Sales order is generated when the seller converts the sales quote approved by the customer into a Sales Order (SO).

Suffice it to say that a sales order (SO) is an internal document generated by the seller, indicating that the customer is now ready to purchase products and services. It is a confirmation document that authorises the sale of listed items for the given amount. The document gives a clear understanding of what the customer has decided to buy. SO is often considered a legal contract that makes it mandatory for the seller to sell products at the agreed upon price. The seller generates SO when the sales quote sent to the customer is approved.

The generation of SO implies confirmation of sale and no additional charges resulting from increased labour or transportation cost will be included in the document. So once the SO is created, the seller will have to sell the products at the agreed upon price quoted with no further cost to be incurred by the buyer. In case, the sellers want to make any changes in SO document; it is necessary to take prior consent from the buyer.

While a Sales Order confirms a sale, an invoice indicates that the customer is legally bound to pay for the products that have been delivered to him. Sales order authorises the products & services that customer wants to buy from the seller. On the other hand, the invoice is the bill for the products that the customer has purchased from the seller.

Here are the steps from quotation/estimate to invoice

Fig. 89

Let's do that in QuickBooks Online, shall we?

To begin the process, click on the create (+) button as illustrated in the figure below.

Fig. 90

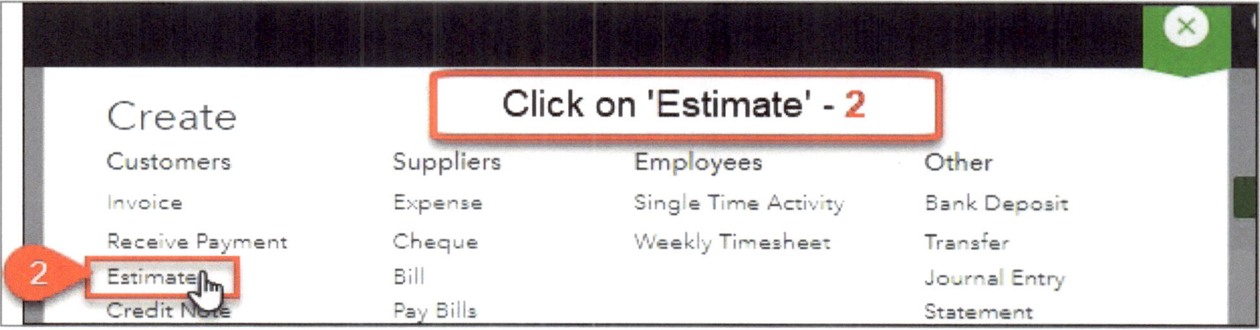

Fig. 91

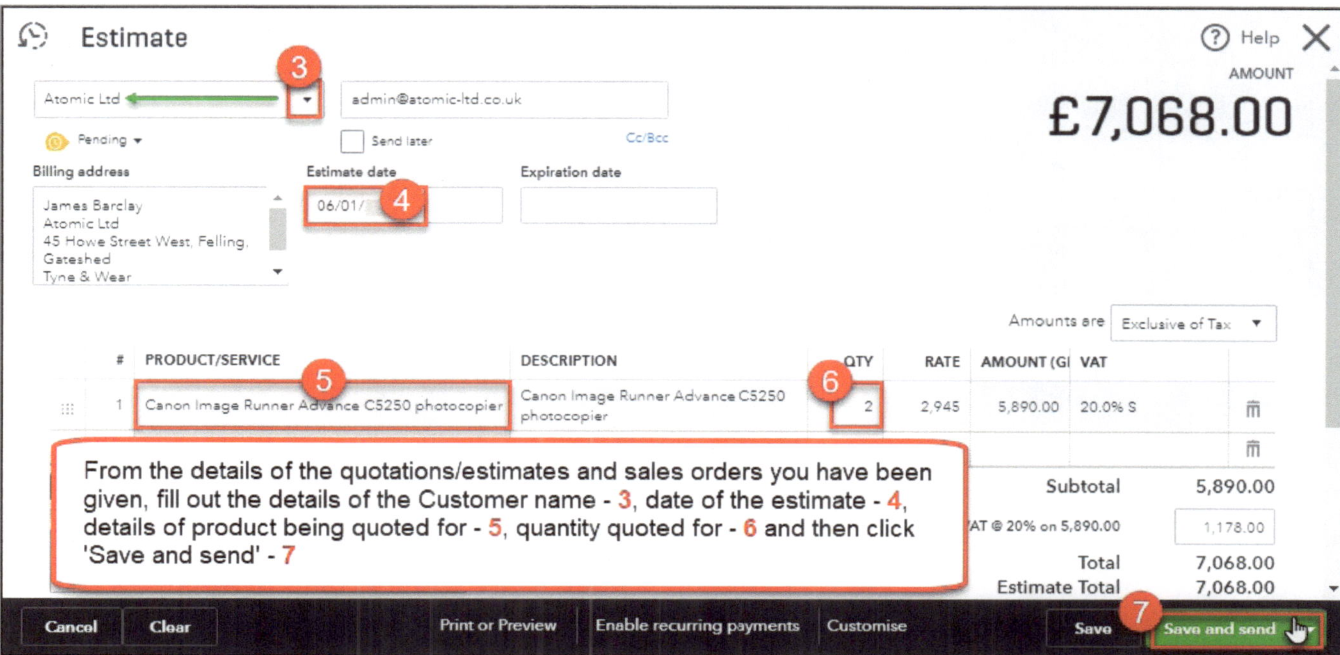

Fig. 92

This space is for notes

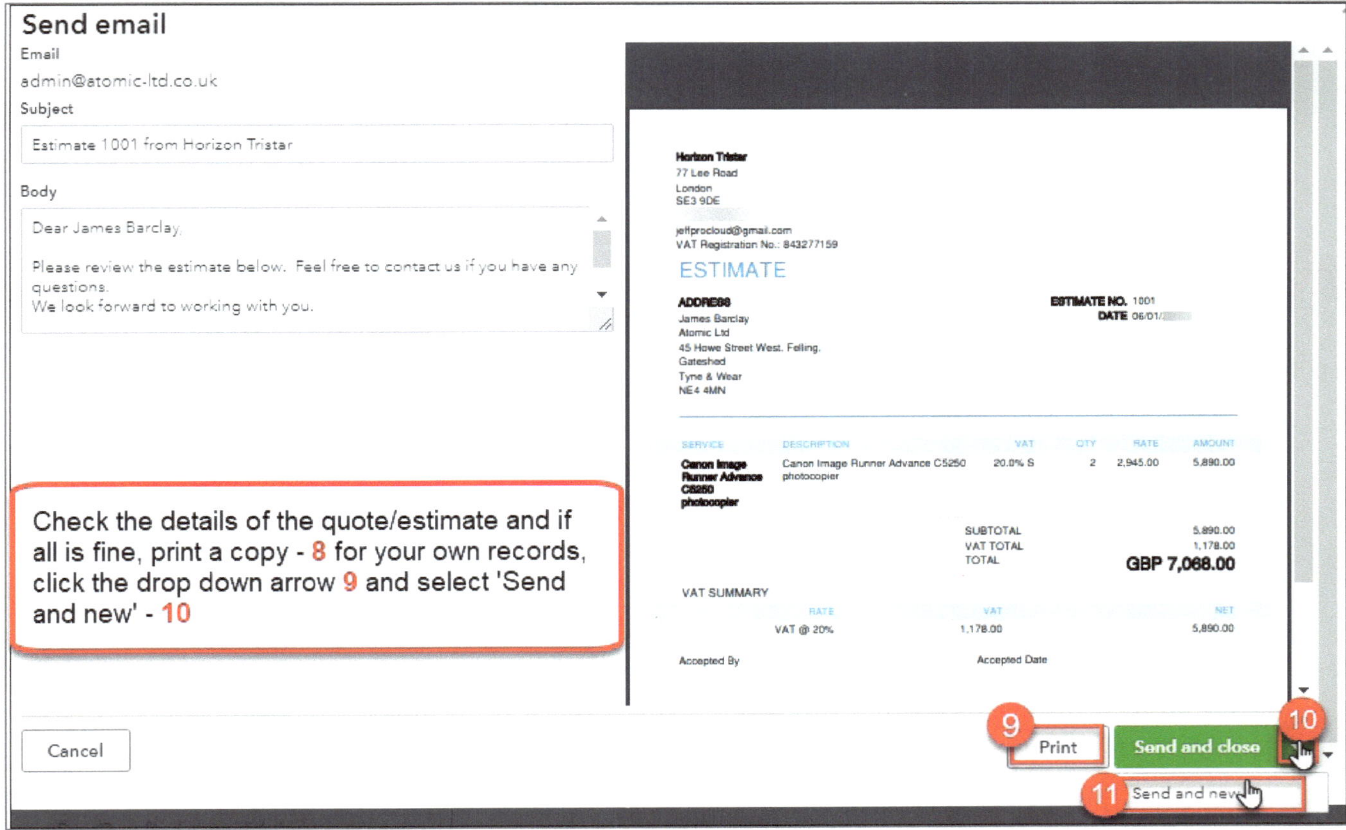

Fig. 93

After step 11 as illustrated in the figure above, fill out the details of the quotation/estimate for Golden Goose Ltd – see figure 177.

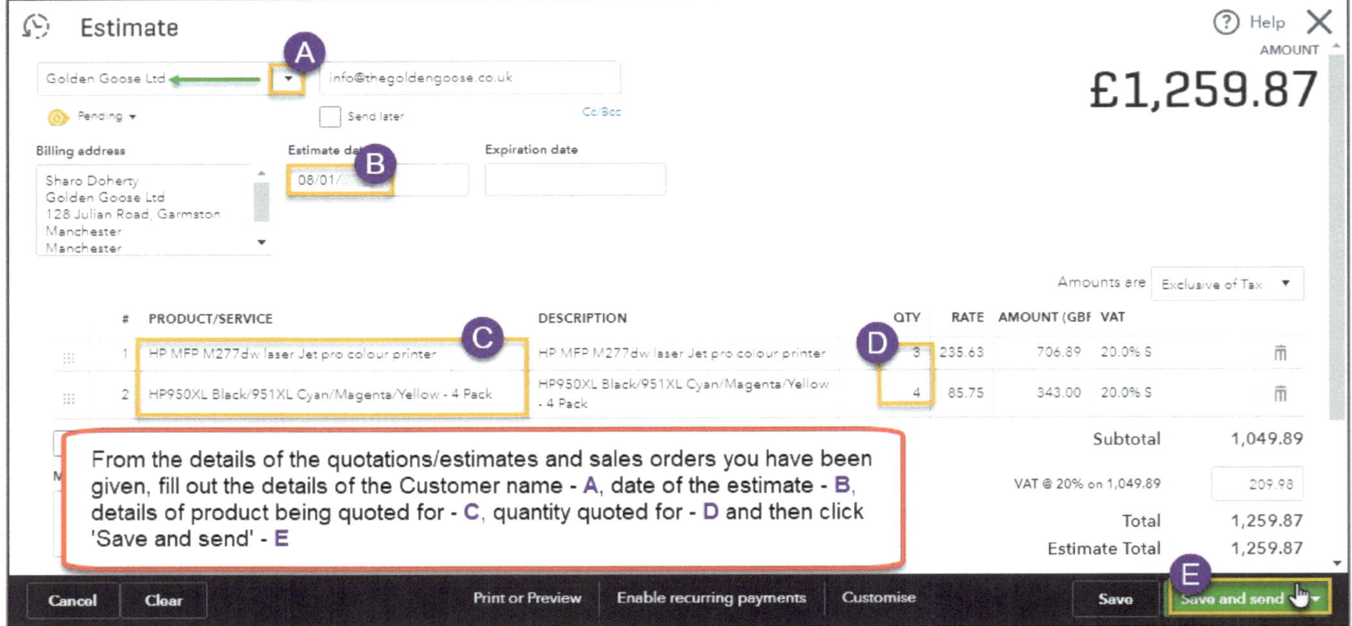

Fig. 94

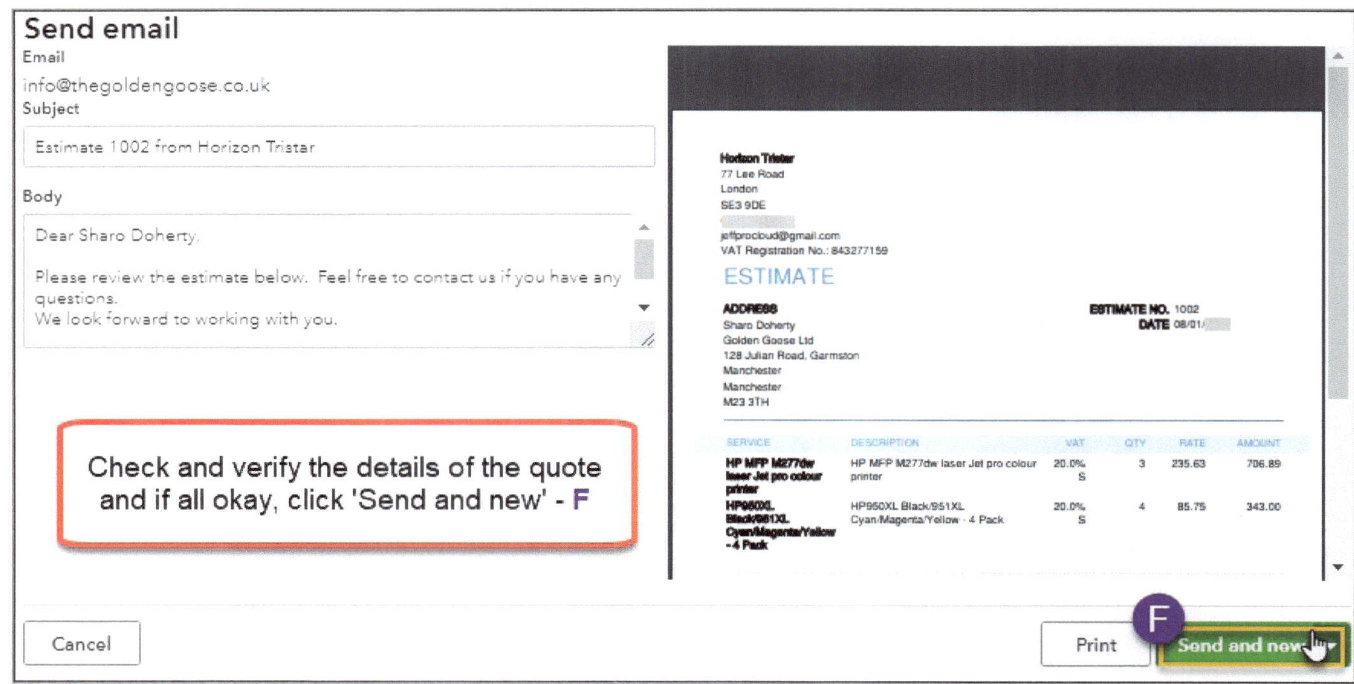

Fig. 95

And for A2Z Enterprises, here is how the quotation/estimate should look like on your screen.

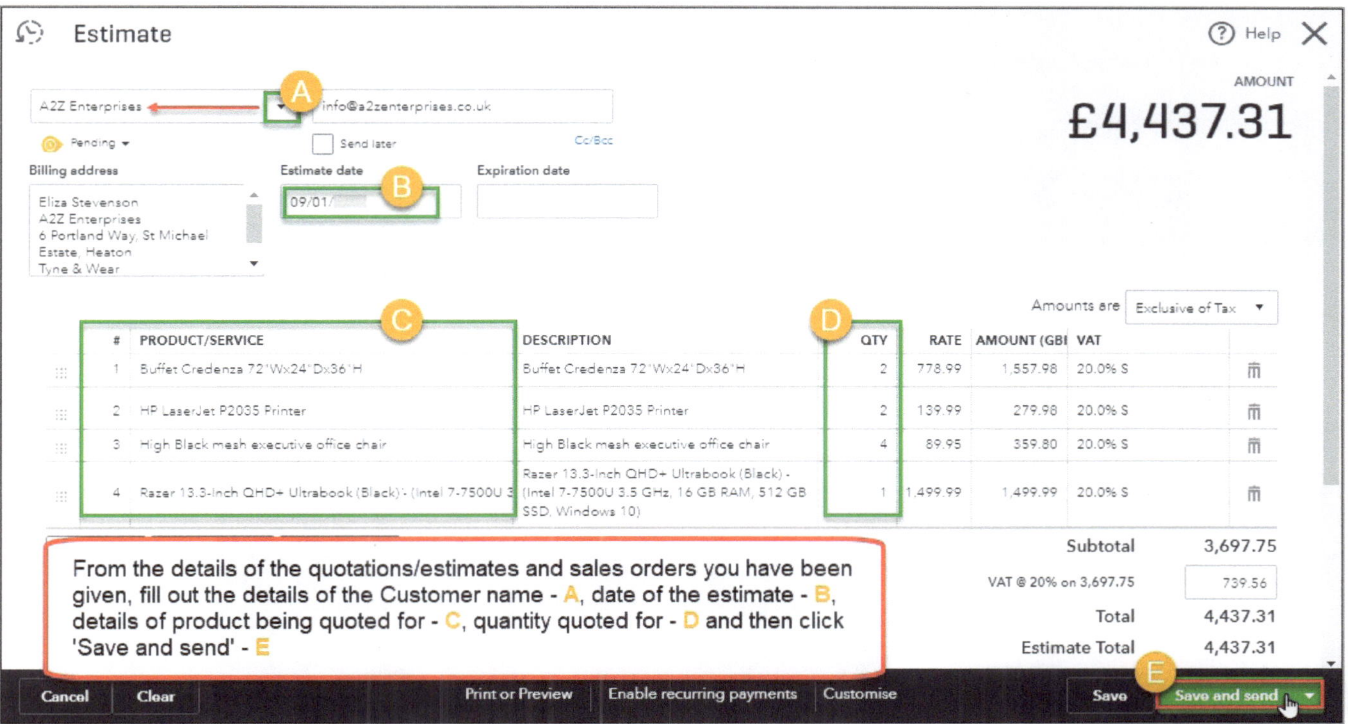

Fig. 96

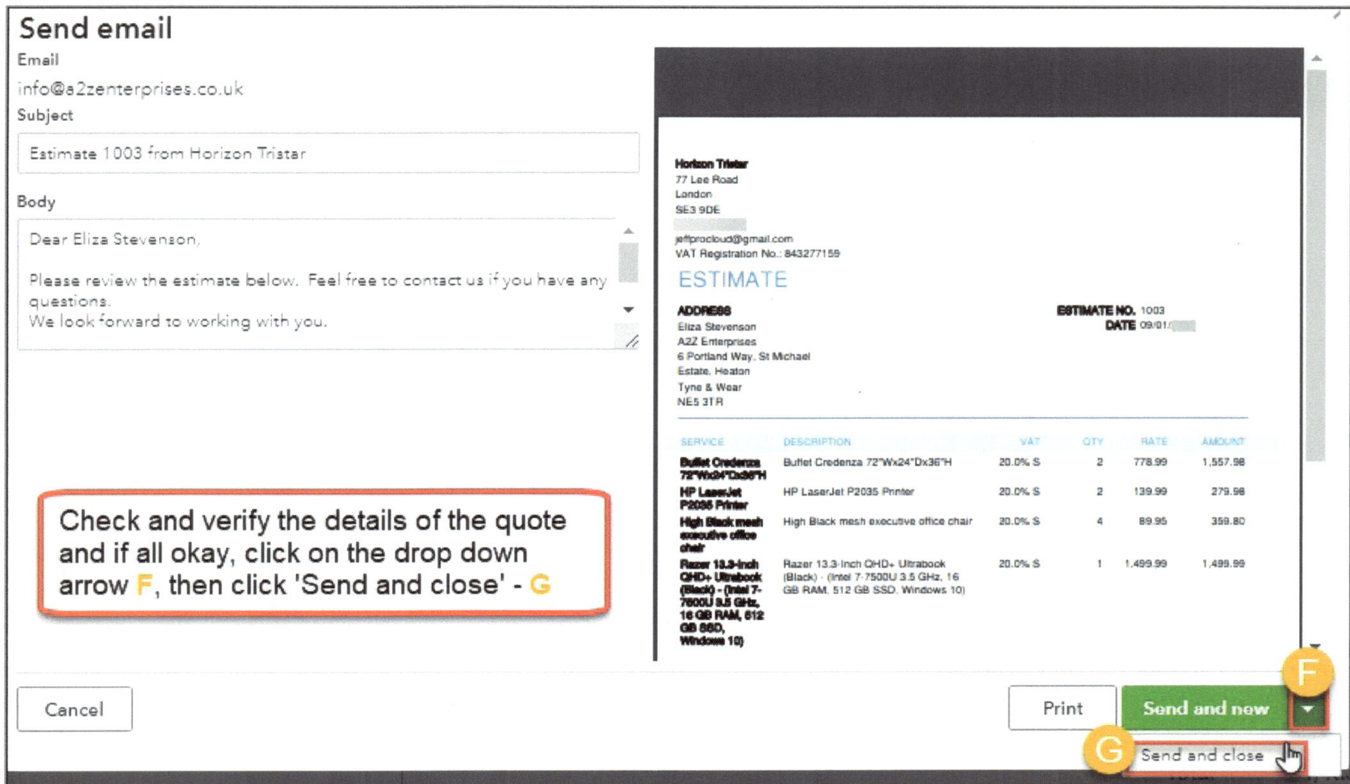

Fig. 97

Processing a customer sales invoice from sales orders.

Let's raise the first invoice Atomic Ltd. Click on the Create (+) button, then click on Invoice

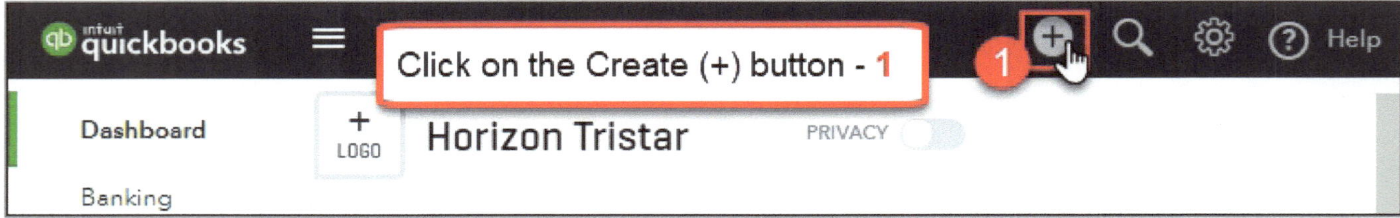

Fig. 98

Fig. 99

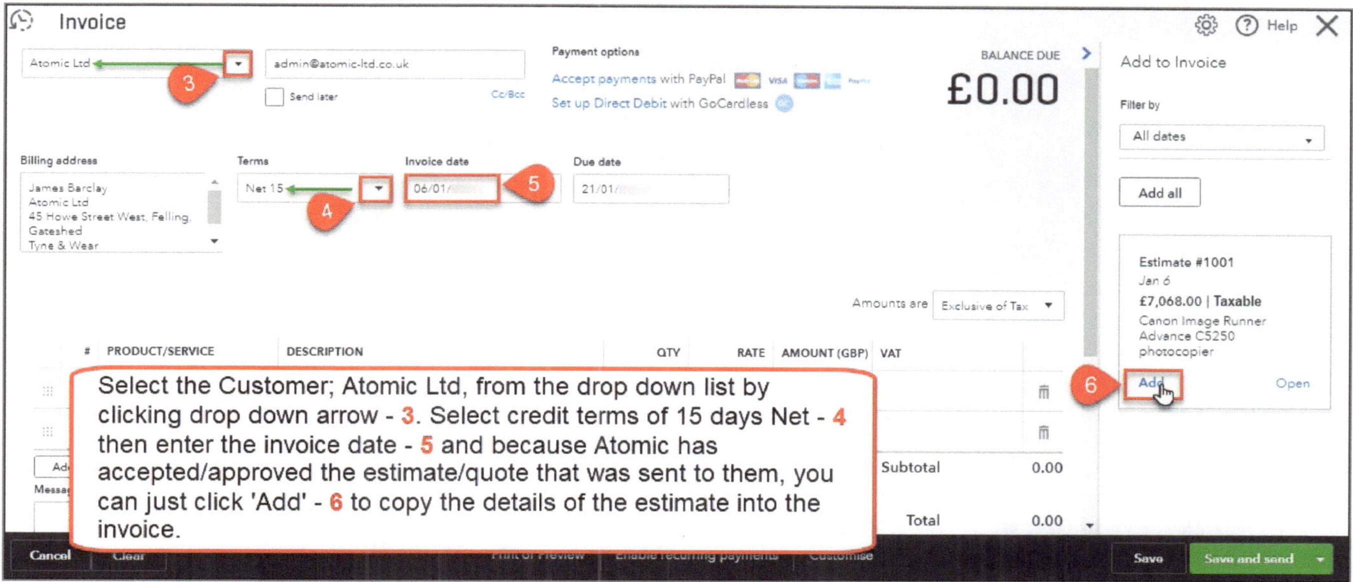

Fig. 100

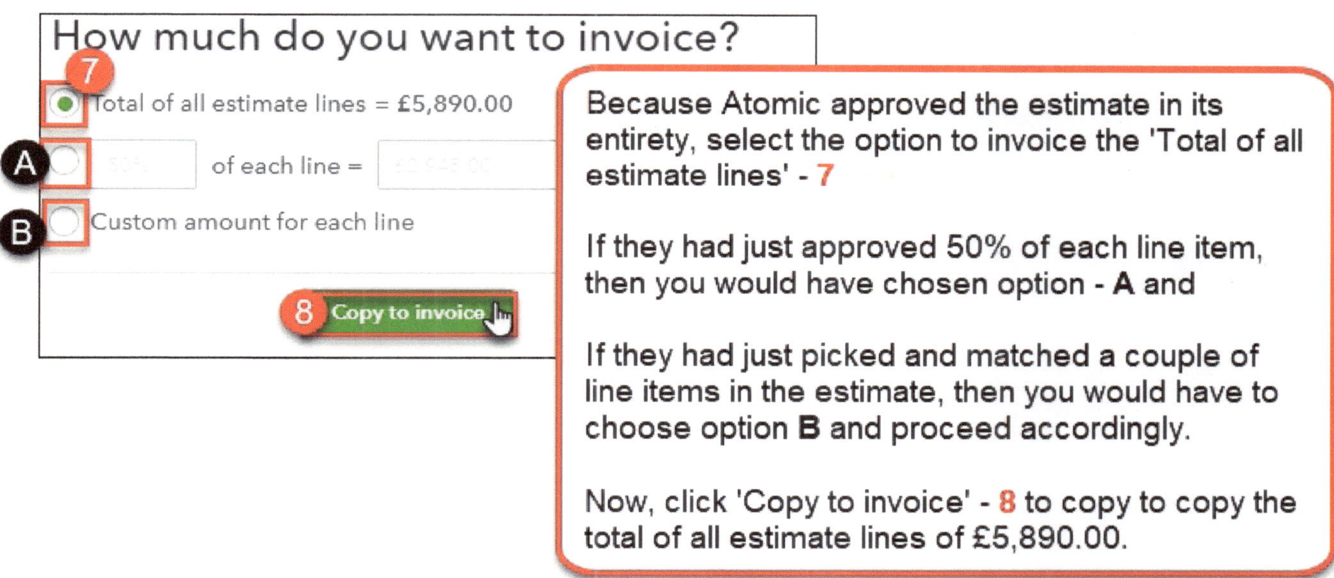

Fig. 101

This space is for notes

Invoice
Help
Atomic Ltd
admin@atomic-ltd.co.uk
1 linked transaction
9
Send later
Cc/Bcc
Payment options
Accept payments with PayPal
Set up Direct Debit with GoCardless
BALANCE DUE
£7,068.00
Billing address
James Barclay
Atomic Ltd
45 Howe Street West, Felling,
Gateshead
Tyne & Wear
Terms
Net 15
Invoice date
06/01/
Due date
21/01/
Amounts are
Exclusive of Tax
PRODUCT/SERVICE DESCRIPTION DUE QTY RATE AMOUNT (GBP) VAT
1 Canon Image Runner Advance Canon Image Runner Advance C5250 photocopier 5,890.00 of 5,890.00 2 2,945 5,890.00 20.0% S
9
Confirm that all the details of the estimate have been copied over to the invoice and 9 shows you that there is a linked transaction to this invoice. If you click on that hyperlink in 9, you will find out that it is the estimate.
Click 'Save and send' - 10
Subtotal 5,890.00
VAT @ 20% on 5,890.00 1,178.00
Total 7,068.00
Balance due 7,068.00
10
Cancel
Clear
Print or Preview
Enable recurring payments
Customise
Save
Save and send

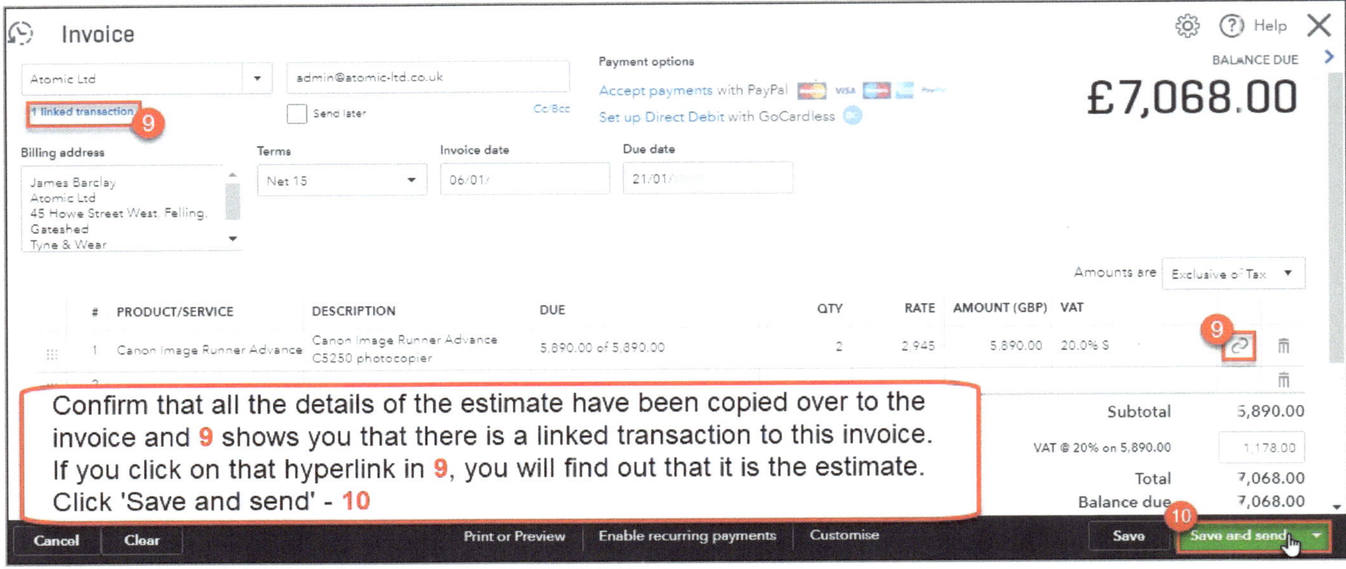

Fig. 102

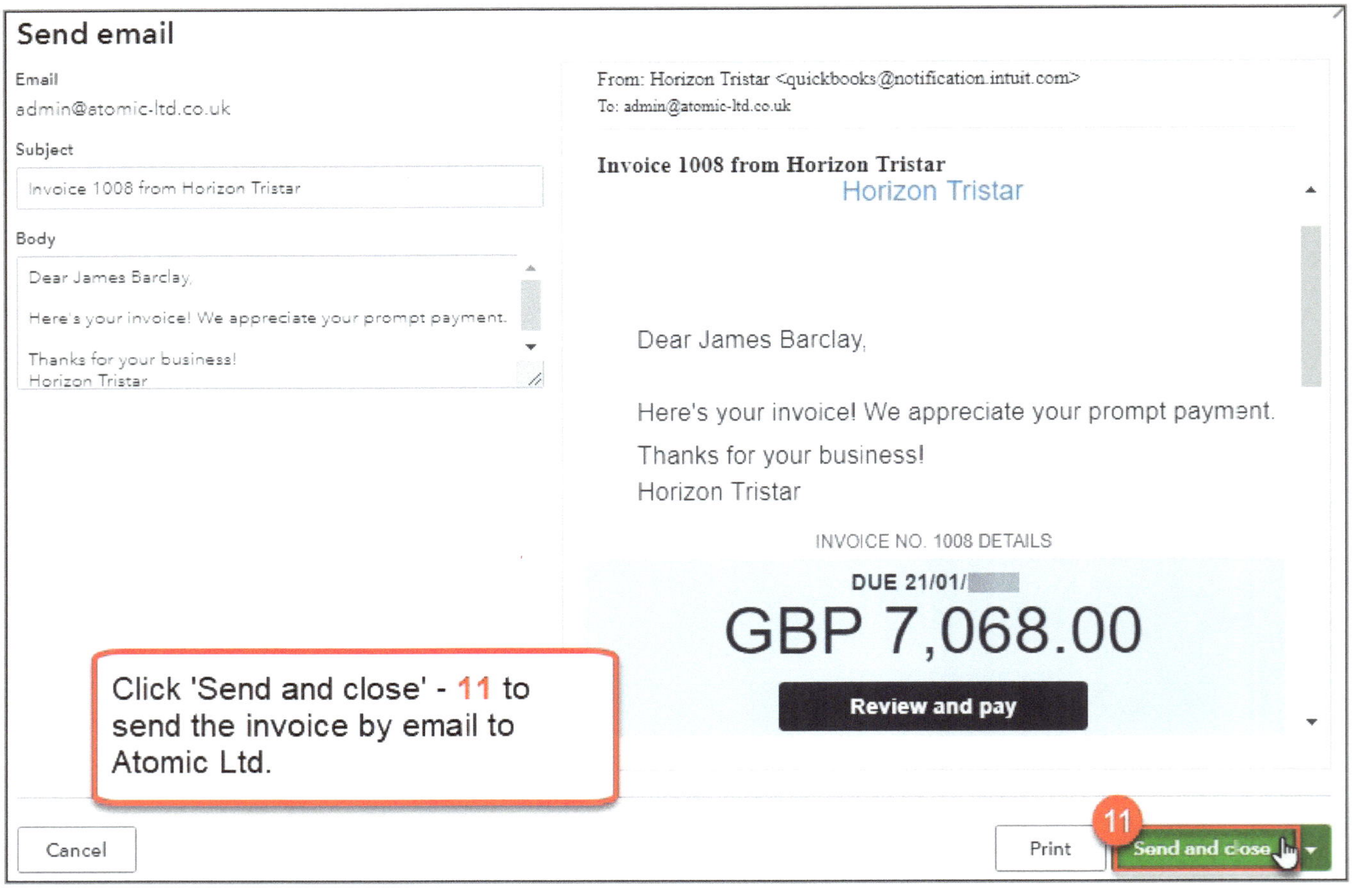

Send email
Email
admin@atomic-ltd.co.uk
Subject
Invoice 1008 from Horizon Tristar
Body
Dear James Barclay,
Here's your invoice! We appreciate your prompt payment.
Thanks for your business!
Horizon Tristar
From: Horizon Tristar <quickbooks@notification.intuit.com>
To: admin@atomic-ltd.co.uk
Invoice 1008 from Horizon Tristar
Horizon Tristar
Dear James Barclay,
Here's your invoice! We appreciate your prompt payment.
Thanks for your business!
Horizon Tristar
INVOICE NO. 1008 DETAILS
DUE 21/01/
GBP 7,068.00
Review and pay
Click 'Send and close' - 11 to send the invoice by email to Atomic Ltd.
Cancel
Print
11
Send and close

Fig. 103

For the Invoice for Golden Goose Ltd, see below.

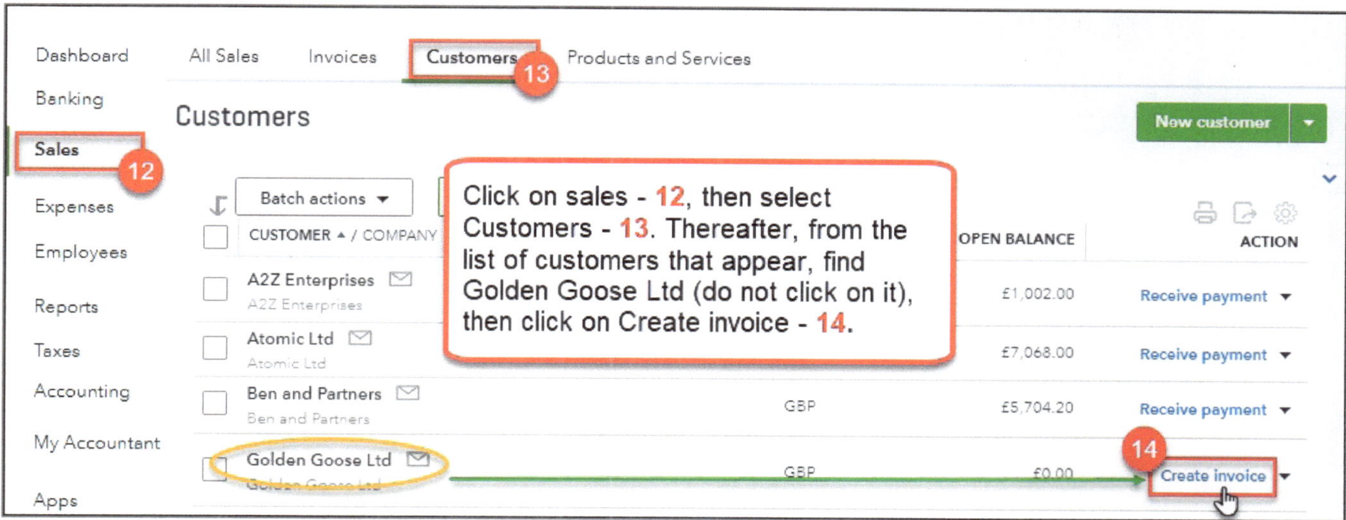

Fig. 104

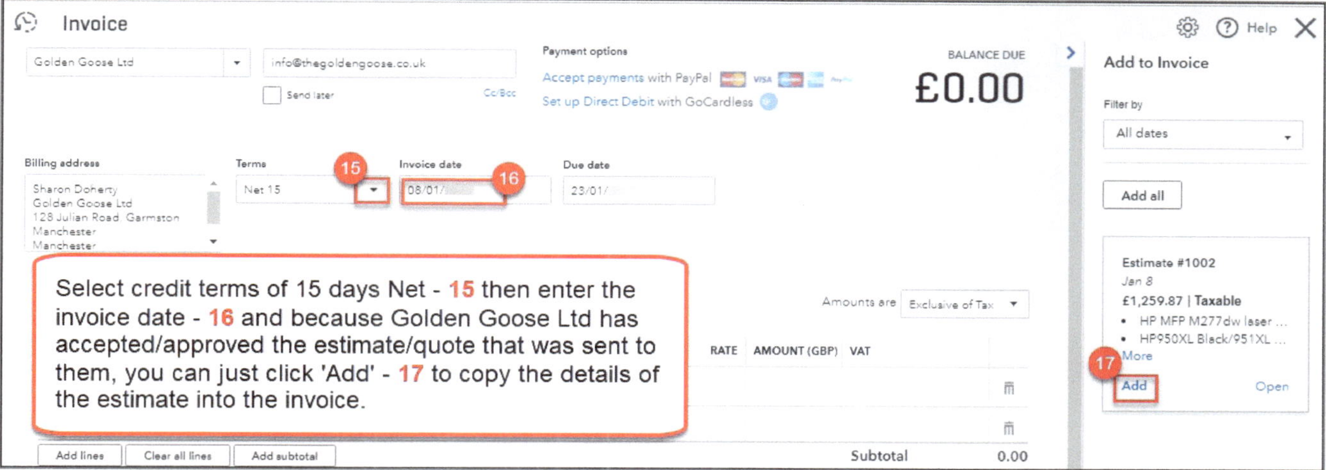

Fig. 105

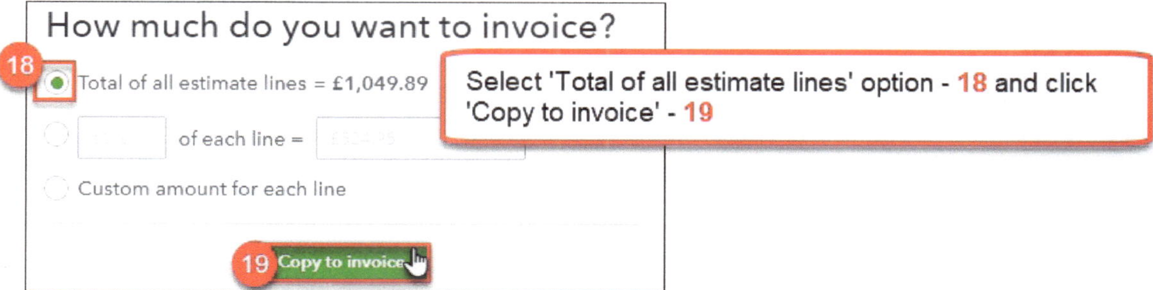

Fig. 106

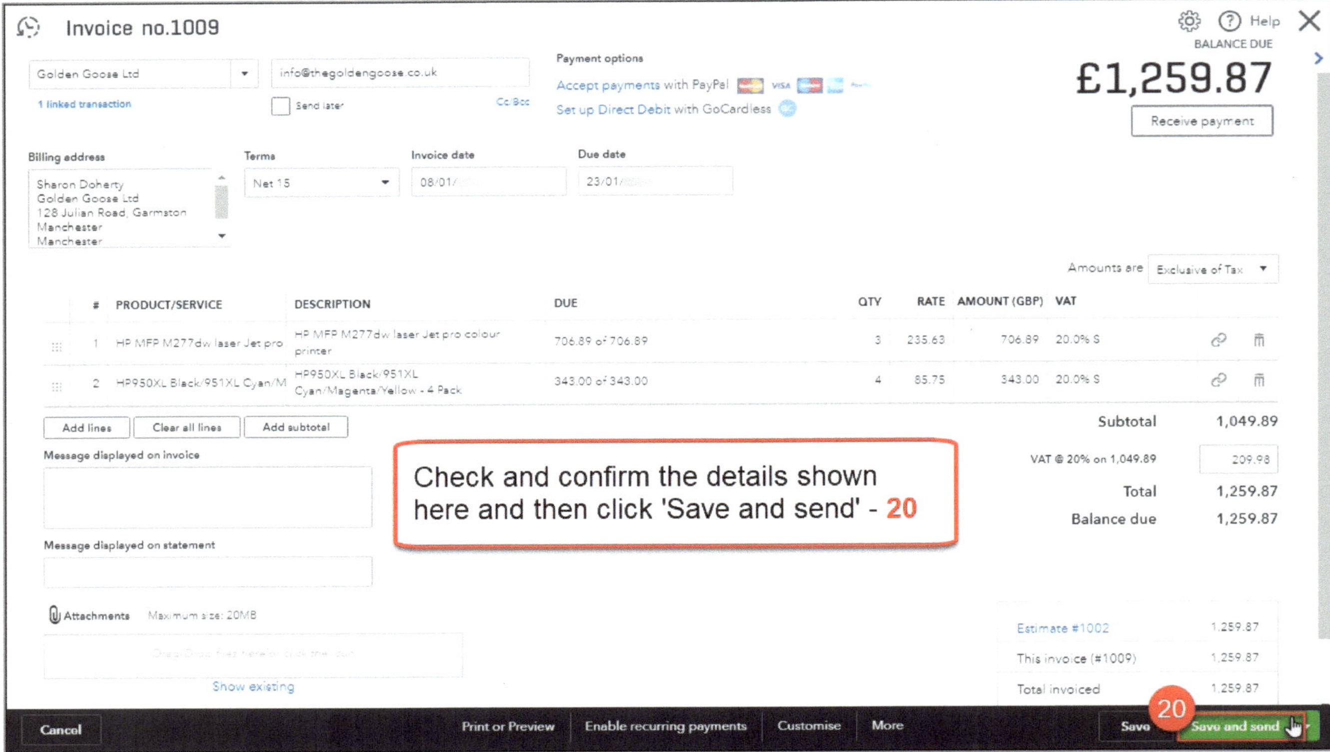

Fig. 107

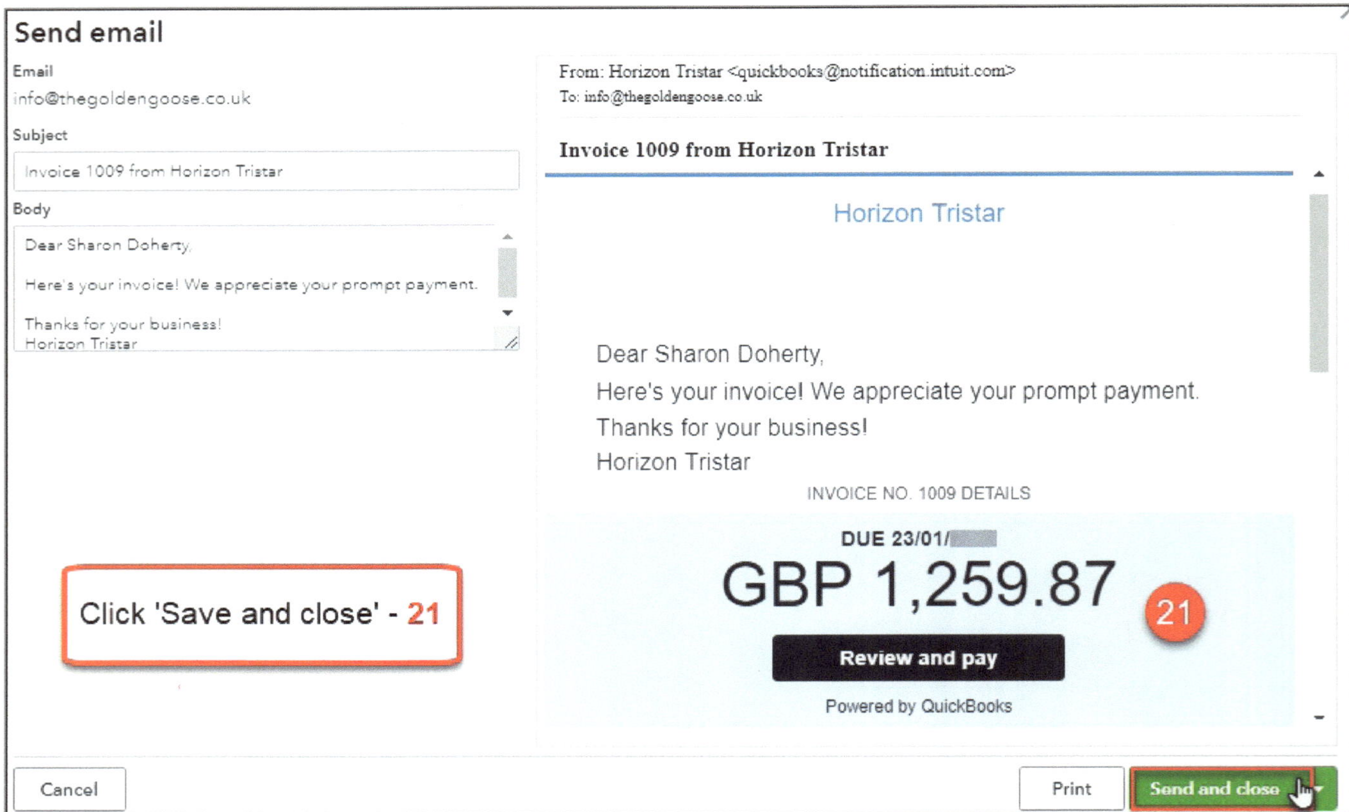

Fig. 108

Invoice for A2Z Enterprises

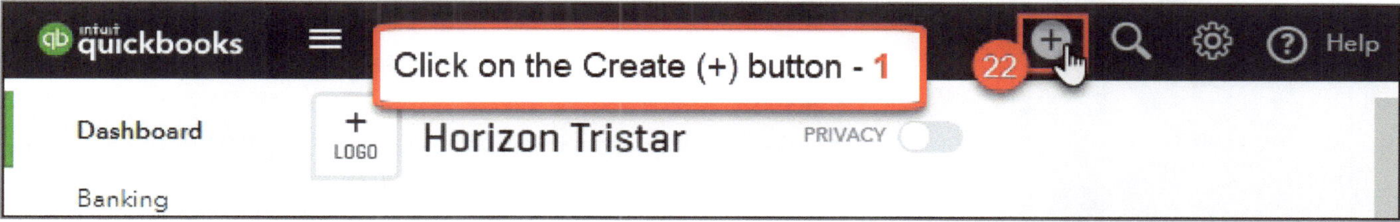

Fig. 109

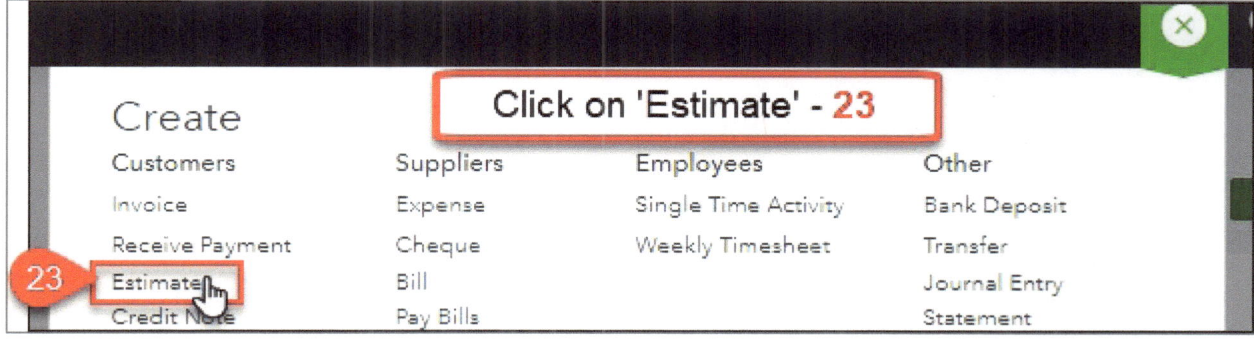

Fig. 110

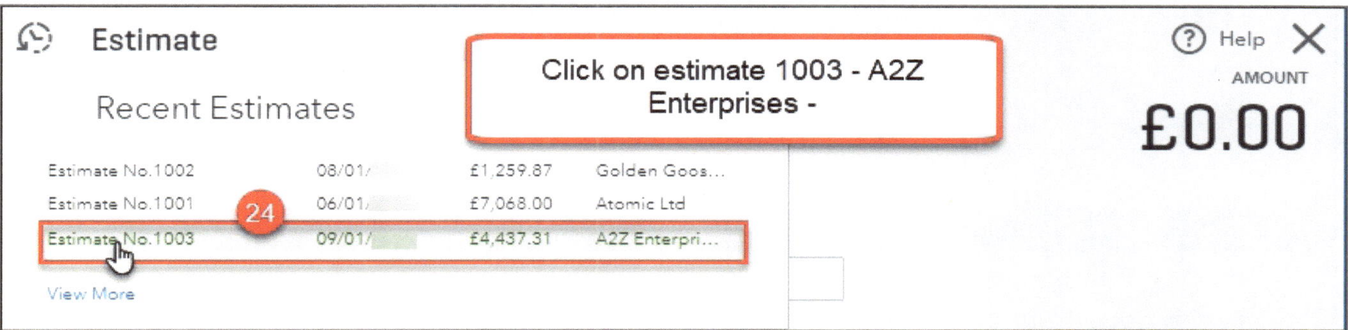

Fig. 111

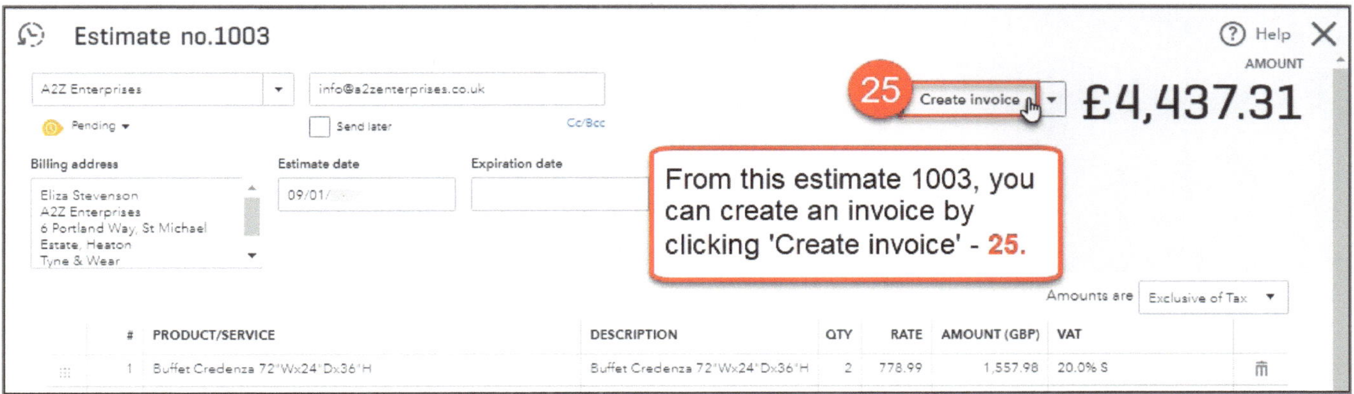

Fig. 112

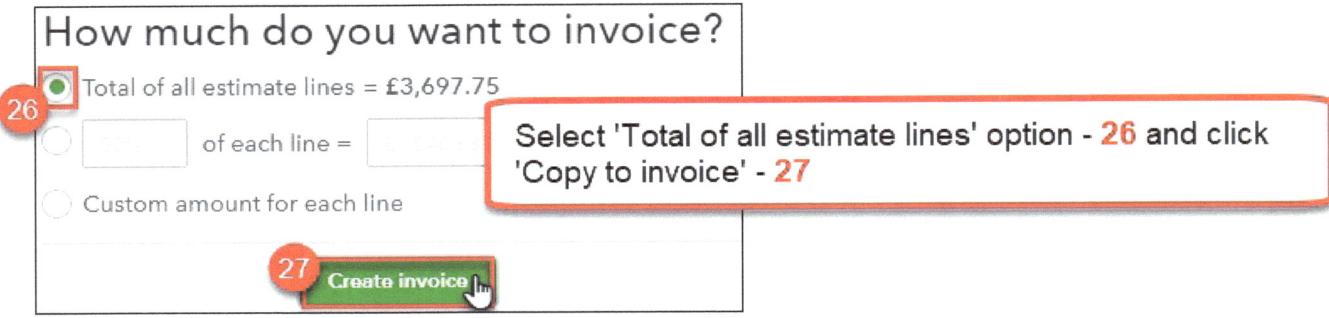

Fig. 113

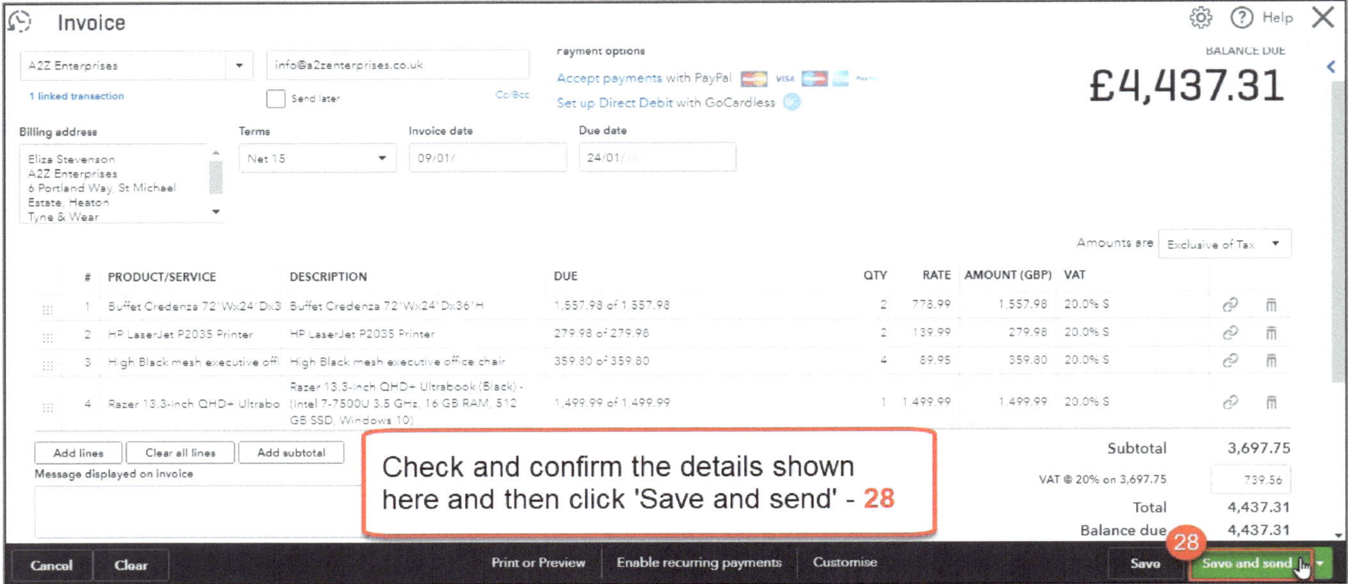

Fig. 114

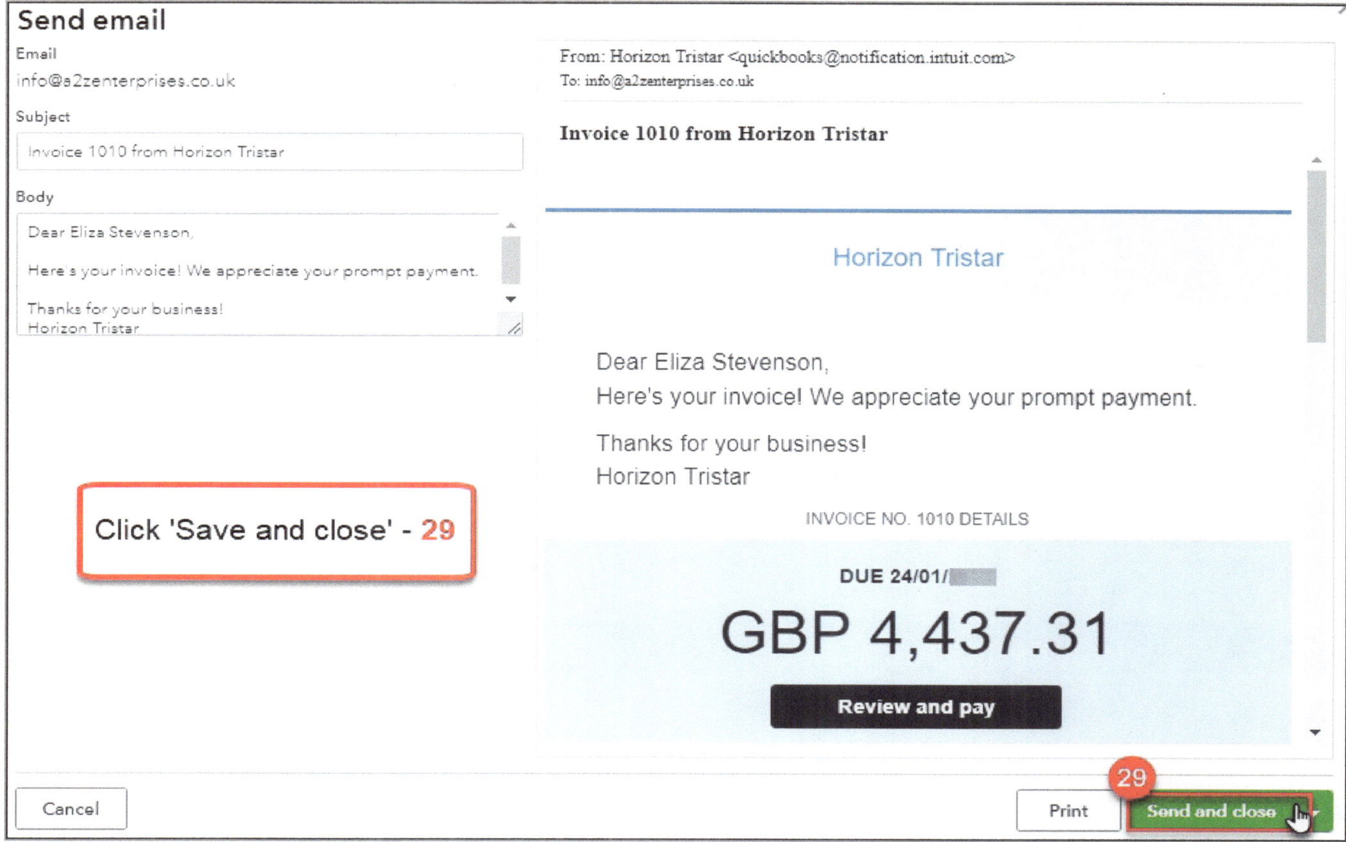

Fig. 115

In the next task, you will have to raise the sales invoice directly from the software instead of going through the sales order/estimate route like we did in the previous sales invoices.

Here is how to do it;
Click on the Create (+) button, then click on Invoice

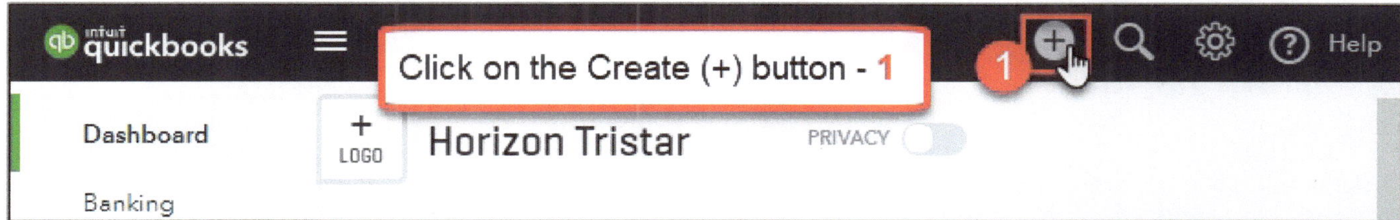

Fig. 116

Fig. 117

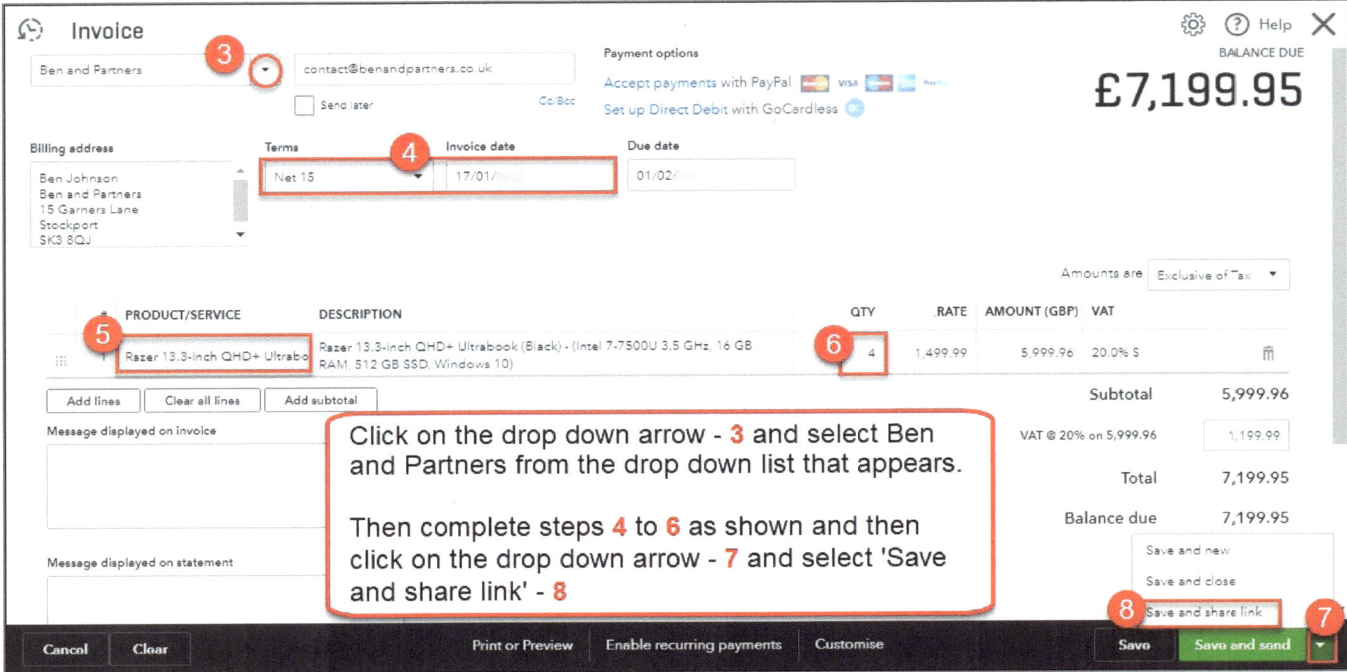

Fig. 118

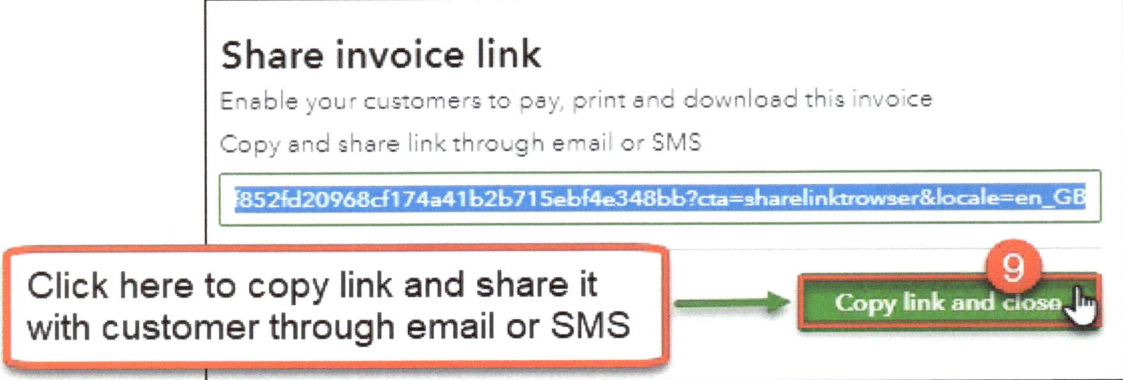

Fig. 119

Click the X at the top right to close the current window and then follow the steps 1 and 2 above to record the next invoice after you have sent the link to the customer for the invoice you have just raised in the previous steps.

Your next invoice window should look like the figure shown on page 81.

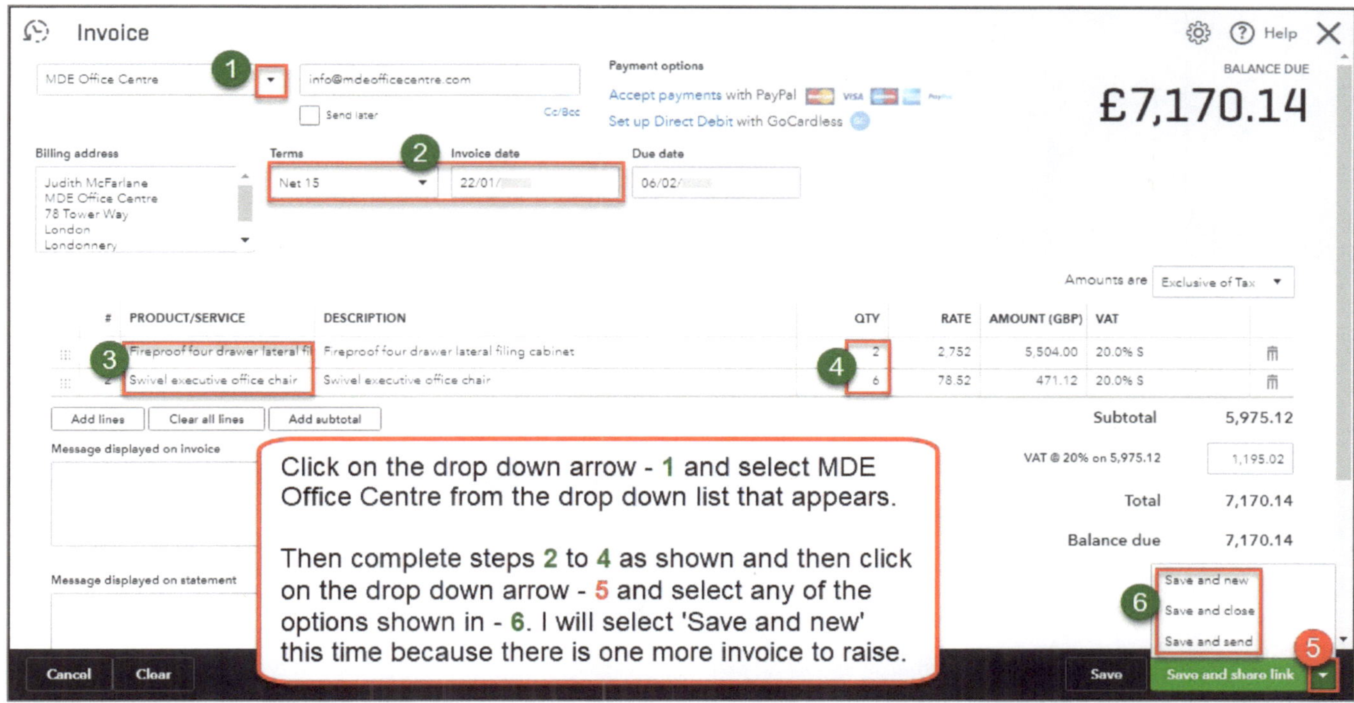

Fig. 120

The next window for the invoice for Peacock Interiors is as shown in figure below.

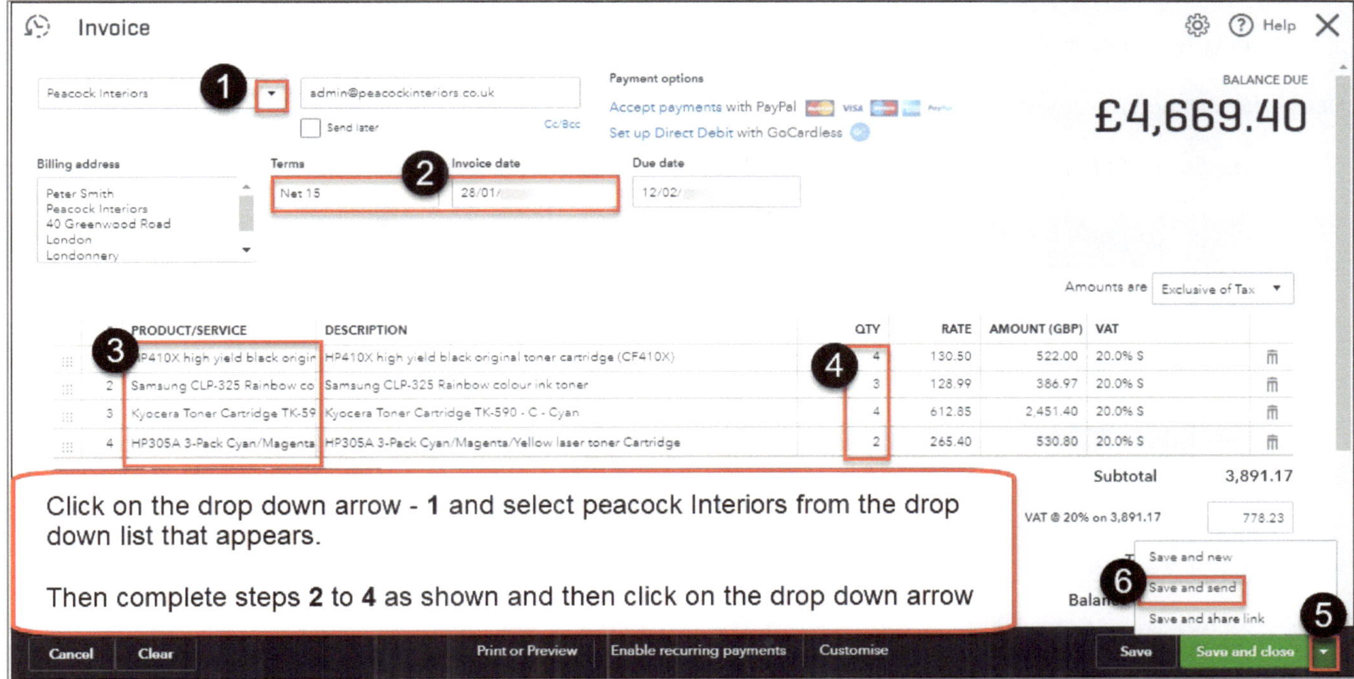

Fig. 121

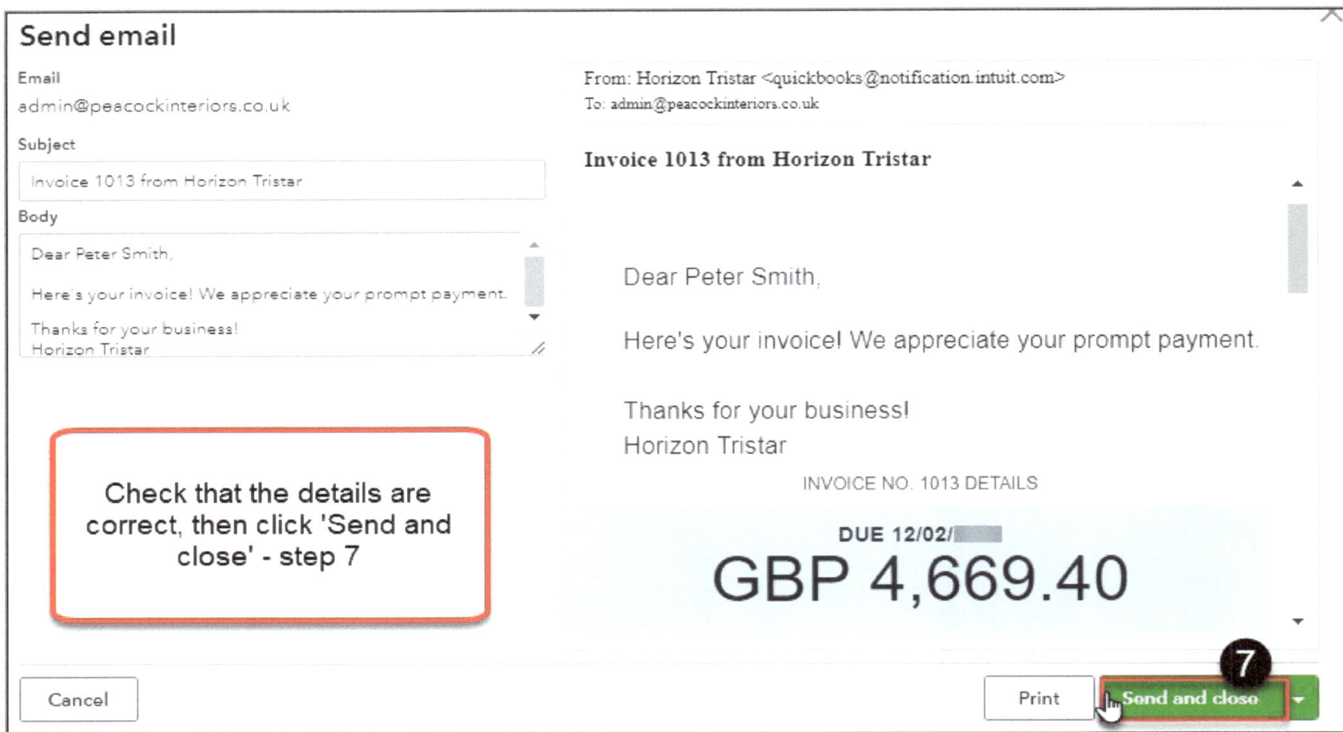

Fig. 122

Raising a sales credit note

A credit note is a posting transaction which can be applied to a Customer's invoice as a payment or reduction.

Here is how to do it in QuickBooks online;

Click on the Create (+) button, then click on 'Credit Note'.

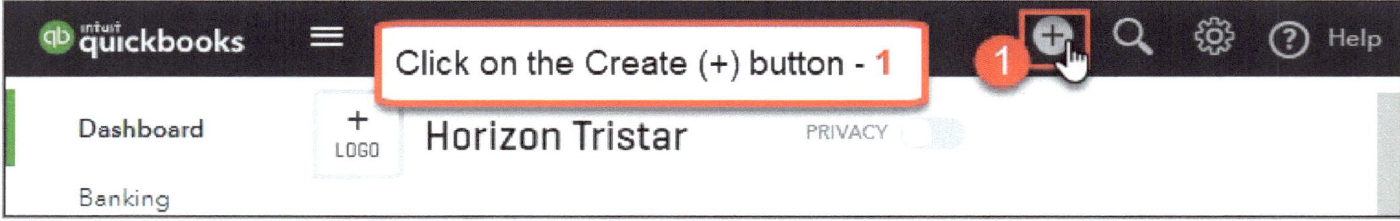

Fig. 123

Fig. 124

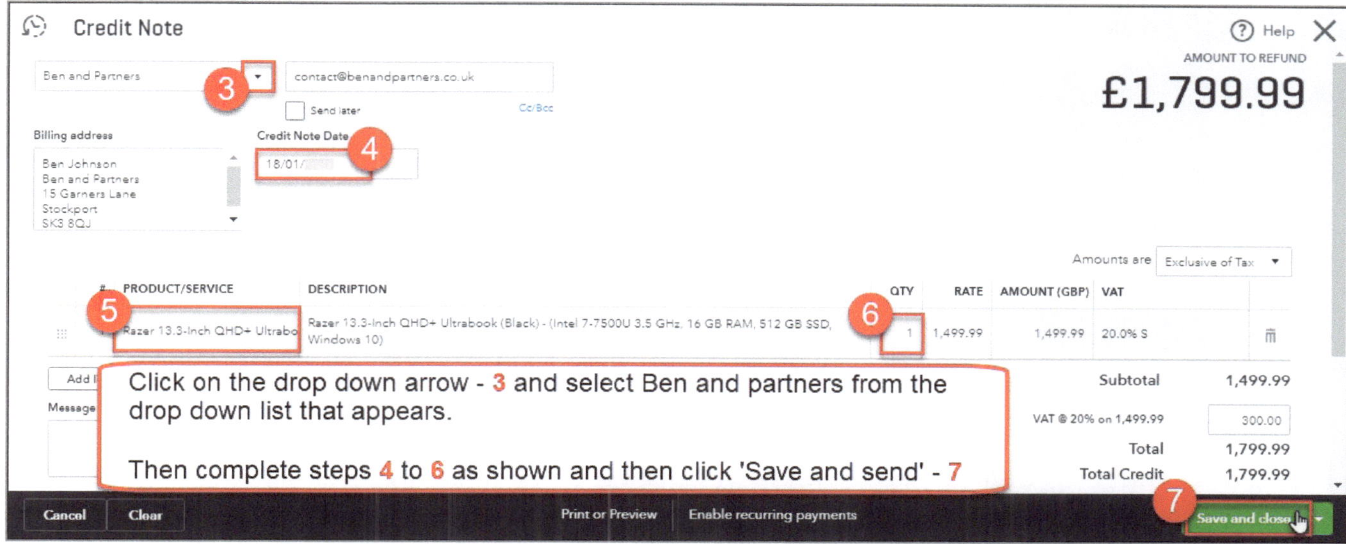

Fig. 125

You now need to apply the credit note you have just raised to the customer invoice to which the returned product relates to. You should do this because just raising a credit note as you did will affect the customer's overall balance, but will not affect a customer's invoice until it is applied to the invoice concerned.

So, here is how to do it.

Click on the Create (+) button, then click on Refund receipt

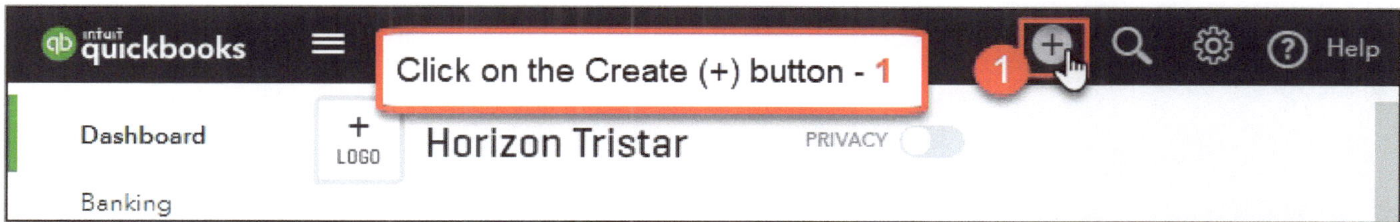

Fig. 126

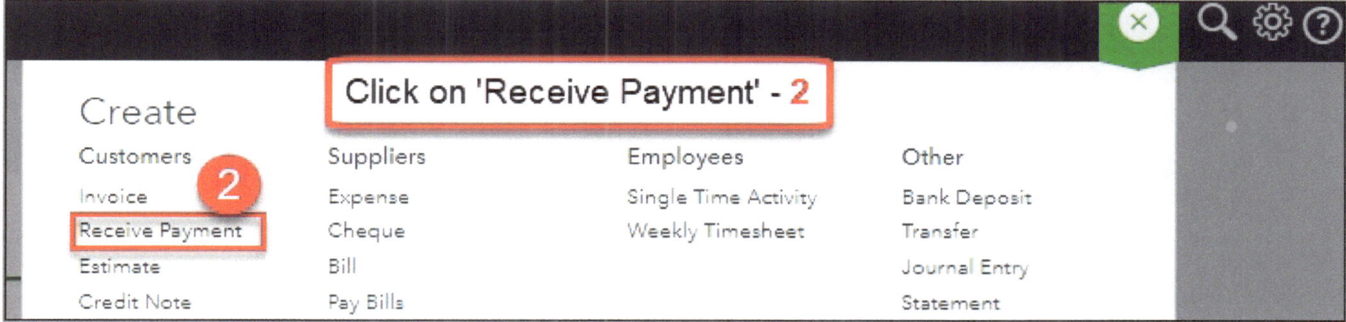

Fig. 127

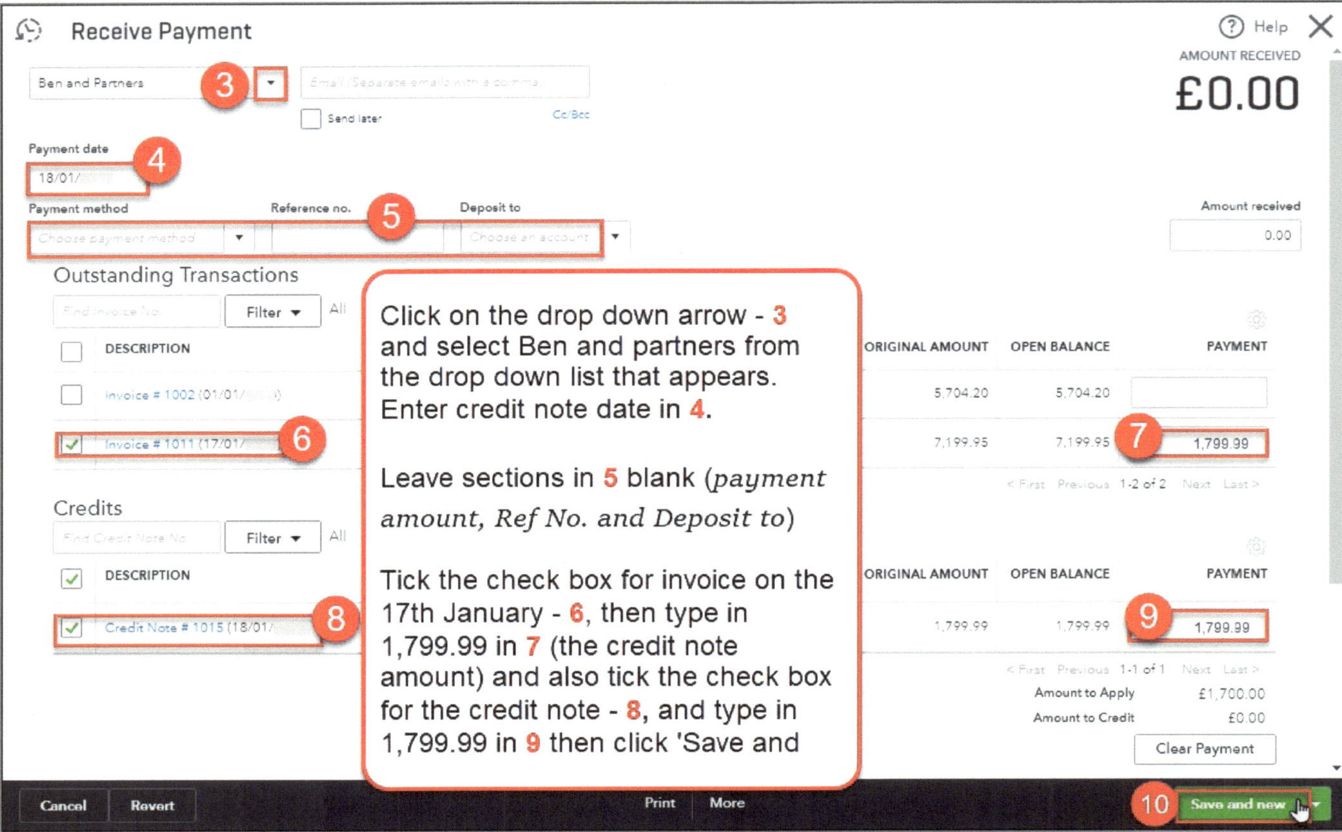

Receive Payment
Help
AMOUNT RECEIVED
£0.00
Ben and Partners
Send later
Cc/Bcc
Payment date
18/01/
Payment method
Reference no.
Deposit to
Amount received
0.00
Outstanding Transactions
Filter
All
DESCRIPTION
Invoice # 1002 (01/01/
Invoice # 1011 (17/01/
ORIGINAL AMOUNT
OPEN BALANCE
PAYMENT
5,704.20
5,704.20
7,199.95
7,199.95
1,799.99
Credits
Credit Note # 1015 (18/01/
1,799.99
1,799.99
1,799.99
Amount to Apply
£1,700.00
Amount to Credit
£0.00
Clear Payment
Cancel
Revert
Print
More
Save and new
Click on the drop down arrow - 3 and select Ben and partners from the drop down list that appears. Enter credit note date in 4.
Leave sections in 5 blank (payment amount, Ref No. and Deposit to)
Tick the check box for invoice on the 17th January - 6, then type in 1,799.99 in 7 (the credit note amount) and also tick the check box for the credit note - 8, and type in 1,799.99 in 9 then click 'Save and

This space is for notes

Fig. 128

How to analyse a financial - Invoice.

Let's do this task by analysing one of the invoices received by Horizon Tristar Ltd.

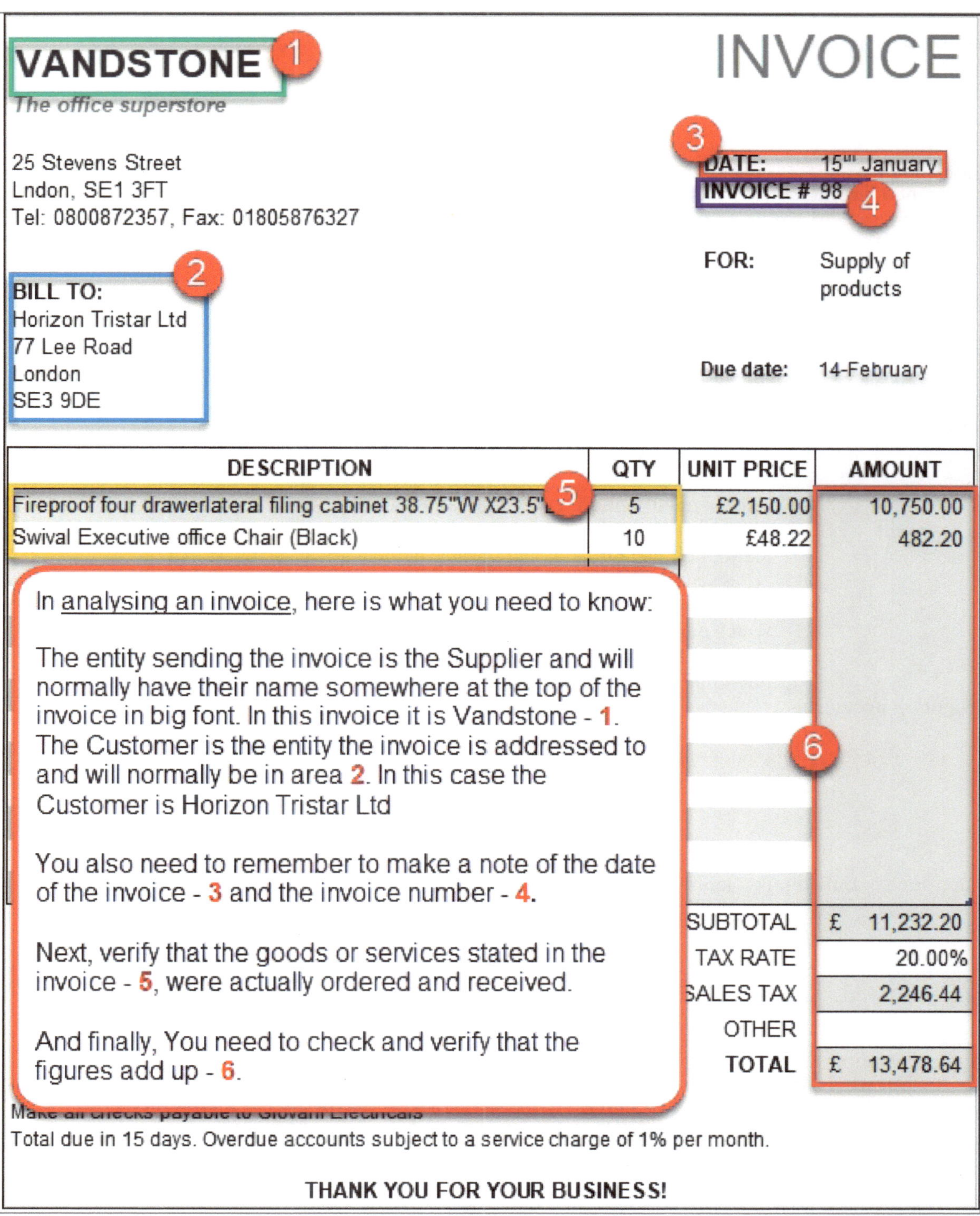

VANDSTONE
The office superstore

INVOICE

25 Stevens Street
Lndon, SE1 3FT
Tel: 0800872357, Fax: 01805876327

DATE: 15th January
INVOICE # 98

FOR: Supply of products

BILL TO:
Horizon Tristar Ltd
77 Lee Road
London
SE3 9DE

Due date: 14-February

DESCRIPTION	QTY	UNIT PRICE	AMOUNT
Fireproof four drawerlateral filing cabinet 38.75"W X23.5"L	5	£2,150.00	10,750.00
Swival Executive office Chair (Black)	10	£48.22	482.20
		SUBTOTAL	£ 11,232.20
		TAX RATE	20.00%
		SALES TAX	2,246.44
		OTHER	
		TOTAL	£ 13,478.64

In analysing an invoice, here is what you need to know:

The entity sending the invoice is the Supplier and will normally have their name somewhere at the top of the invoice in big font. In this invoice it is Vandstone - 1. The Customer is the entity the invoice is addressed to and will normally be in area 2. In this case the Customer is Horizon Tristar Ltd

You also need to remember to make a note of the date of the invoice - 3 and the invoice number - 4.

Next, verify that the goods or services stated in the invoice - 5, were actually ordered and received.

And finally, You need to check and verify that the figures add up - 6.

Make all checks payable to Giovani Electricals
Total due in 15 days. Overdue accounts subject to a service charge of 1% per month.

THANK YOU FOR YOUR BUSINESS!

Fig. 129

Task 3b: Recording Customer receipts and a non-customer recept

Two customers; Ben and Partners, and Atomic have made BACS payments and have sent over remittance advice notes. You are now required to update the sales ledger with these details.

But before you that, let's have a look at three ways a customer can make payment for outstanding amounts.

Regardless whether it is customers making payments of their outstanding invoices or the company making payments to its suppliers, there basically three options available to do so:

1. Full payment of an outstanding invoice
2. Part payment of an outstanding invoice
3. Payment on account to reduce any outstanding balance (more like when you pay the minimum balance on your credit card)

See table below for a brief explanation of this a bit further

Payment option	What it means
1. Full payment	In this payment option, an outstanding invoice is paid in full. This payment method is specific in that; there is a specific outstanding invoice which the customer is paying for when they send a remittance.
2. Part payment	This payment option is similar to a full payment option in that there is specificity as to what invoice is being paid, except on this occasion, not the full amount of the outstanding invoice is being paid but just part of it.
3. Payment on account	In this payment option, a customer will just make payment but will not specify which particular outstanding invoice he/she is paying for. It is then left to the accounts receivable department to allocate the payment to the Customers outstanding invoices perhaps with the oldest ones cleared first. Think of the way most credit card bills are paid, most of those payments are payments on account – just to reduce the credit card bill amount each month. The credit card company then makes the payment allocations according to the terms they agreed with you when you signed up for the credit card.

Let's see how this done in QuickBooks Online – see figures 128 to 135

A quick note

To help you keep track of money coming in and manage your cash flow it's important that you record your customer receipts.

The Customer Receipt window helps you easily record receipts and allocate them to the relevant invoices. You can see what the oldest outstanding invoices are so that you can clear these invoices first or you can even spread the receipt value over multiple invoices.
From here you can also allocate outstanding credit notes and outstanding payments on account to invoices.

3b(i) Recording customer receipts

Full payment

Click on the Create (+) button, then click on 'Receive Payment.'

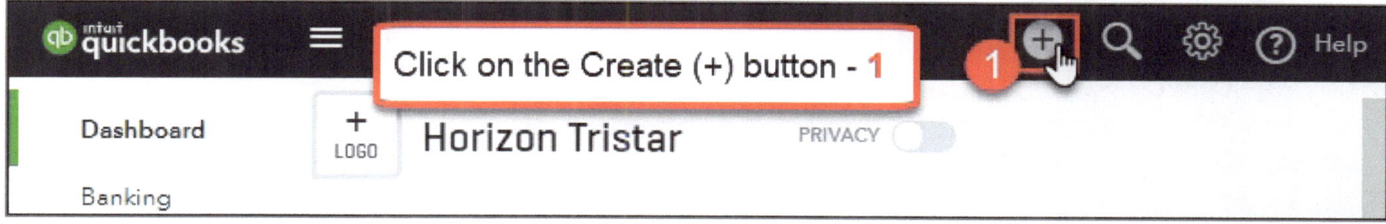

Fig. 130

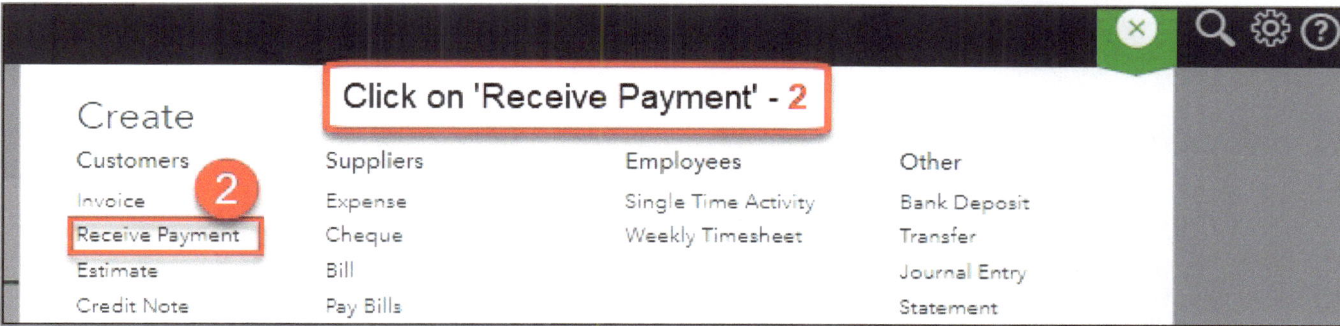

Fig. 131

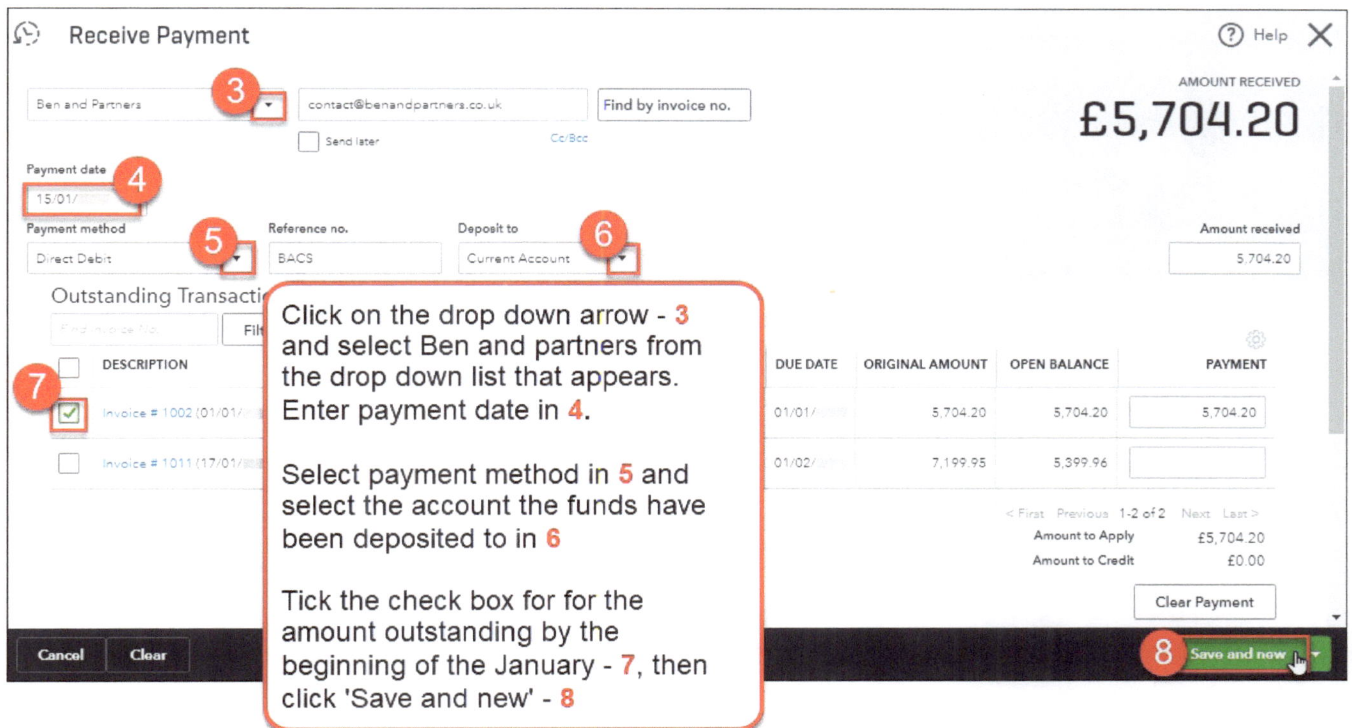

Fig. 132

The next payment is also a full payment by the customer – Atomic Ltd, and your screen should look like figure 131

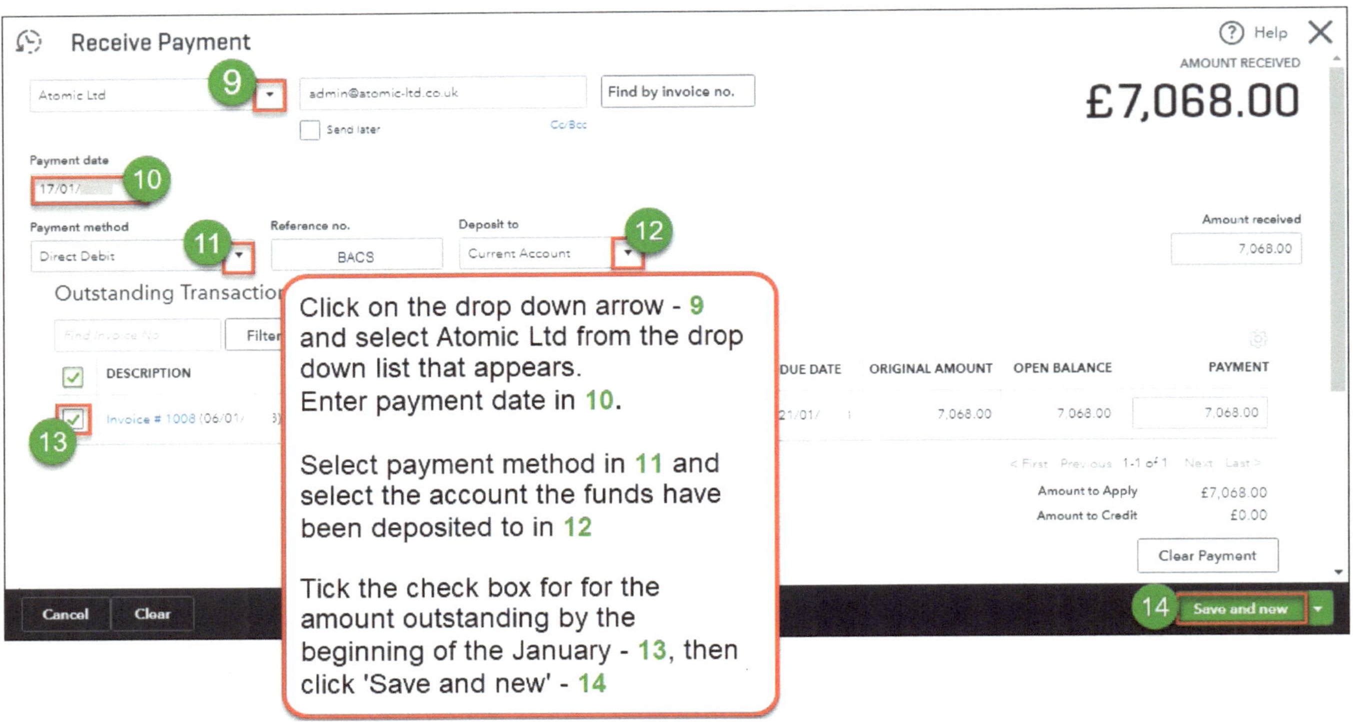

Fig. 133

The next payment from the customer is a part payment of the outstanding invoice and continuing from the window that appears after step 14 above, here is how your work should look like:

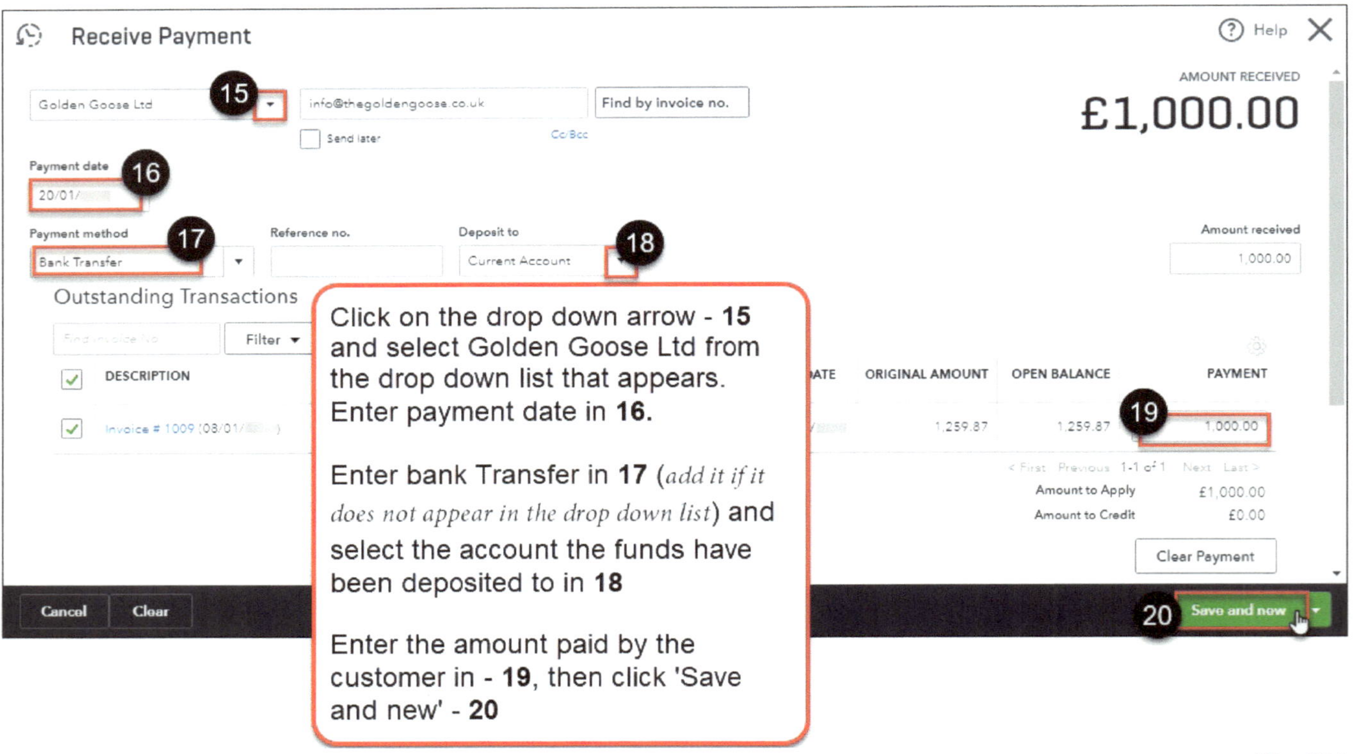

Fig. 134

Follow through with the next part payment from Ben and Partners.

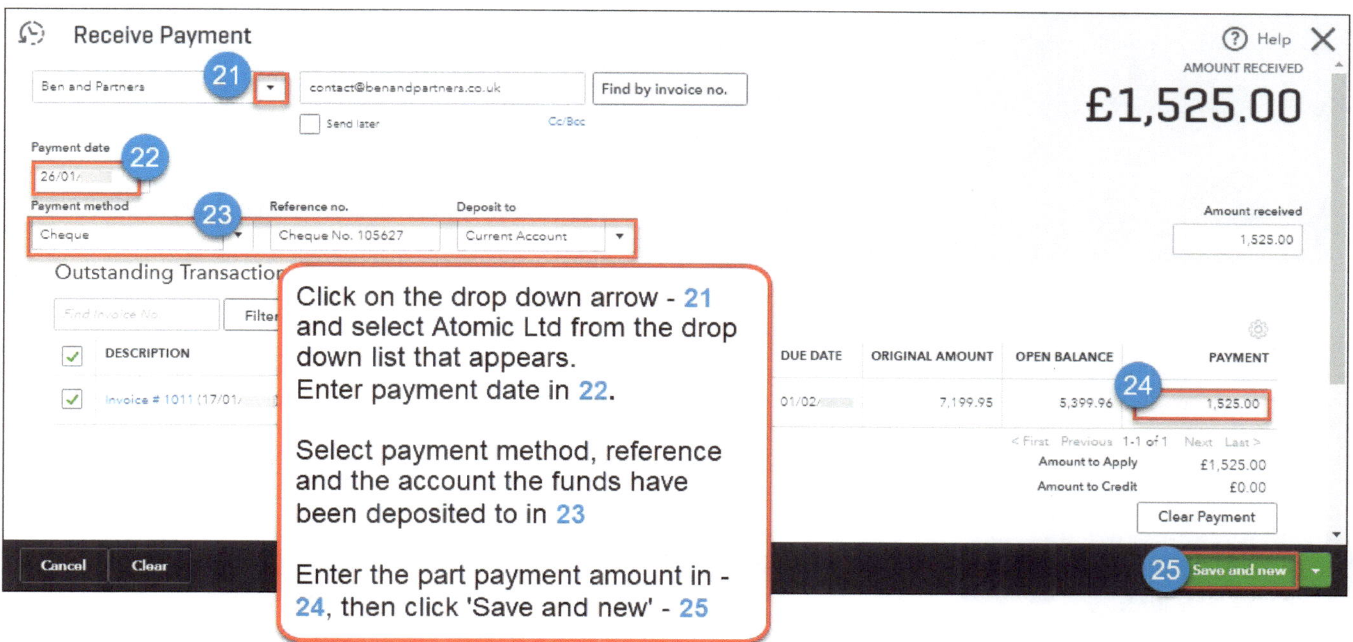

Fig. 135

The next payment made by the customer – A2Z Enterprises is a payment on account and here is how to record it.

From the window following step 25 in the previous task, here is how your screen should look like;

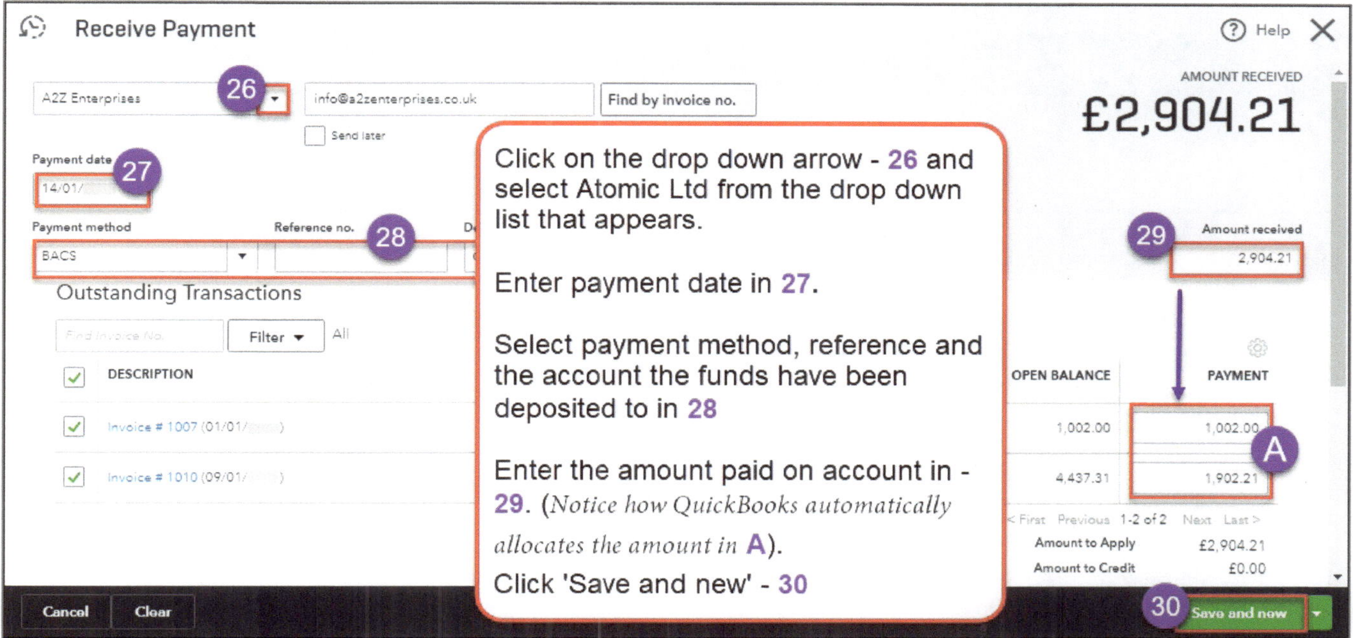

Fig. 136

We are also told that, A2Z also sent a cheque (without specifying which invoice they were paying for) and this cheque was deposited to the bank account on the 22nd January this year. So, you have to record that transaction too.

Here is how your work should look like;

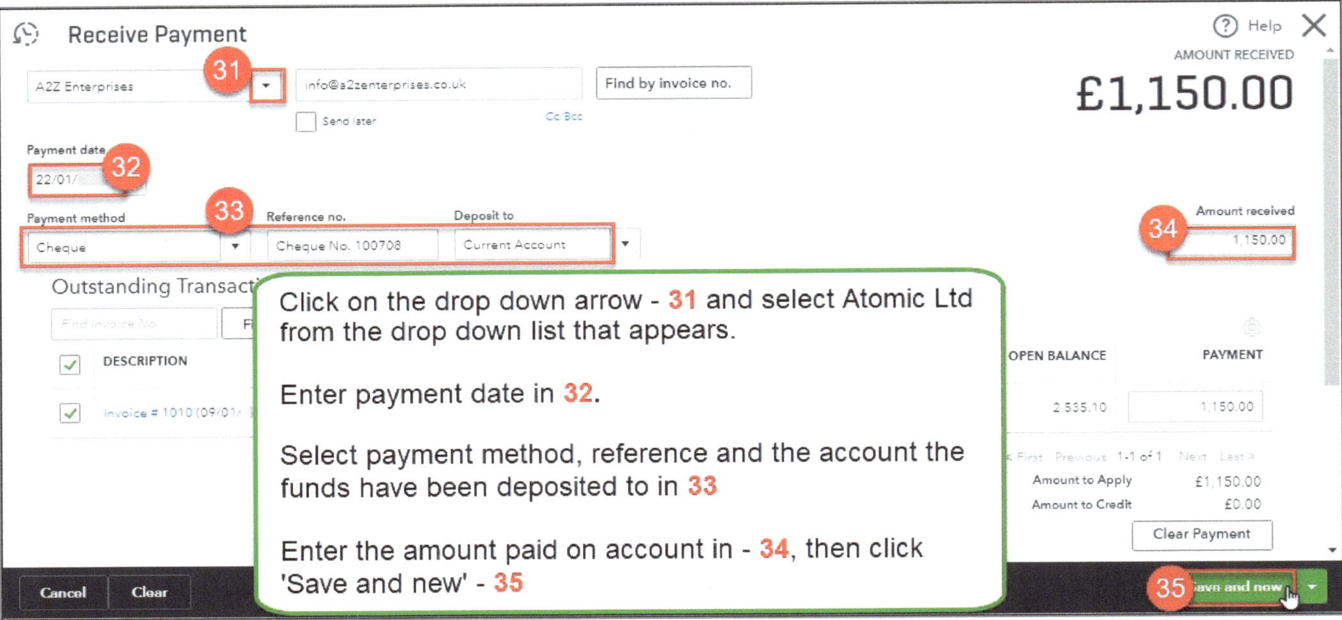

Fig. 137

3b.(ii) Recording non-customer receipts

Recording a VAT refund from HMRC (Tax Authority)

Fig. 138

Fig. 139

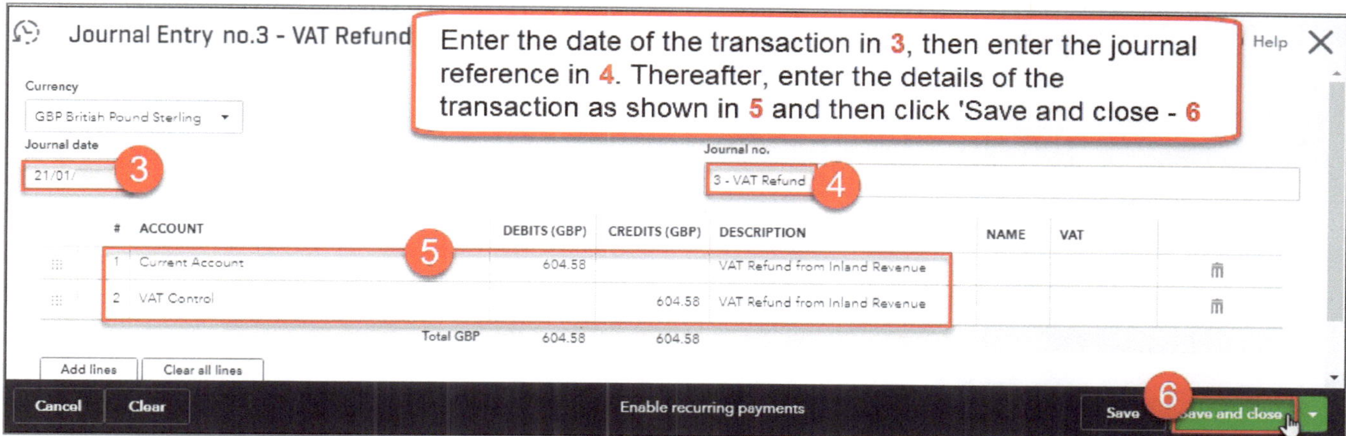

Fig. 140

Recording sales receipts

Fig. 141

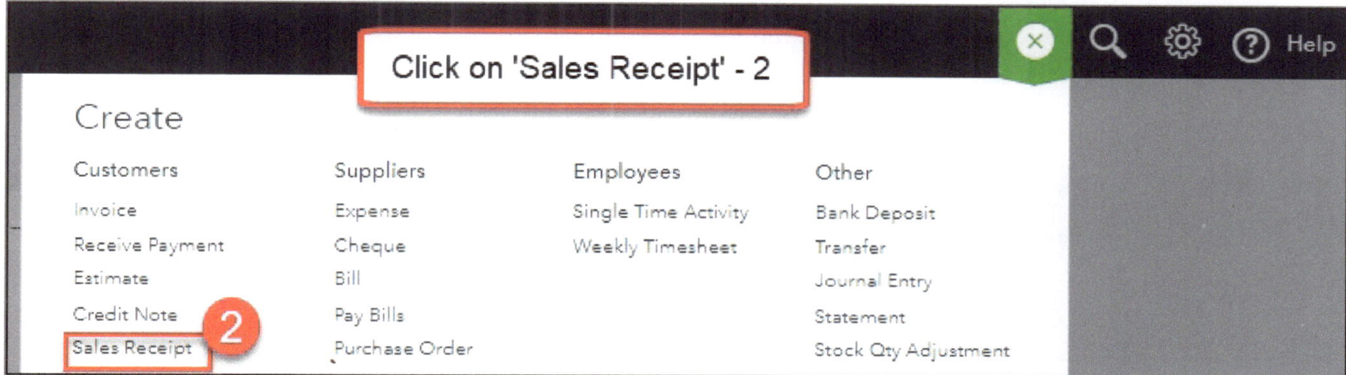

Fig. 142

This space is for notes

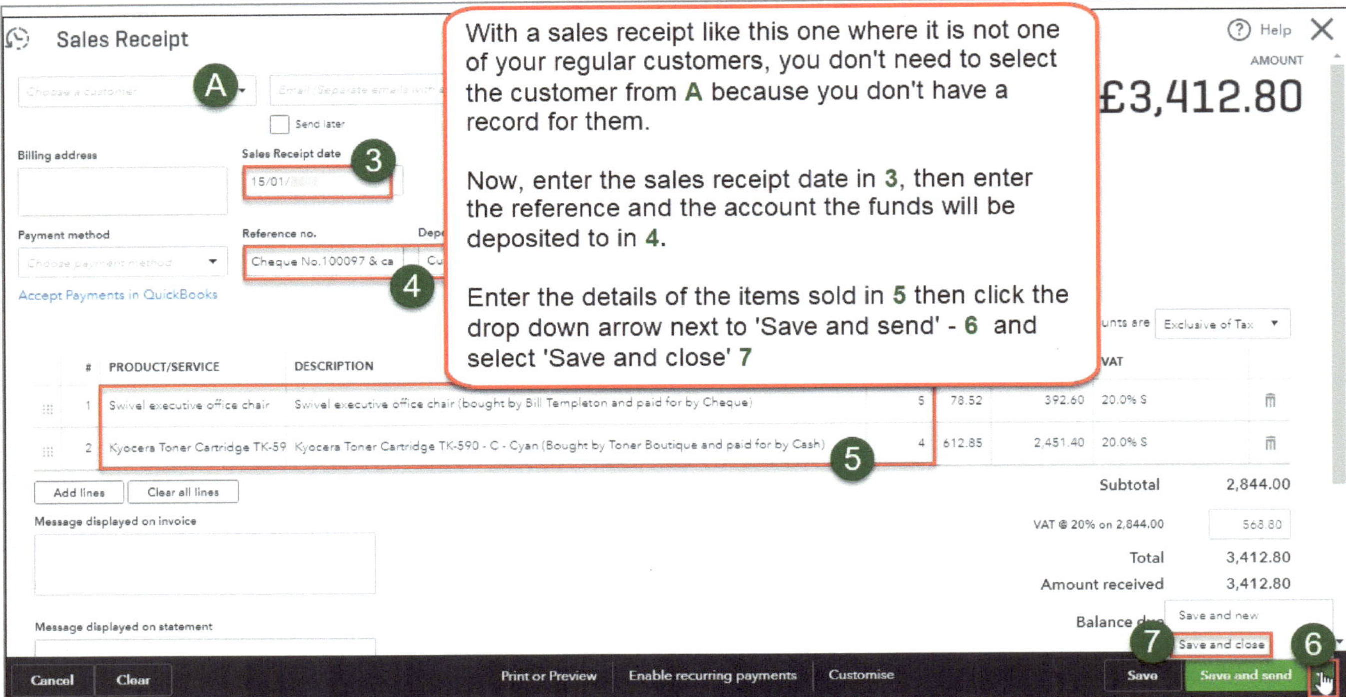

Fig. 143

Recording a drop shipping transaction.

If I am a supplier and a customer comes to me to buy something, and it so happens that I don't have that thing in stock, if I order that item from my supplier ask him to supply it directly to my customer, that would be termed as drop shipping.

We have a situation like that in our work experience to deal with – J. James' transaction. Let's deal with it.

Fig. 144

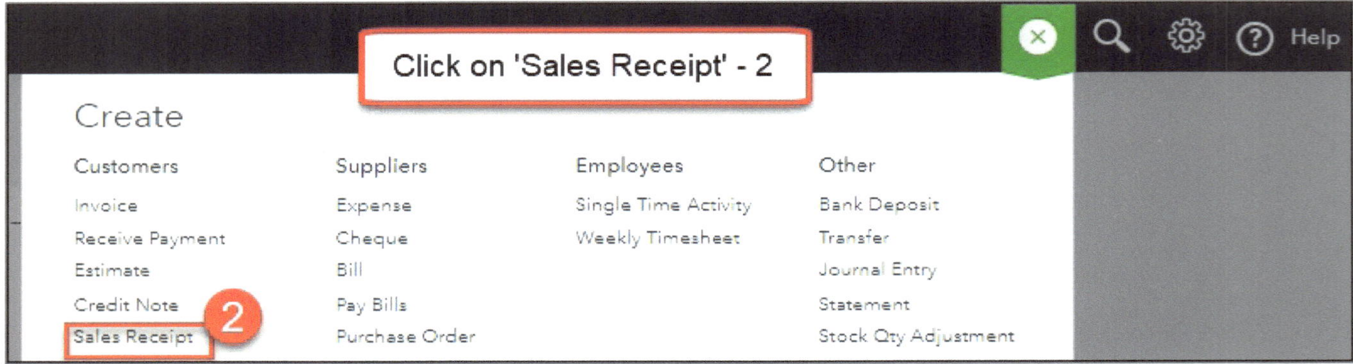

Fig. 145

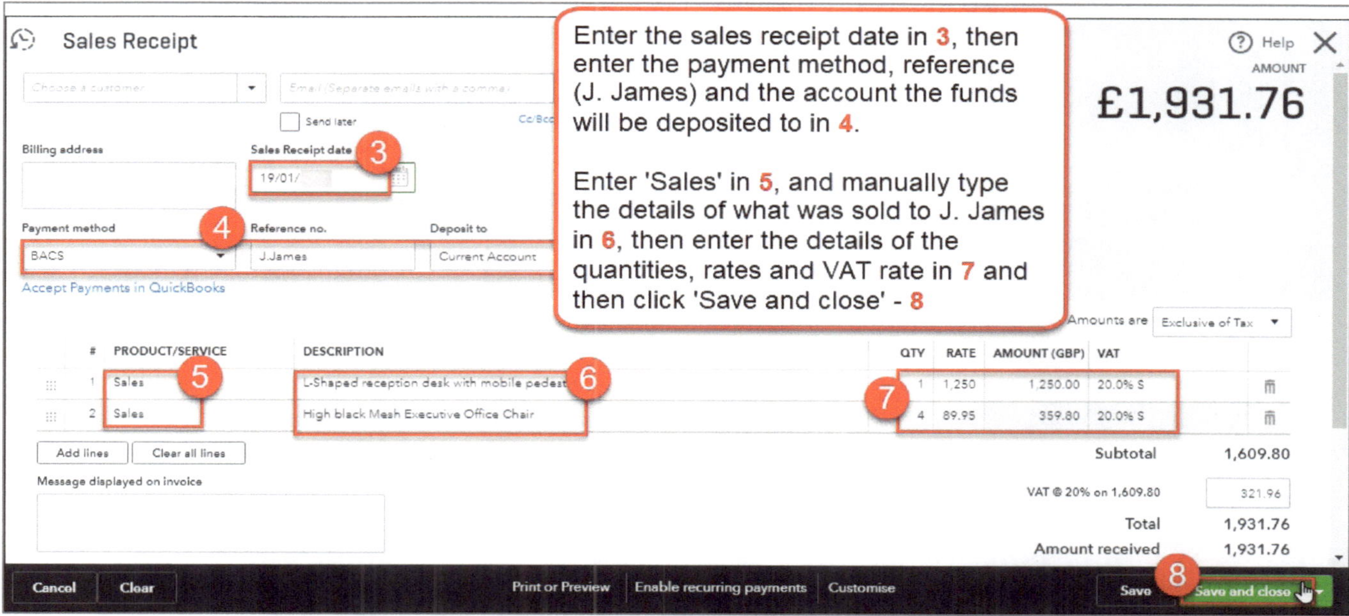

Fig. 146

Remember the items J. James paid for were delivered directly to him from Horizon Tristars supplier – Vandstone plc. The supplier has now sent n invoice for those items and therefore, you need to update the purchase ledger.

Here is how to do it.

Step **1**, click on the plus button - , then select "Bill" under the heading of 'Suppliers.'

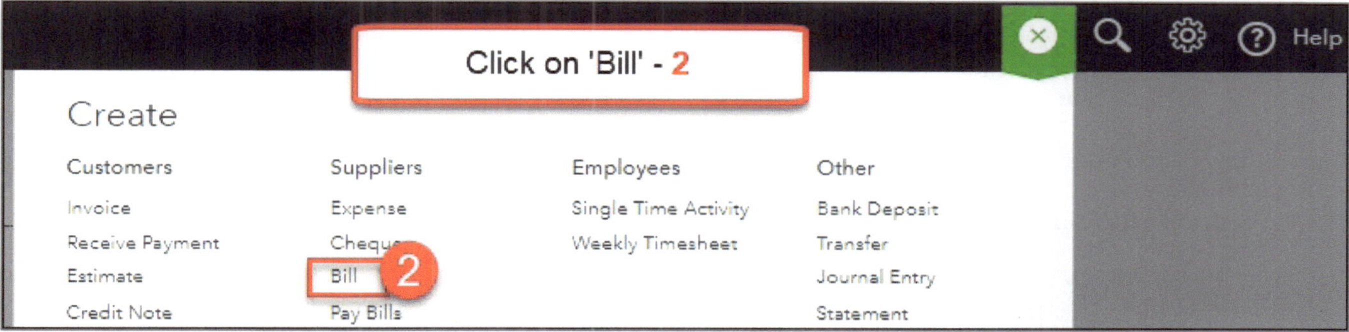

Fig. 147

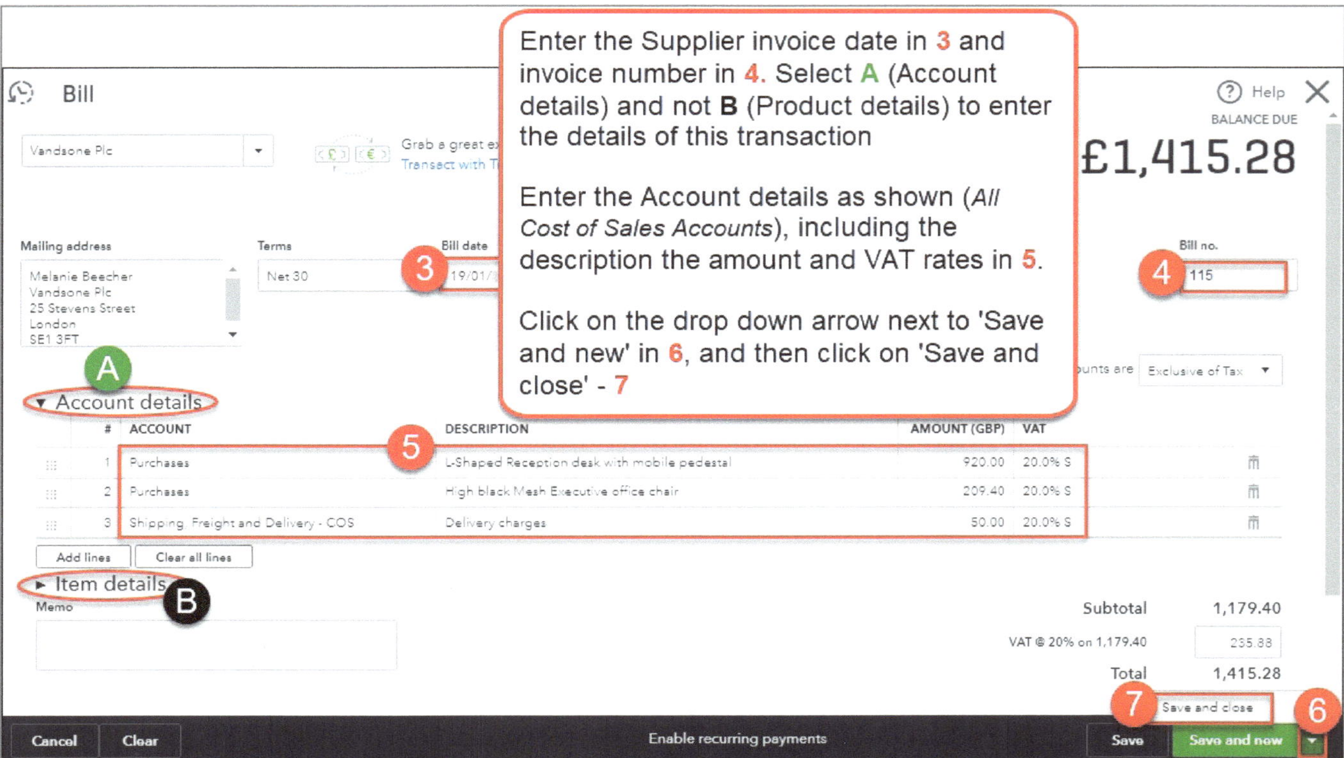

Fig. 148

Task 3c: How to update dishonoured cheques and returned goods.

3c(i): Dishonoured cheque

How do you deal with cheques that the bank has cleared either insufficient funds or mistake on the cheque and how do you update the accounts when customers return goods and want a refund?

Here is how to enter these type of transactions in Quickbooks online.

Step 1, click on the plus button - and under Suppliers select 'Cheque.'

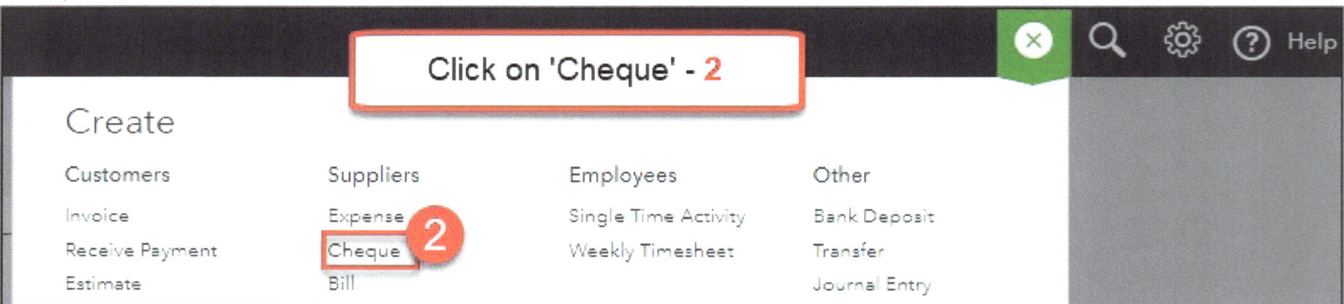

Fig. 149

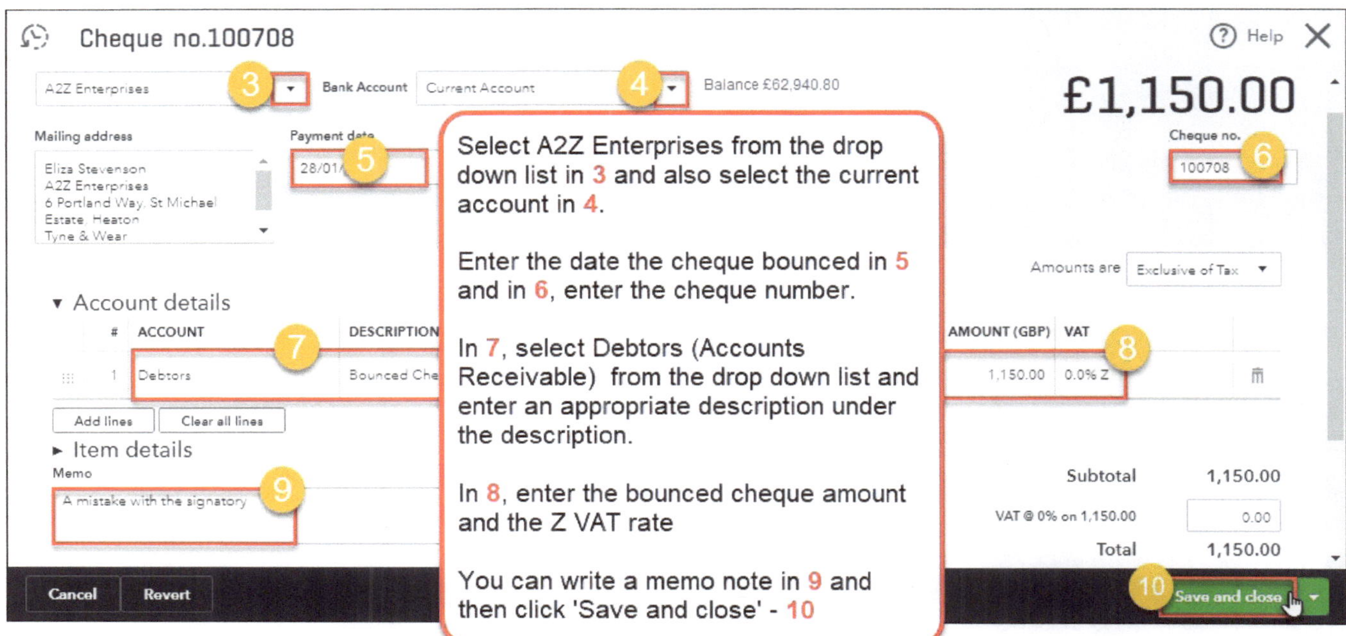

Fig. 150

The bounced cheque is now recorded.

What is a Bounced Check/Cheque

A bounced check/cheque is slang for a check/cheque that cannot be processed because the account holder has nonsufficient funds (NSF). Banks return, or bounce, these checks/cheques, also known as rubber checks/cheques, rather than honouring them, and banks charge the check/cheque writers NSF fees.

Source: *https://www.investopedia.com/terms/b/bouncedcheck.asp*

The next step is to record the service charge from the bank for the bounced/dishonoured cheque.

Step **11**, click on the plus button - , and under Suppliers select 'Expense.'

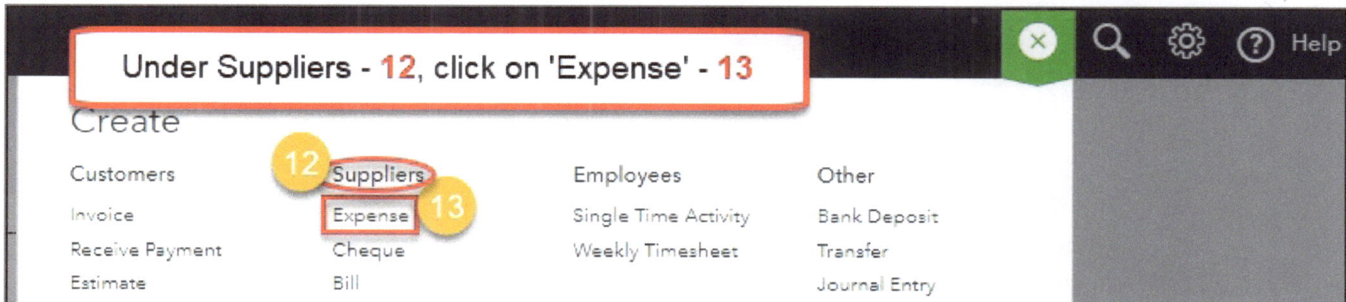

Fig. 151

This space is for notes

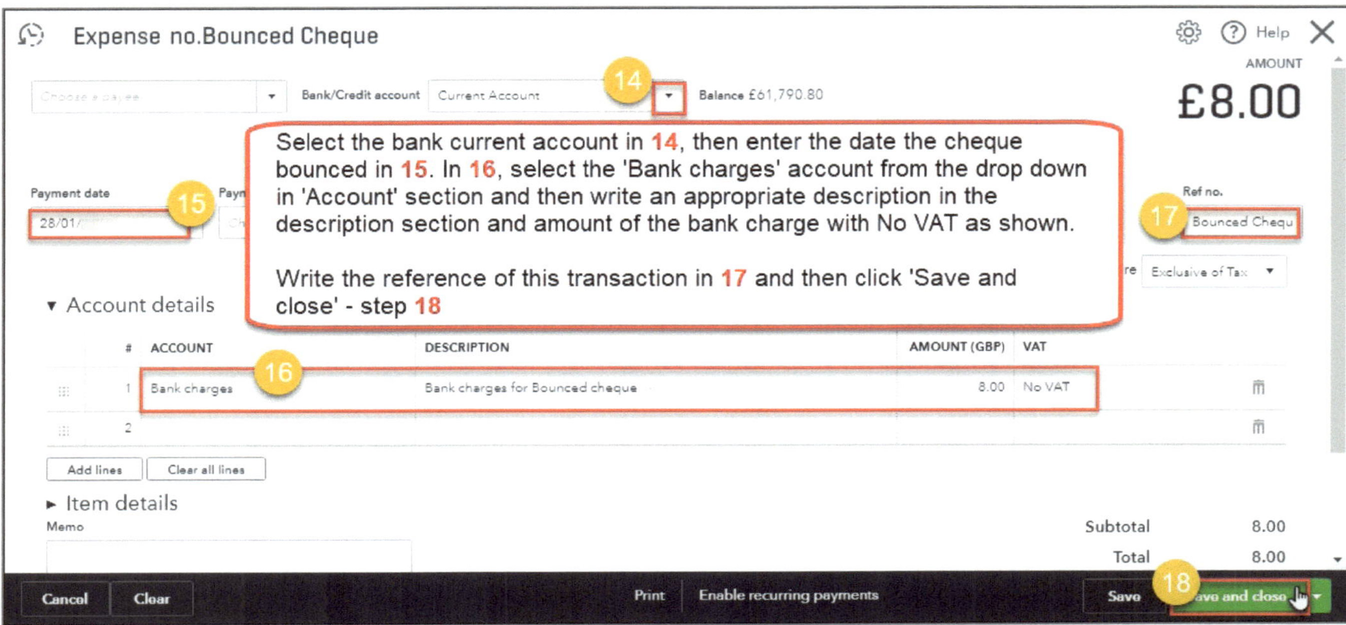

Fig. 152

Now, you need to invoice the customer for the bank charge that the bank charged the company for this bounced cheque.

Here is how to do it.

Next step, click on the plus button - , and under Customers select 'Invoice.'

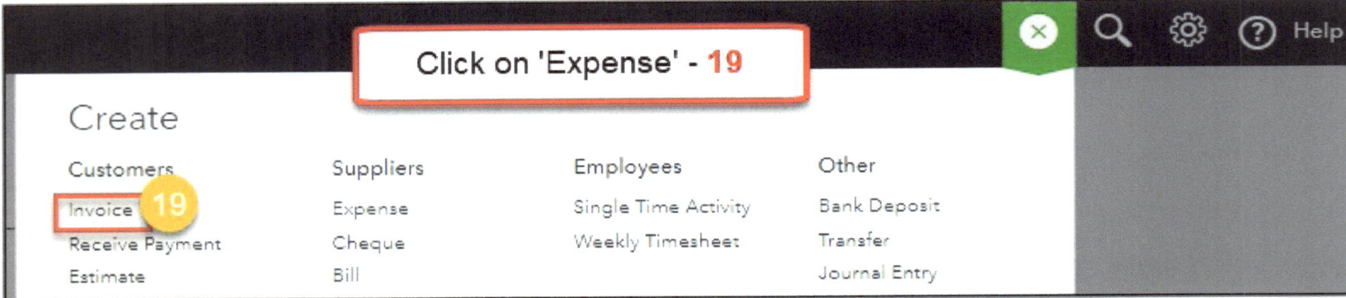

Fig. 153

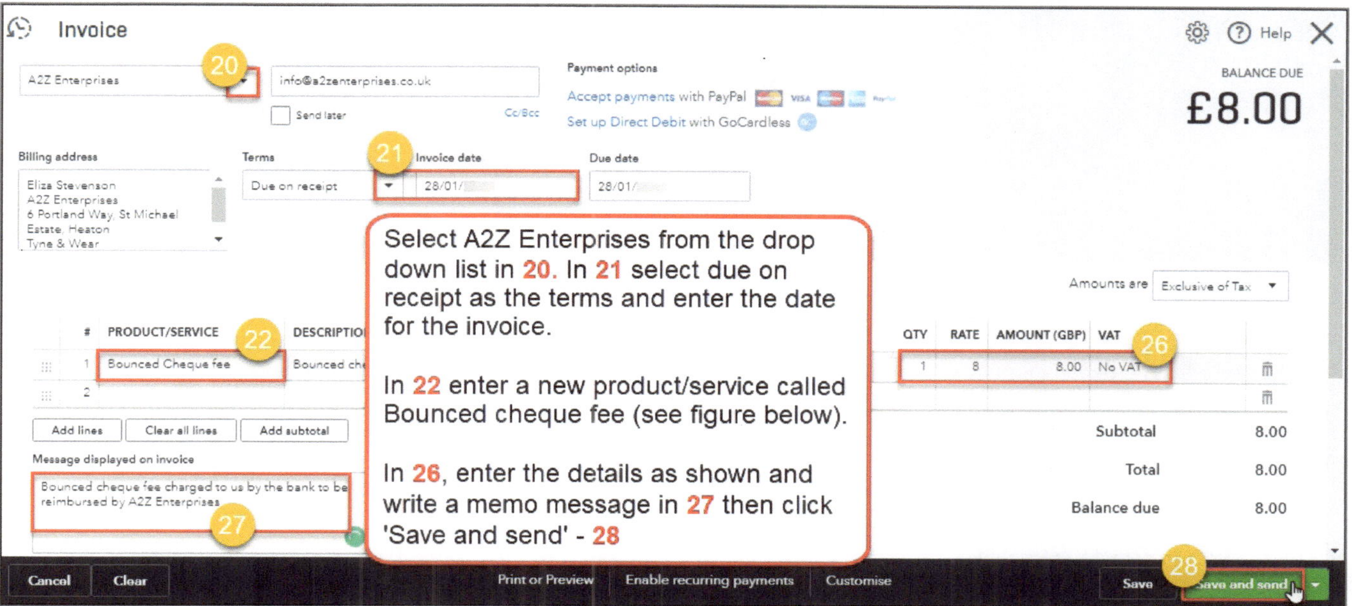

Fig. 154

Step 22 above

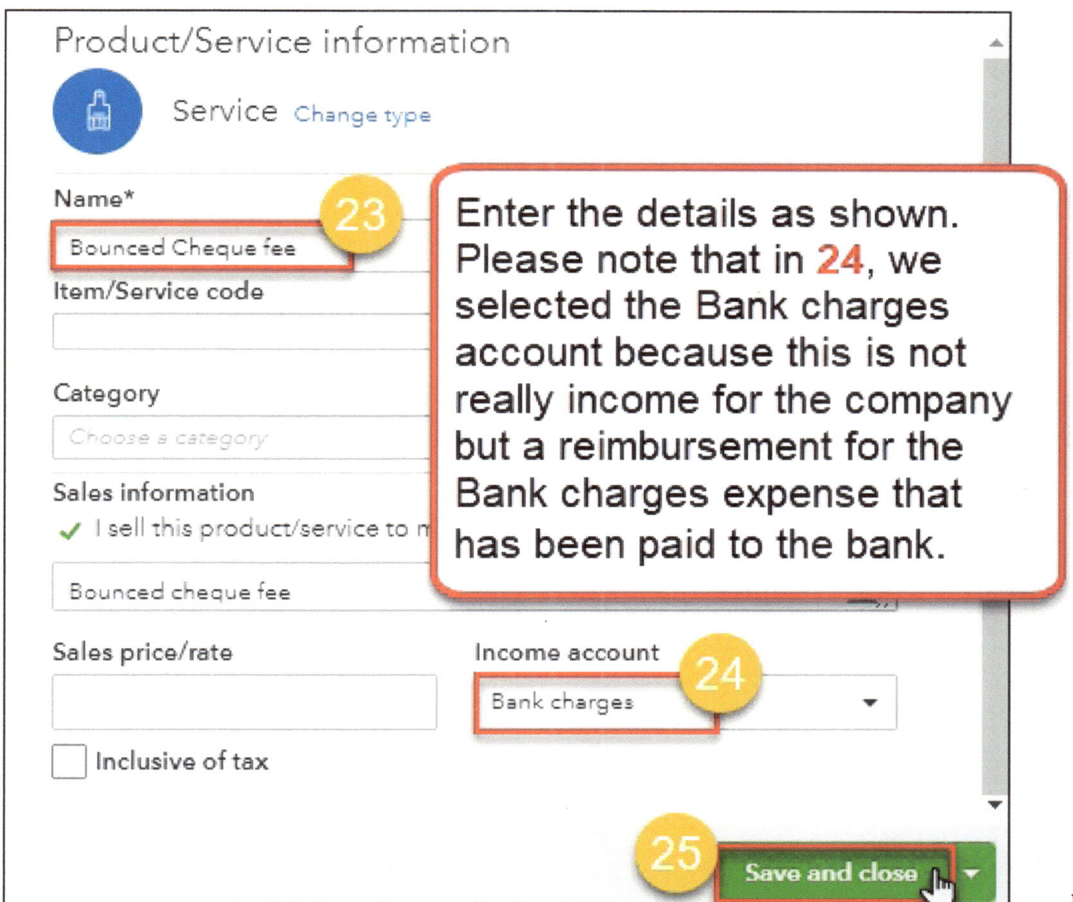

Fig. 155

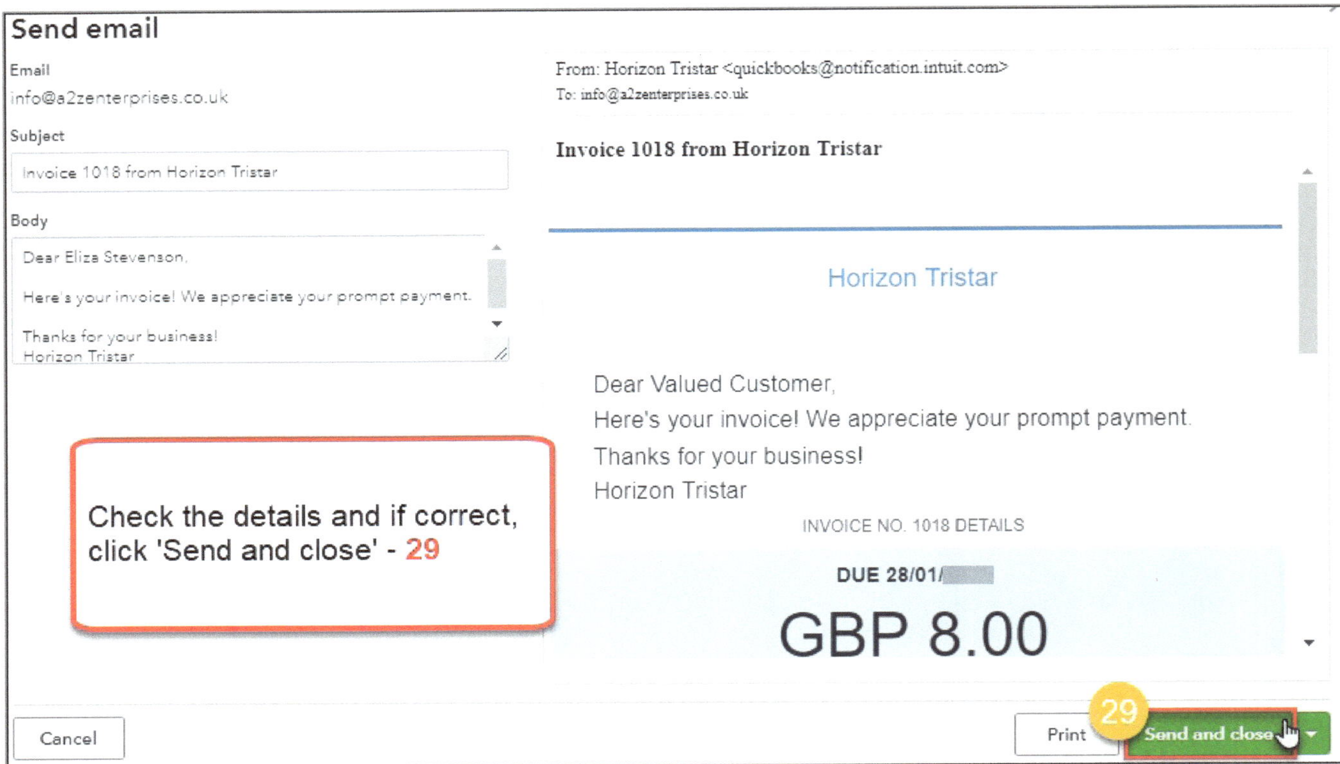

Fig. 156

Task 3c(ii): Dealing with returns in

In this task, you need to record a refund of the sales receipt for the items returned by J. James and also update the stock.

Let's get right to it.

Step 1, click on the plus button - , and under Customers select 'Refund receipt'

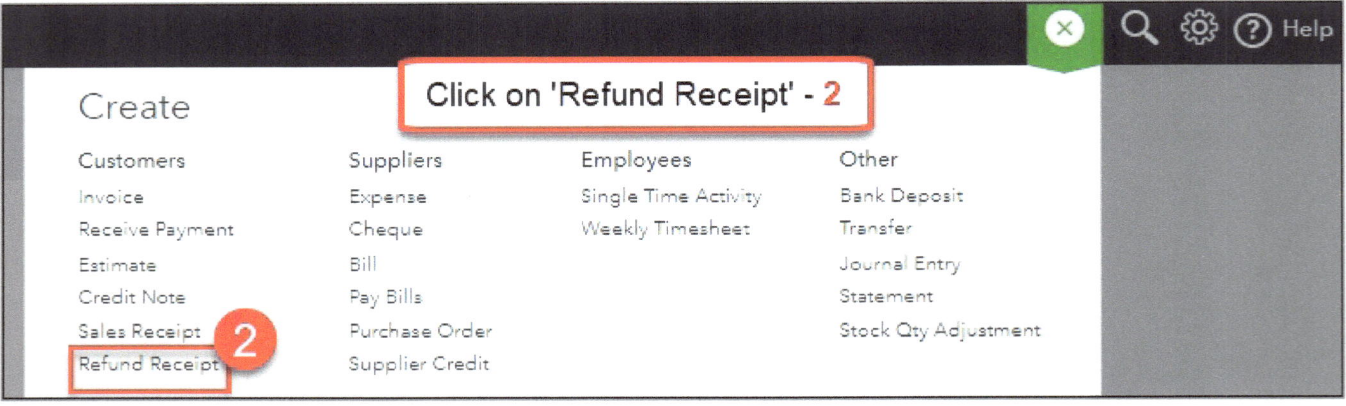

Fig. 157

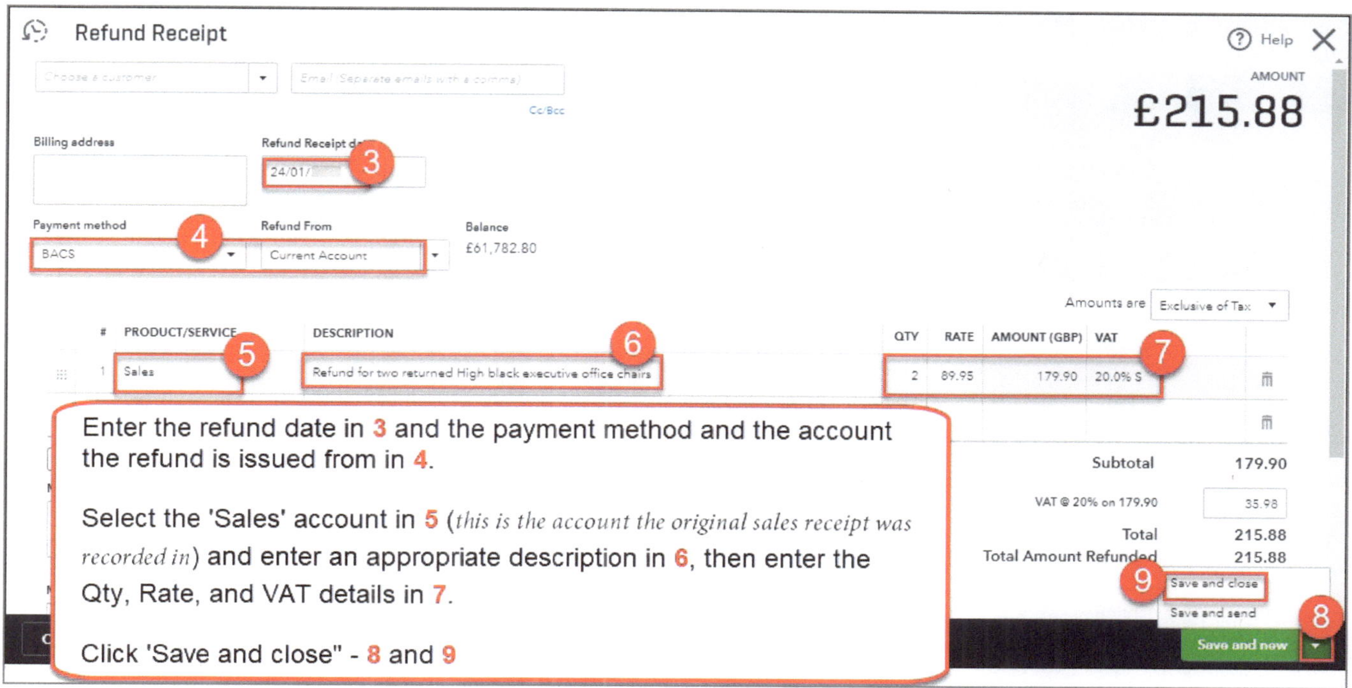

Fig. 158

Here is the confirmation message that the refund has been processed.

Fig. 241

Let's now update the stock with the chairs that were returned.

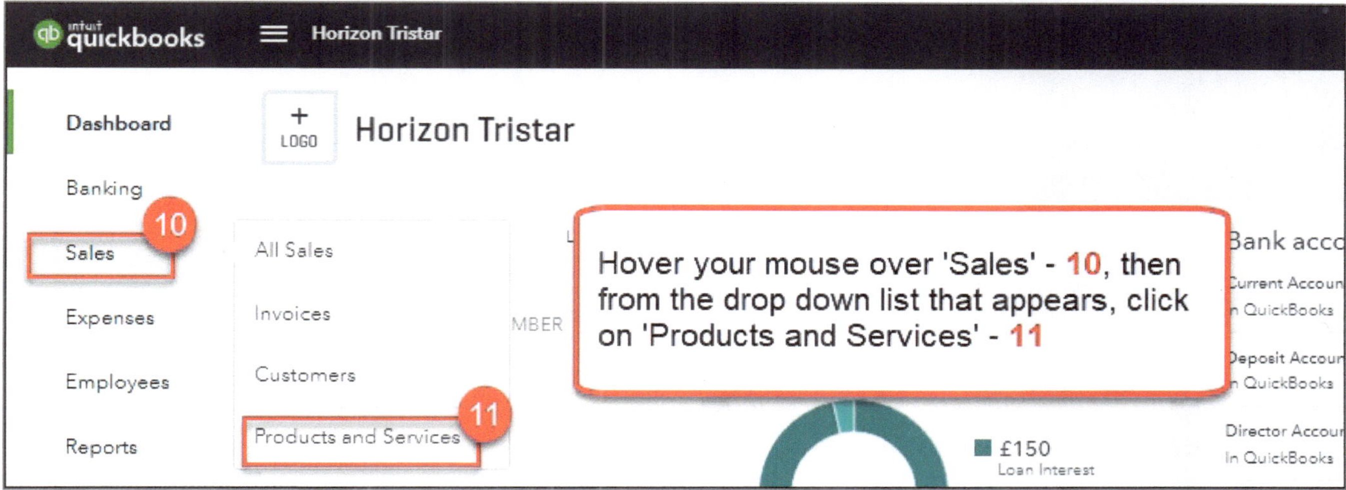

Fig. 159

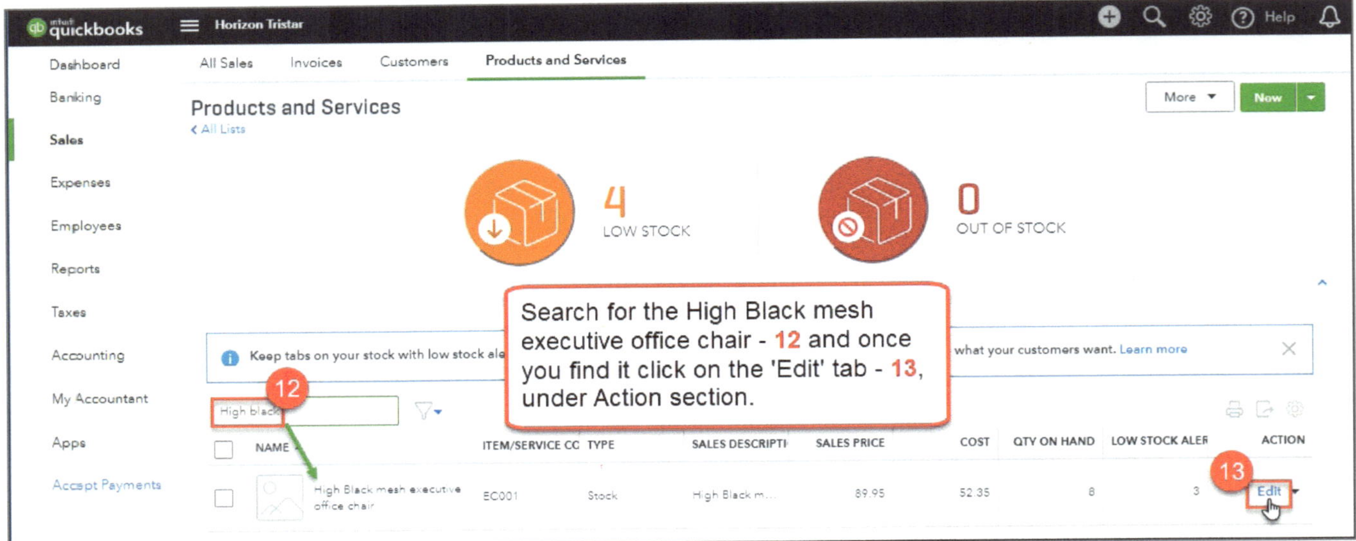

Fig. 160

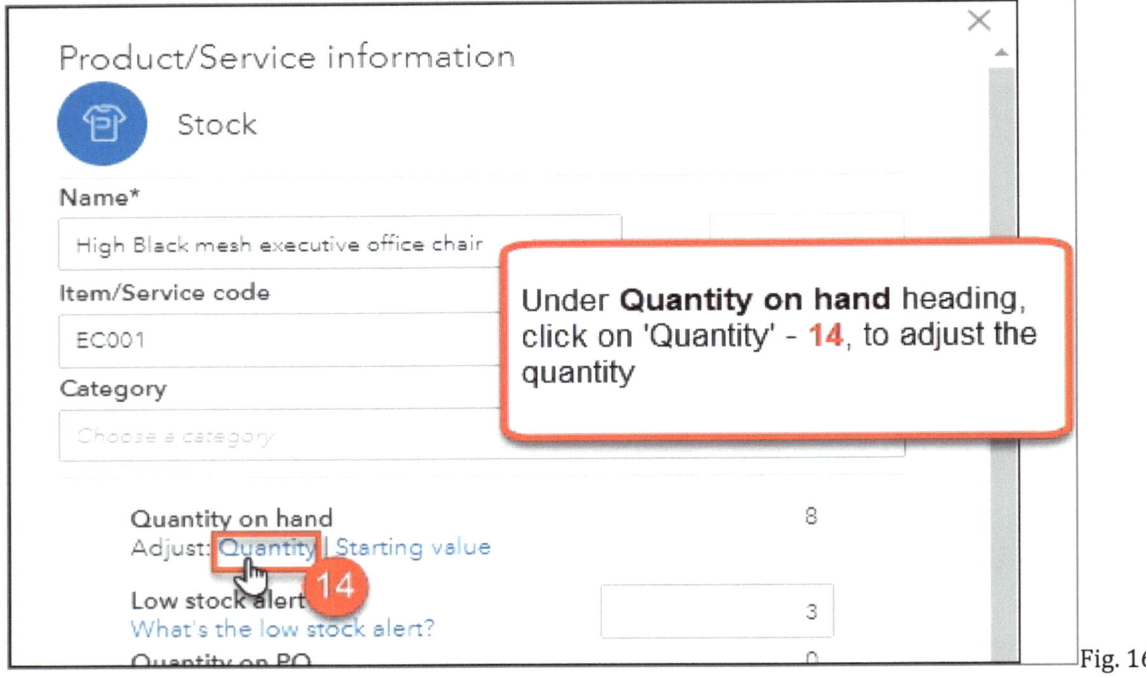

Fig. 161

Note about Online, mail and phone order sales

Online, mail and telephone order customers have the right to cancel their order for a limited time even if the goods aren't faulty. Sales of this kind are known as 'distance selling'.

You must offer a refund to customers if they've told you within 14 days of receiving their goods that they want to cancel. They have another 14 days to return the goods once they've told you.

You must refund the customer within 14 days of receiving the goods back. They don't have to provide a reason.

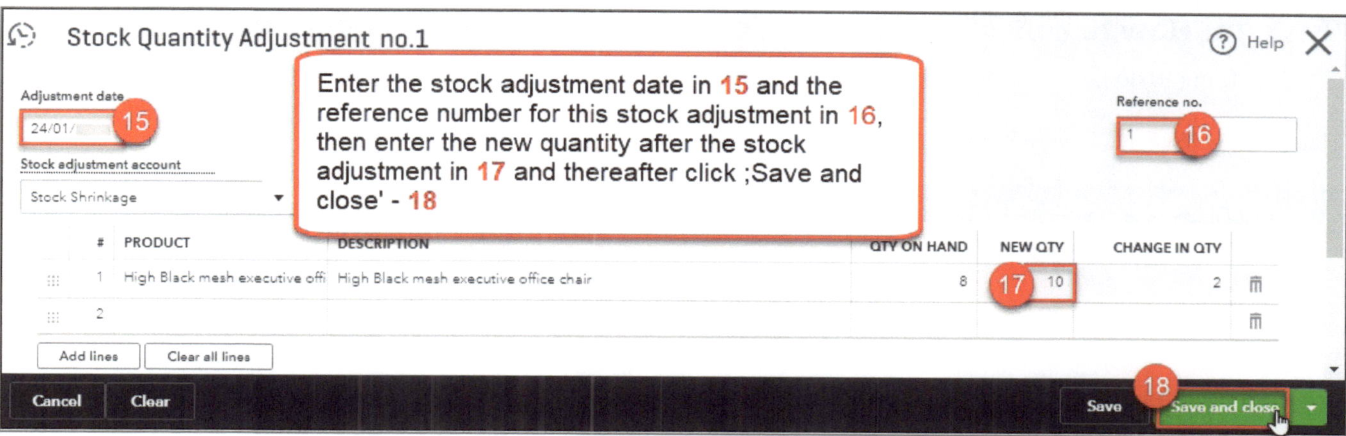

Fig. 162

What the law says about refunds - UK

You must offer a full refund if an item is faulty, not as described or doesn't do what it's supposed to. Under the Consumer Rights Act 2015, consumers may be entitled to a refund, replacement, repair and/or compensation where goods are faulty or not as described; they are also entitled to a refund and/or compensation where the seller had no legal right to sell the goods.

When you don't have to offer a refund

You don't have to refund a customer if they:

- knew an item was faulty when they bought it
- damaged an item by trying to repair it themselves or getting someone else to do it (though they may still have the right to a repair, replacement or partial refund)
- no longer want an item (e.g. because it's the wrong size or colour) unless they bought it without seeing it

You have to offer a refund for certain items only if they're faulty, such as:

- personalised items and custom-made items, e.g. curtains
- perishable items, e.g. frozen food or flowers
- newspapers and magazines
- unwrapped CDs, DVDs and computer software

This space is for notes

Task 3d: How to collect outstanding debtor amounts – part of credit control.

The first thing to do here is to generate a collection report for the accounts that are past their due dates.

Here is how to do it.

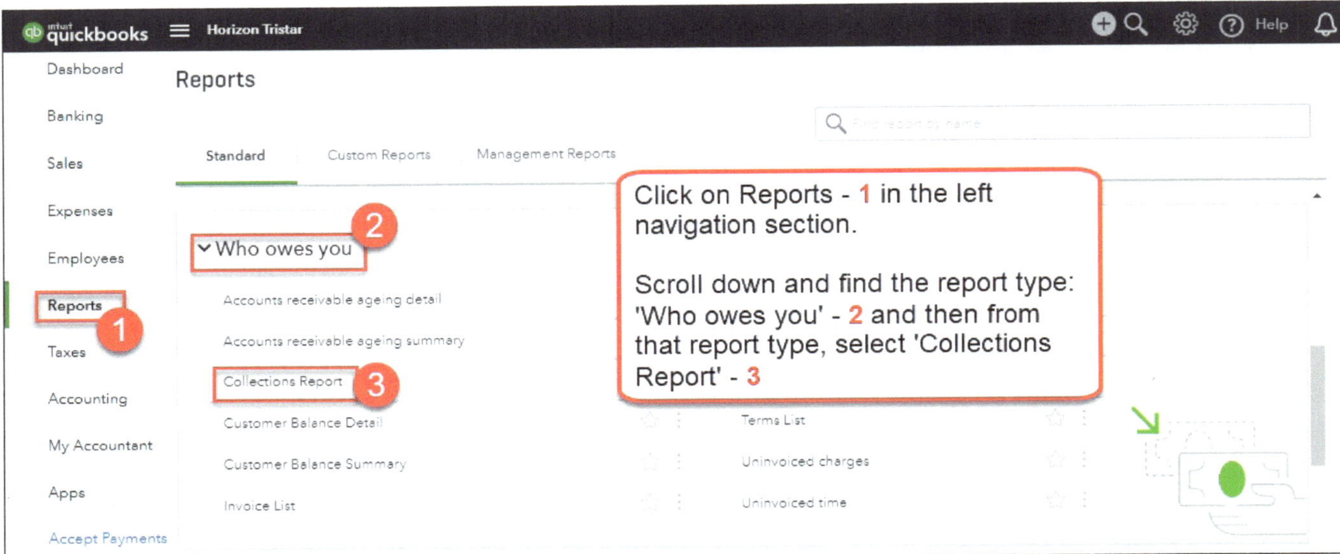

Fig. 163

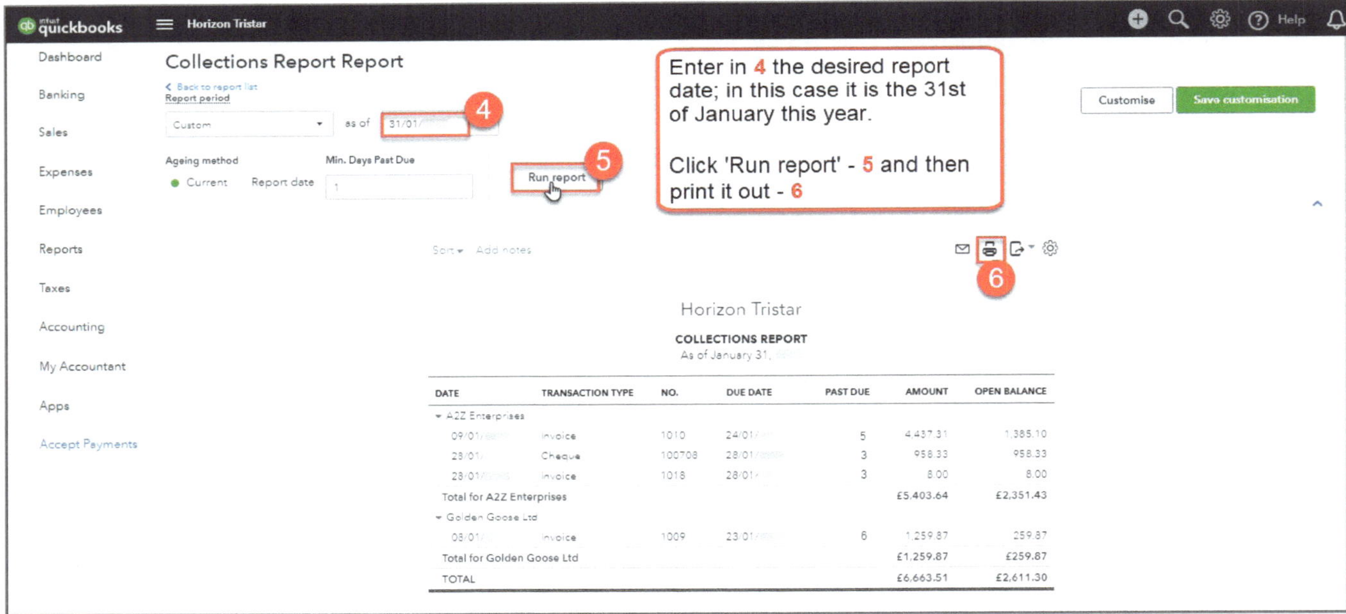

Fig. 164

Once you have the printed report, use the following debt collection procedure to collect the overdue accounts.

14 steps to take to collect outstanding debts from debtors

1. *Send the customer a current account statement or gentle reminder.*

2. *Five working days after sending the statement check to see whether the amount has been paid.*
3. *If the amount has not been paid, telephone the client and discuss the reason for non-payment, remind them of their credit terms, and agree on a payment date.*
4. *Write a letter to the client summarising the telephone conversation and noting the agreed payment date.*
5. *Make a note on the system of the date payment should be received. Use the communication tab on customer record window from Sage to make a note.*
6. *If payment is not received by the agreed date telephone the client and remind them of your previous discussion.*
7. *Agree on a date for payment (or direct debit/credit card if applicable).*
8. *Write a letter to the client summarising the telephone conversation and noting the agreed payment date.*
9. *Make a note on the system of the date payment should be received.*
10. *If payment is not received by the agreed date telephone the client.*
11. *Write a letter to the client summarising the telephone conversation and noting the date court proceedings will commence.*
12. *Make a note on the system of the date payment should be received.*
13. *If payment is not received within the specified time, then continue with the County Court procedure.*
14. *Make arrangements to attend court.*

I do not like to state my opinion on matters unless I know the precise facts

Albert Einstein

"Don't mistake movement for achievement. It is easy to be faked out by being busy. Here is a question to ask yourself if you are always busy: Busy doing what?

Sterling Libs

TASK 4: JOURNAL ENTRIES AND DOUBLE ENTRY REVIEW

Task 4a: Posting a journal on issue of share capital.

12,000 £1.00 ordinary shares were issued for a cash consideration of £2.70 each, and there were £1,000 of brokers fees to pay.

Here is what to do to enter this transaction in QuickBooks online;

Step 1, click on the plus button - , and under Other, select 'Journal Entry'

Fig. 165

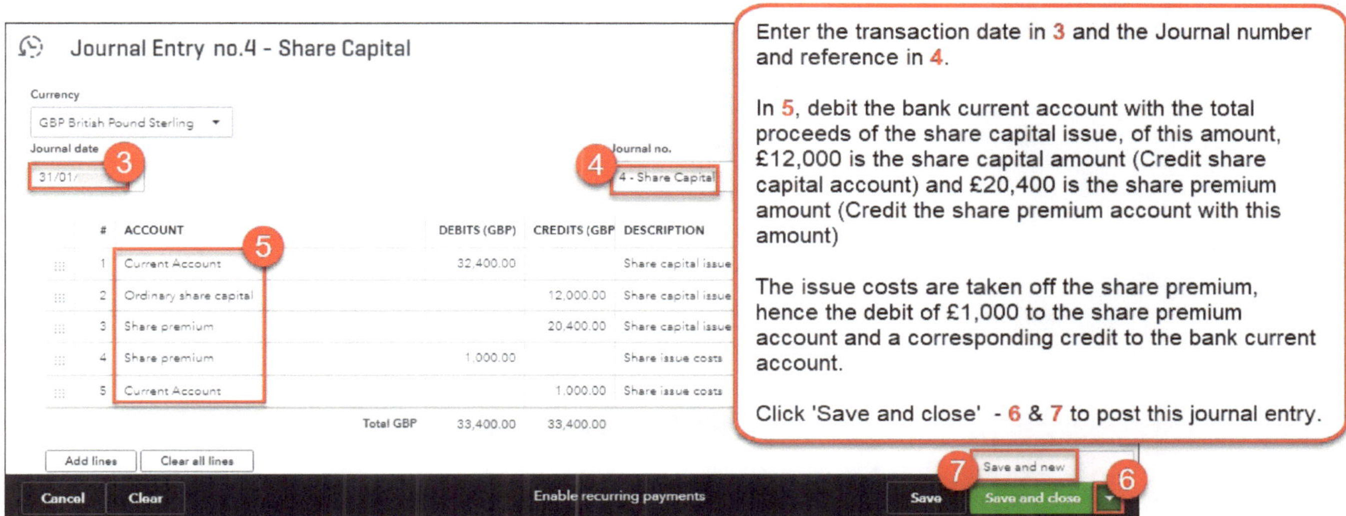

Fig. 166

A brief note about journals

In manual accounting or bookkeeping systems, business transactions are first recorded in a journal...hence the term journal entry.

A manual journal entry that is recorded in a company's general journal will consist of the following:

- the appropriate date
- the amount(s) and account(s) that will be debited
- the amount(s) and account(s) that will be credited
- a short description/memo
- a reference such as a check number

These journalised amounts (which will appear in the journal in order by date) are then posted to the accounts in the general ledger.

Today, computerised accounting systems will automatically record most of the business transactions into the general ledger accounts immediately after the software prepares the sales invoices, processes receipts from customers, etc. The result is, we will not see journal entries for most of the business transactions.

However, we will need to process some journal entries in order to record transfers between bank accounts and to record adjusting entries. For example, it is likely that at the end of each month there will be a journal entry to record depreciation. (This will include a debit to Depreciation Expense and a credit to Accumulated Depreciation.) In addition, there will likely be a need for journal entry to accrue interest on a bank loan. (This will include a debit to Interest Expense and a credit to Interest Payable.)

Task 4b: Double entry review.

Task 4b(i): Double entry to record a cash sale paid for by cash and bank transfer.

Step 1, click on the plus button - , and under Customers, select 'Sales Receipt.'

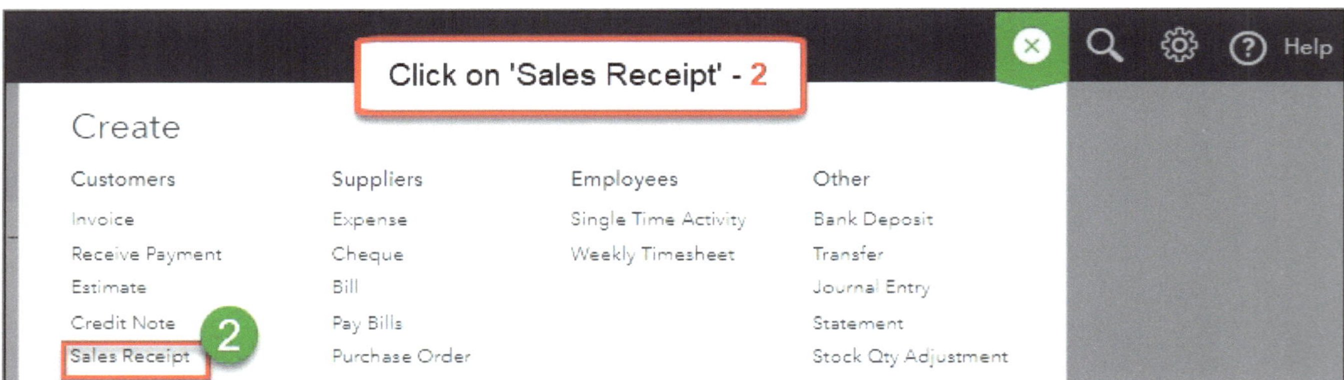

Fig. 167

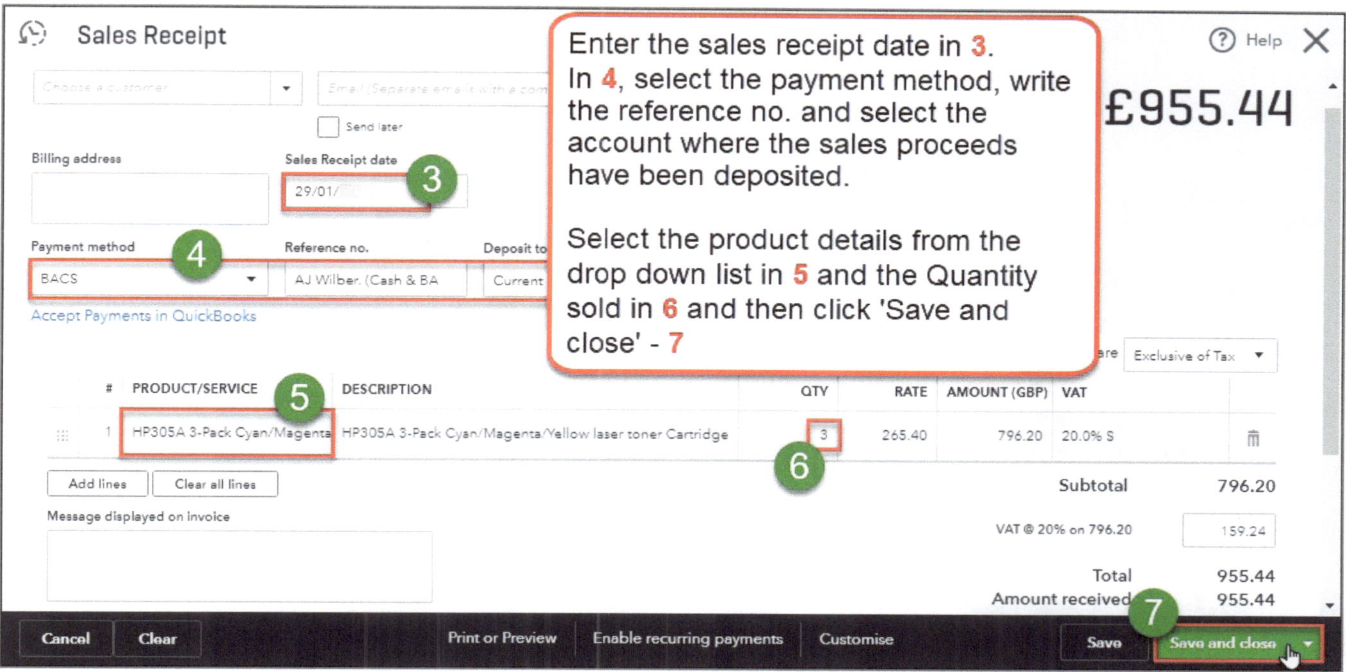

Fig. 168

Task 4b(ii): Double entry to record a Credit sale.

Step 8, click on the plus button - , and under Customers, select 'Invoice.'

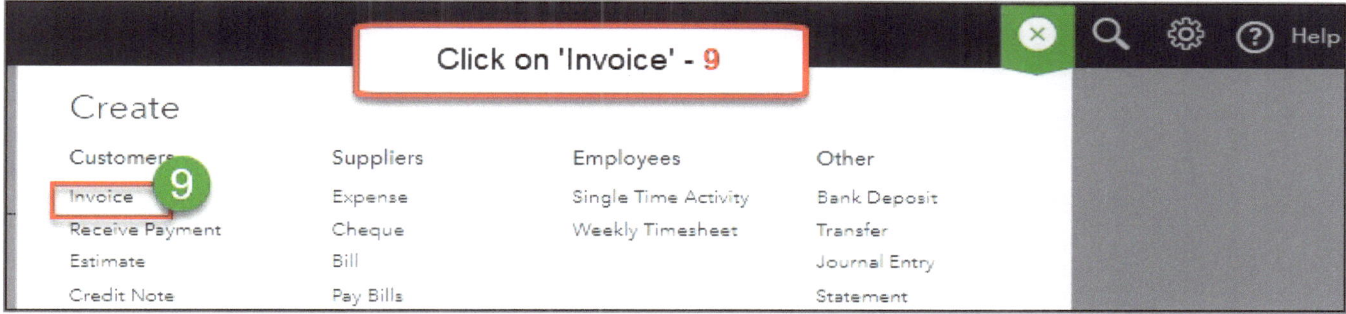

Fig. 169

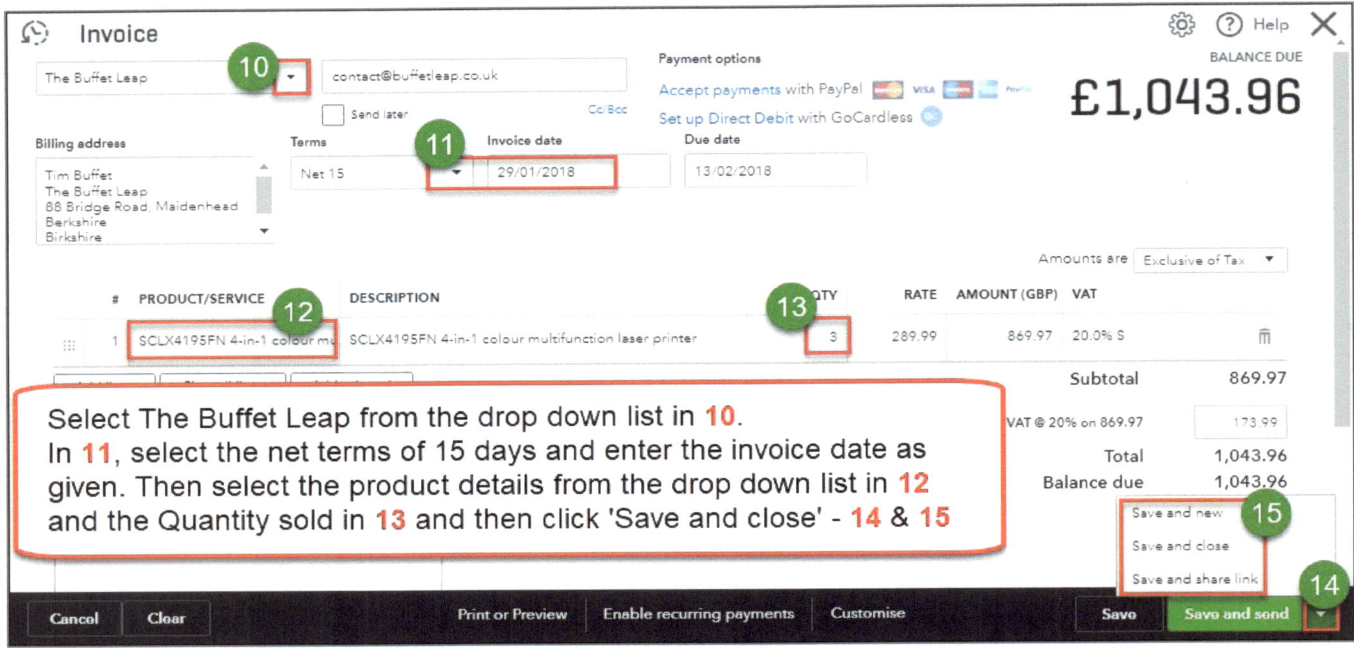

Fig. 170

> "If you want to live a happy life, tie it to a goal and not on people or objects"
>
> **Albert Einstein**

"Wherever you are and in whatever you do in life, don't go against or violate your Conscience. It is never a good idea"
Sterling Libs

TASK 5: HOW TO ENSURE SECURITY OF ACCOUNTING DATA

Task 5a: How to change your password in QuickBooks online.

Here is how to do it.

Step 1, click on the gear icon - , then select 'User profile.'

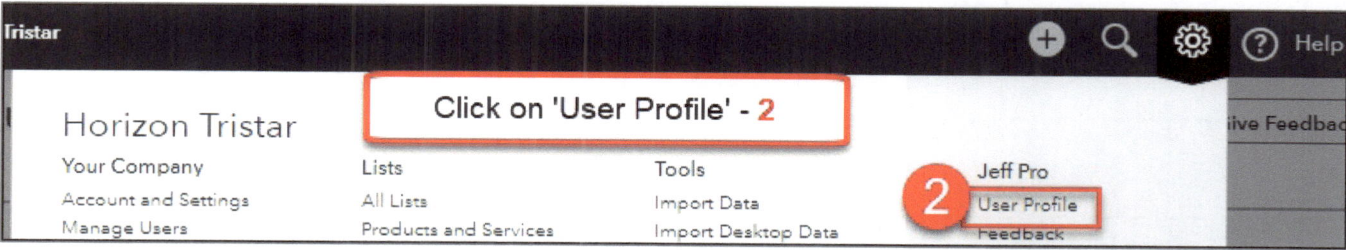

Fig. 171

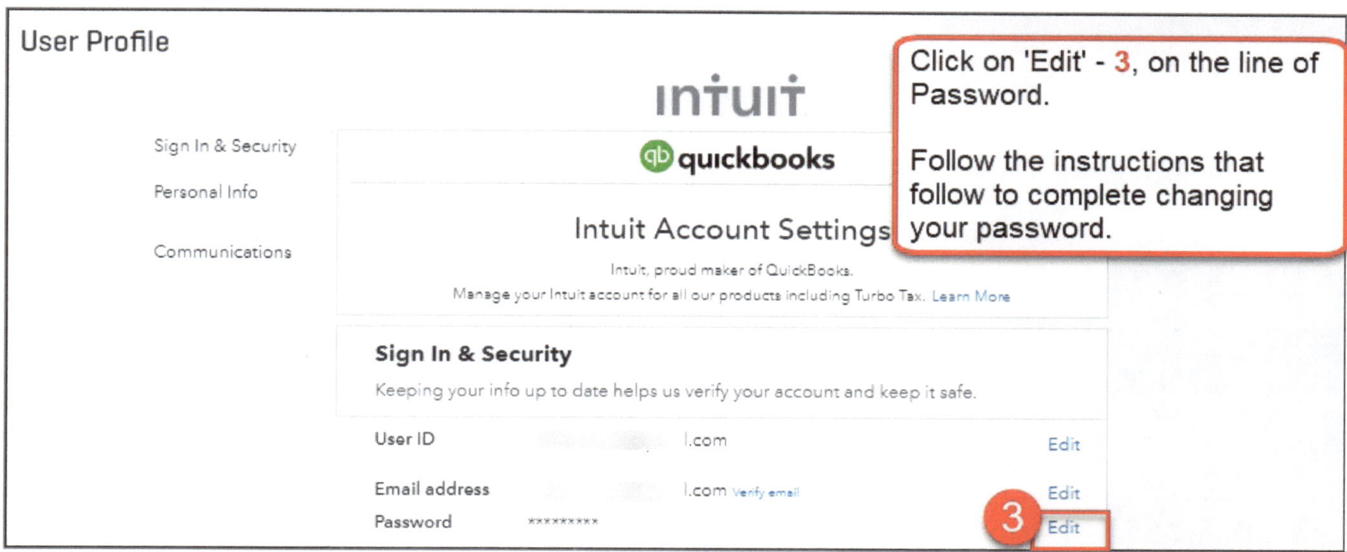

Fig. 172

Task 5b: How to add a new user in QuickBooks online.

We are adding a new user - Caroline McFarlane. Here is how to do it.

Step 1, click on the gear icon - , then under 'Your Company' select 'Manage Users'

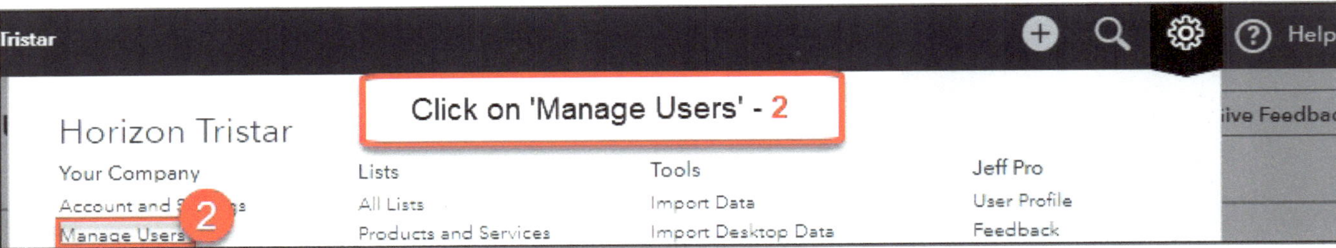

Fig. 173

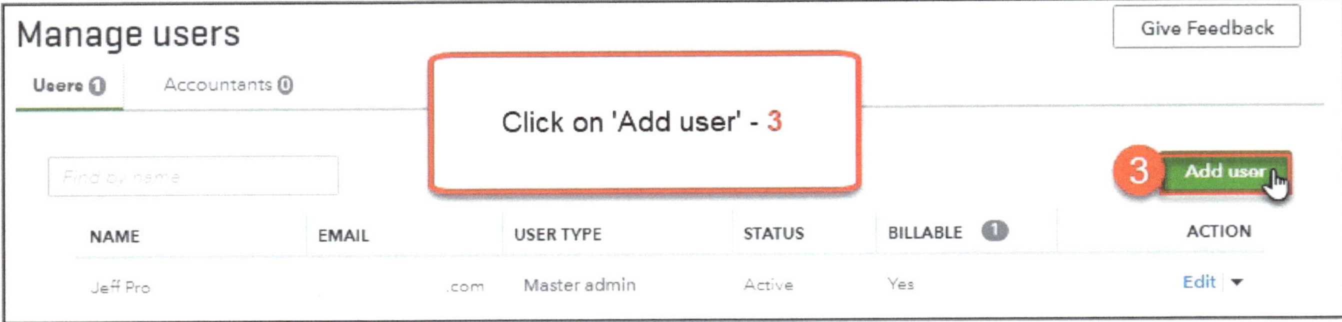

Fig. 174

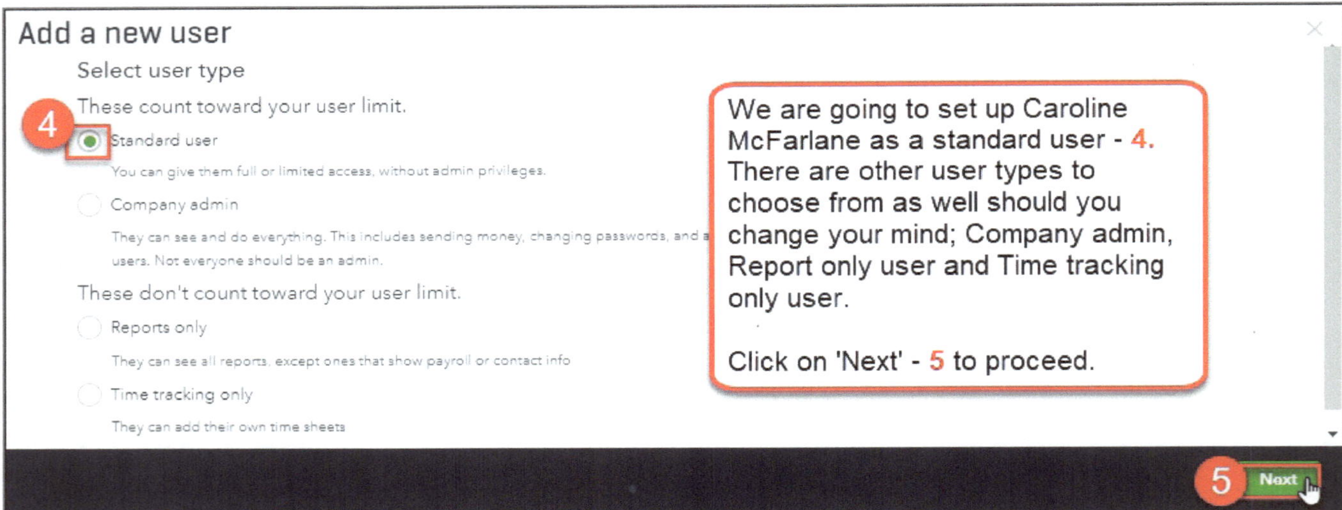

Fig. 175

This space is for notes

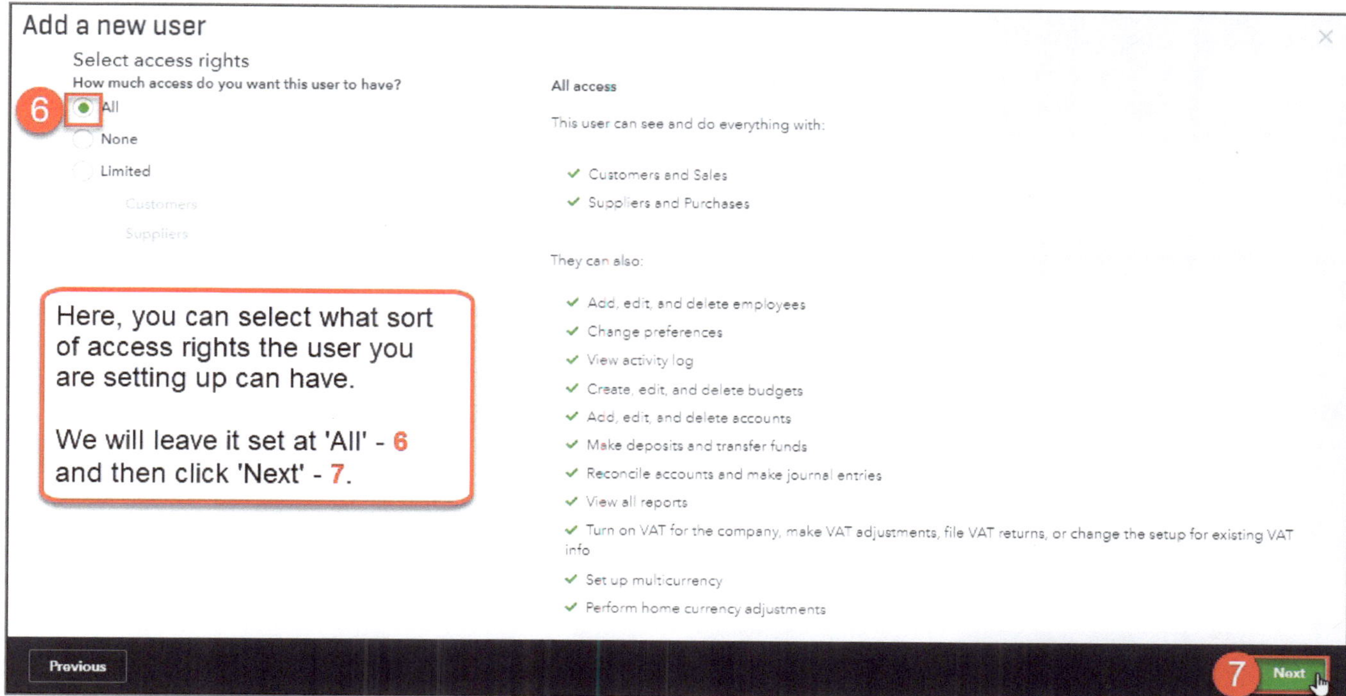

Fig. 176

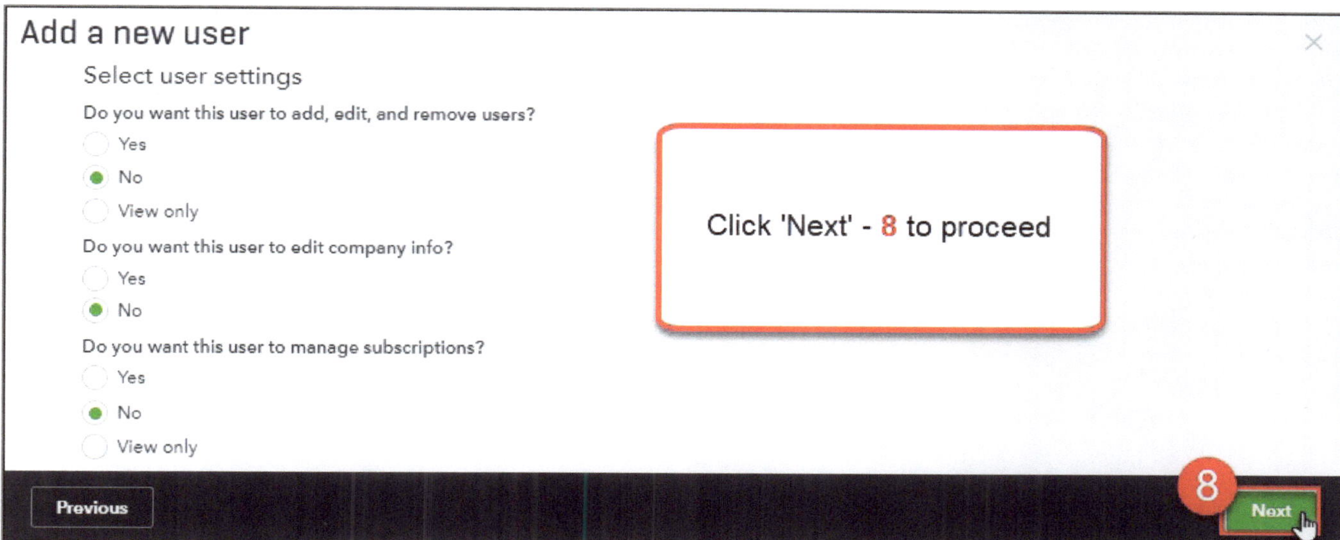

Fig. 177

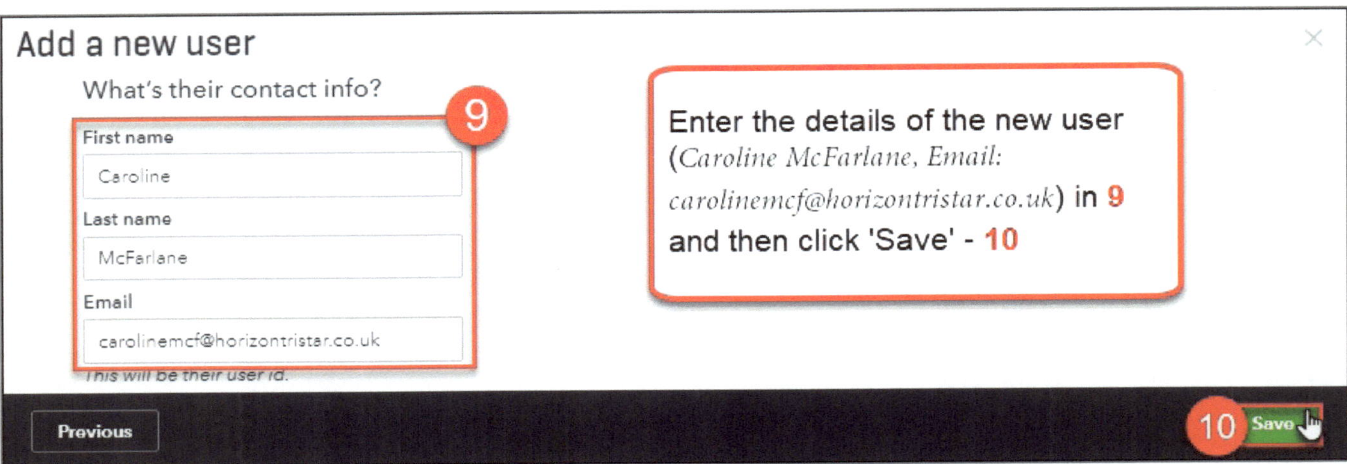

Fig. 178

"Alone we can do so little, together we can do so much"

Helen Keller

ABOUT THE AUTHOR

Sterling Libs FCCA trained as a Chartered Accountant and has written several practical accounting books that have helped many accounting students and graduates in their accounting career journeys to getting accounting jobs. He studied and qualified for his professional accountancy career in London England and is now a Fellow of the Association of Chartered Certified Accountants. He currently lives and works in London, United Kindom.

Sterling is pragmatic, motivational and hard working. He has been very instrumental in training many accounting students, and graduates in gaining work-based practical accounting experience and many of his trainees have been able to get accounting jobs in the UK and abroad. His passion for practical accounting and training is profound, and he loves mentoring individuals to discover, develop and deploy their talents and gifts to make the world a better place for all.

He is passionate about inspiring confidence for work, and life in general, among all those he meets and interacts with.

The Author can be contacted by sending an email to sterling@sterlinglibs.com

www.ingramcontent.com/pod-product-compliance
Lightning Source LLC
LaVergne TN
LVHW070214110826
845147LV00003B/573

* 9 7 8 1 9 1 1 0 3 7 1 4 9 *